THE TEGETTHOFF CLASS DREADNOUGHTS

1909-1925

ANDY SOUTH

AMAZON.CO.UK

Copyright © 2019 Andrew South, Andrew Wilkie & Zoltan Takacs

All rights reserved

No part of this book may be reproduced, or stored in a retrieval system, or transmitted in any form or by any means, electronic, mechanical, photocopying, recording, or otherwise, without express written permission of the publisher.

ISBN: 9781093932492

Cover design by: Andrew Wilkie
Library of Congress Control Number: 2018675309
Printed in the United States of America

Title Page
Copyright
PART ONE: THE CONCEPTION
CHAPTER 1: THE DREADNOUGHT CLUB.   1
CHAPTER 2: CASH AND SCHEMING   24
CHAPTER 3: OF RUMOURS AND SPIES.   27
CHAPTER 1: THE SZENT István & VIRIBUS UNITIS.   32
CHAPTER 2: DESIGN, DIMENSION, DISPLACEMENT & POWER   38
CHAPTER 3: GUNS, TORPEDOES AND MINES.   59
CHAPTER 4: ARMOUR AND MINE PROTECTION   116
CHAPTER 5: THE SHIPS CONNING TOWER, BRIDGE & FIRE CONTROL. 127
CHAPTER 6: SHIP COLOURS.   145
CHAPTER 7: FIXTURES AND FITTINGS.   149
CHAPTER 8: THE SHIPS BOATS.   187
PART THREE: THE HISTORY   216
CHAPTER 1: STEEL & RIVETS.   217
CHAPTER 2: TIMES OF PEACE (PRE-WAR)   244
CHAPTER 3: THE PATH TO WAR   255
CHAPTER 4: COMBAT (1915)   267
CHAPTER 5: BOREDOM & MUTINY.   274
CHAPTER 6: SZENT IŚTVAN   290
CHAPTER 7: THE ENQUIRY, BLAME & THE WRECK.   324
CHAPTER 8: THE LAST YEAR OF WAR   330
CHAPTER 9: LOSS OF THE YUGOSLAVIA   335

CHAPTER 10: TO CONCLUDE.	350
APPENDICES	355
APPENDIX A: THE MYTH OF A UNUSABLE GUN TOWER: LEGEND OR REALITY?	356
APPENDIX B: THE 'COMPETITION' ENTRIES.	363
APPENDIX C: THE MILTARY HISTORY MUSEUM, VIENNA (ILLUSTRATIONS).	389
APPENDIX D: THE PHOTOGRAPH ALBUM	395
APPENDIX E: THE FILM ARCHIVE	408
APPENDIX F: THE PLUMBING	414
APPENDIX G: CAPTAIN'S OF THE SZENT ISTVÁN & THE DESIGNER	416
LITERATURE & SOURCES	418
Books By This Author	425

S.M.S. VIRIBUS UNITIS

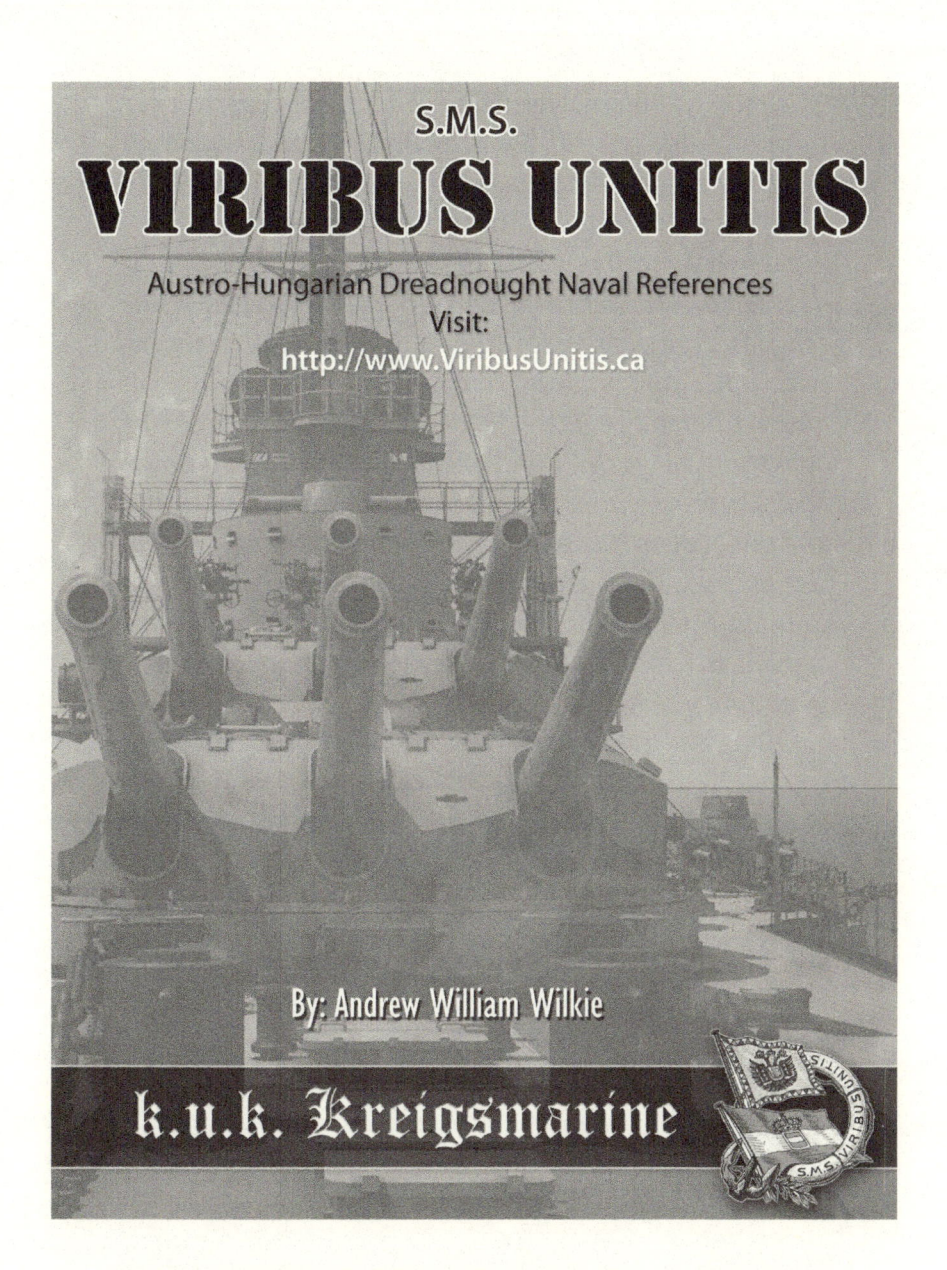

Austro-Hungarian Dreadnought Naval References
Visit:
http://www.ViribusUnitis.ca

By: Andrew William Wilkie

k.u.k. Kreigsmarine

Andrew Wilkie's passion for ships began at a very young age of 5 years old, his first love, the R.M.S. Titanic. His passion spread from ocean liners to the battleships of WWI and WWII, heavily favouring the British and Italian Navies, with special interest in the obscure, forgotten nations like Austria-Hungary. Having an art-

istic talent, Andrew wanted to combine his passion for ships with his passion for drawing. He embarked on re-creating the little known Austro-Hungarian battleship S.M.S Viribus Unitis in stunning 3D detail on his computer, a project that would span three years. Eventually, he created her sister ship Szent István in 3D, all the while collaborating with historians, magazines, museums, institutions, film studios, and diving associations on many different projects. His art has graced the covers of books and magazines and eventually creating his own book. Andrew shares his passion for the Viribus Unitis and the Austro-Hungarian Navy in the form of his website at www.ViribusUnitis.ca. Be sure to visit the site to learn the history around these ships, the preliminary battleship/battlecruiser designs, photos, drawings, plans and much, much more.

THE TEGETTHOFF CLASS

2nd Edition

Austria-Hungary's Dreadnoughts 1909-1925

BY: ANDY SOUTH

3D Model: Andrew Wilkie

PREVIOUS PAGE: THE ALTERNATIVE COVER CREATED BY ANDREW WILKIE. BOTH ARE STUNNING IMAGES AND I FLUCTUATED BETWEEN THE TWO. BUT BOTH DEMAND THEIR PLACE IN THE SPOTLIGHT AS BOTH ARE STUNNING AND BOTH ARE COPYRIGHTED. THANK YOU, ANDREW.

PHOTOGRAPHS, TRANSLATIONS & ERRORS.

A brief note (and an apology) concerning a small number of the images within this 'E' book. They are off a poor quality and their inclusion means no higher resolutions were available to me. I decided after much thought to include them and thereby tell the complete tale. I felt their omission would leave out more than their submission would bring to the telling of the history. I hope the reader will both bear with me and forgive me.

Secondly having worked with Hungarian, Serbian, and Croatian source material, I had to resort to Googles translations services. If the text does not 'flow' within these parts I am sorry, but I was reluctant to tamper with languages I do not read or speak.

Finally, this volume has been proofread and checked by three people, myself included. However, I am not naive enough to think it will emerge free of errors. If you find any, please do not post a bad review but drop me an email and I will correct any mistakes. This volume is the result of hundreds of hours work, so allow me the chance to make amendments. Once again I hope the reader will both bear with me and forgive me.

Andy South
(andyuknaval@gmail.com)

MAPS

VIRIBUS UNITIS STERN ORNAMENTS

THE ADRIATIC

500 MILES (800 KM) LONG WITH AN AVERAGE WIDTH OF 100 MILES,

A=LOSS OF THE WIEN BAY OF MUGGIA, 19/12/17.
B= VENICE, ITALIAN PORT.
C= LOSS OF JUGOSLAVIJA 01/11/18
D= LOSS OF THE SZENT ISTVAN 10/06/18
E= BOMARDMENT OF ANCONA 05/15
F= VIRIBUS UNITIS 06/14
G= ROUTE OF COFFINS 06/14
H= OTRANTO BARRAGE

ALL PLACEMENTS ARE APPROXIMATE.
NATIONAL FLAG DONATES NAVAL BASE.

XII

THE PORT OF POLA

A= THE MAIN NAVAL BASE WITHIN POLA
B= THE SITE OF THE YUGOSLAVIA LOSS
C= FLEET GUNNERY EXERCISE LOCATION.

THE DISTANCE FROM A TO C IS 8 MILES (APPROX.) AND WAS TO BE THE MOST FREQUENTED ROUTE THE DREADNOUGHTS TRAVELLED DURING THEIR WAR SERVICE. ONLY ON A VERY FEW OCCASIONS DID THEY VENTURE FURTHER.

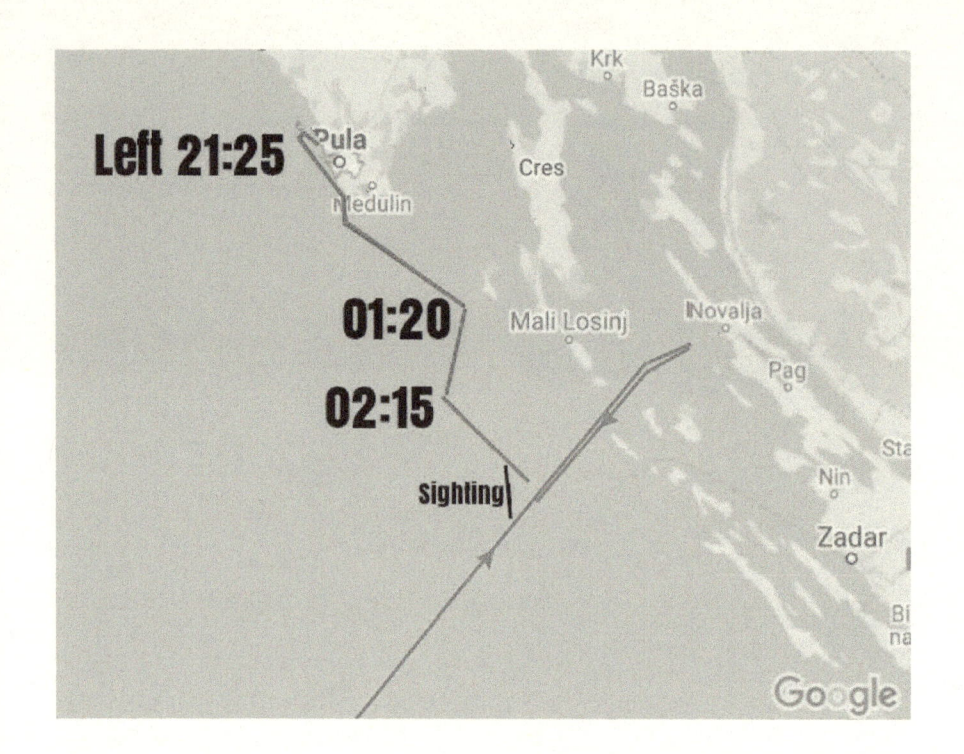

THE SZENT ISTVÁN'S FINAL VOYAGE.

THE RED TRACK DENOTES THE AUSTRIAN-HUNGARIAN FLEET
AND THE GREEN PATH, THE ITALIANS.

(ALL POSITIONS ARE APPROXIMATE)

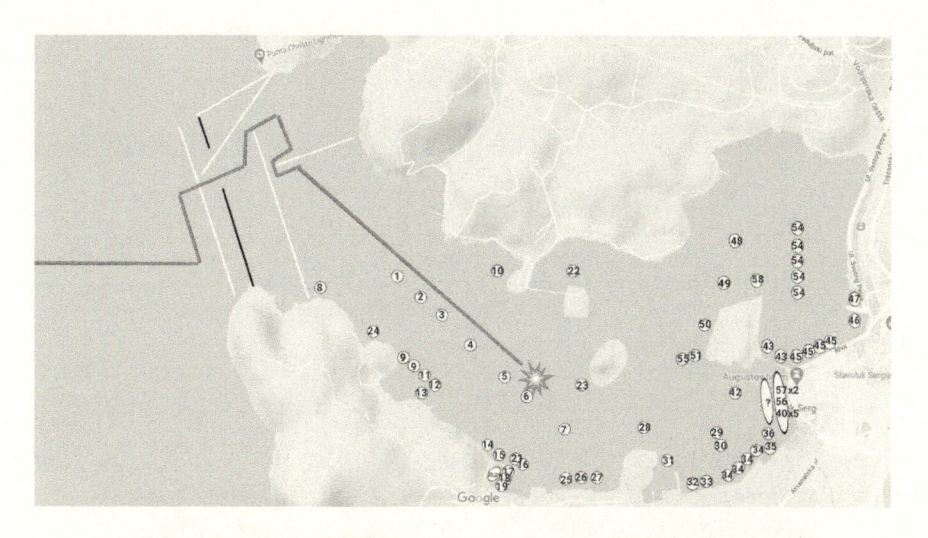

THE AUSTRO-HUNGARIAN FLEET ANCHORAGES

(NOTED ON THE 22ND OCTOBER 1918, BY ITALIAN AIR RECONNAISSANCE).

THE WARSHIPS LOCATIONS ARE MOST UNLIKELY TO HAVE CHANGED
DURING THE DAYS LEADING UP TO THE ITALIAN RAID.
1. ZRÍNYI. 2. RADETZKY 3. ERZHERZOG FRANZ FERDINAND 4. PRINZ EUGEN 5. TEGETTHOFF 6. VIRIBUS UNITIS 7. EMPTY BERTH 8. EMPTY BERTH 9.? 10 BUDAPEST 11.? 12. SMALL WARSHIP 13.? 14. COMET CLASS 15. HABSBURG CLASS 16. HABSBURG CLASS 17. SMS ADRIA 18. KAISERIN UND KONIGIN MARIA THERESIA 19 WIEN 20.? 21. EMPTY BERTH 22. YACHT 23. SMALL WARSHIP 24. OLD WARSHIP 25. SMALL WARSHIP 26. TORPEDO BOAT 27. TORPEDO BOAT 28.? 29. NOVRA CLASS 30. SMALL UNKNOWN WARSHIP 31. EMPTY BERTH 32. STEAMER 33. SMALL UNKNOWN WARSHIP 34. TORPEDO BOAT 35. HUNTING TORPEDO BOAT 36. UNKNOWN WARSHIP 37. EMPTY BERTH 38.? 39.? 40. TORPEDO BOAT 41. HAZAR CLASS 42. SUBMARINE & TORPEDO BOAT 43. SUBMARINE 44. HABSBURG CLASS 45. TORPEDO BOAT 46. STEAMER 47. STEAMER 48. STEAMER 49. NOVARA CLASS 50. SUBMARINE 51. EMPTY DRY DOCK 52. OCCUPIED DRY DOCK 53. BERTH FOR DRY DOCK 54.? 55. OCCUPIED DRY DOCK (SUBMARINE) 56. STEAMER 57. MERCHANT SHIP.

THE RED LINE DENOTES THE ROUTE TAKEN BY THE MAS BOATS. THE WHITE
LINES ARE DEFENCE BOOMS AND BLACK LINE A MOLE OR PIER.
ALL POSITIONS ARE APPROXIMATE,

PART ONE: THE CONCEPTION

THE 21,689 TON S.M.S SZENT ISTVÁN LEAVING HER HOME PORT, IN THE COMPANY OF A LIGHT CRUISER & TORPEDO BOAT ESCORT. (IMAGE CREDIT ANDREW WILKIE WWW.VIRIBUSUNITIS.CA)

CHAPTER 1: THE DREADNOUGHT CLUB.

THE TEGETTHOFF CLASS

In 1906 there was a new club in town. One that only the richest and most powerful of nations could realistically afford to join. Its chief assets were bigger, faster, shapelier, and more powerful than anything that had gone before. Membership of this 'exclusive' club sent the message "don't mess with us". As with all new 'must-haves' those who could not afford to join, 'wanted-in' even more, so they too would be recognized as a 'Great Power'. In 1906 the must have item was the Dreadnought battleship and the Austro-Hungarian Habsburgs wanted in. The *Tegetthoff* Dreadnoughts (often referred incorrectly to, as the *Viribus Unitis* class) was destined to be the only group of Dreadnoughts ever to be built and completed for the Austrian-Hungarian Imperial Navy, (the Kaiserliche und königliche Kriegsmarine, sometimes shortened to K.U.K. Kriegsmarine). The class, (after much scheming and politicking), would be comprised of four ships, the *Viribus Unitis* (pronounced: "Var-e-buss Unit-is"), *Tegetthoff* ("Tea-gee-toff"), *Prinz Eugen,* ("Prinz U-jen") and the *Szent István* ("Scent ist-van") [1]. Three of the four ships were to be built in, what was until 1918, the fourth largest city in the Habsburg Empire, Trieste. The fourth vessel, the Szent István, was constructed in the Empire's Hungarian port of Fiume. [1a] The allocation of the two construction sites was made to ensure that both parts of the Dual Monarchy, (or Empire), benefited from and agreed to provide the funds for these four 'status' symbols.

Vice-Admiral Rudolf Montecuccoli.

Two years prior in September 1904, the Austrian Naval League had been founded and a month later Vice-Admiral Rudolf Montecuccoli was appointed to the two posts of Commander-in-Chief of the Navy and Chief of the Naval Section of the War Ministry. These two events would help set the foundation for what was to be the final expansion of the Austria-Hungarian Navy, it in to one that was deemed worthy of a 'Great Power'. Montecuccoli was to commence his tenure (1904-1913) from day one, by championing the ideas of his predecessor, Admiral Hermann von Spaun, campaigning for an enlarged and a modernized Imperial navy.

There were in addition to Montecuccoli, several other fac-

THE TEGETTHOFF CLASS.

tors that were to help lay the foundation for the proposed naval expansion. The Empire's railway engineers had finally cut through the Austrian Alps, linking both the port of Trieste and the Dalmatian coastline with the rest of the Empire. In addition, lower tariffs in Trieste was to lead to the expansion of the city and a growth in the Austria-Hungarian merchant navy. With these changes came the perceived 'need' for new battleships, replacing the navy's existing Coastal Defence ships. Before the turn of the century, the Empire's Government in Vienna had seen no need for sea power to support the Austrian-Hungarian foreign policy and in addition the public had little interest in a navy. But in September 1902, the situation was to undertake a radical change when the Archduke Franz Ferdinand, heir to the Austria-Hungarian throne and a pro-naval expansionist, was appointed to the position of Admiral at the completion of that years naval manoeuvres. This saw an increase in the importance of the navy in the eyes of both the public and the two Austro-Hungarian Parliaments. The Archduke's interest in the Empire's naval affairs had grown from his belief that a strong navy would be needed if the Empire were to successfully compete with its Italian neighbour. Ferdinand viewed Italy (ironically an ally of the Empire) as Austria-Hungary's greatest threat within the region.

In 1882, Italy had joined the Triple Alliance in company with Austria-Hungary and Germany, who all agreed to fight alongside each other against any possible mutual enemies (which could only really be perceived as France, Great Britain or Imperial Russia). But despite the Treaty, Austria and Italy had retained their mutual rivalry which they would never shed, something that had only been strengthened since the war in 1866. In that year, an Austrian army had defeated an Italian army which was several times larger and the Austrian fleet had in turn defeated the Italian fleet in the battle of Vis (Lissa) on the 20th July. Despite officially being 'Allies', Italy's navy, (the Regia Marina) was to remain the main regional opponent with which Austria-Hungary, often negatively, measured itself against. The gap between the Austria-Hungarian and Italian navies had existed for decades and in the late 1880's Italy could claim to be the world's third-largest fleet, behind the French and Royal Navy. But fourteen years later in 1894, the Imperial German and Russian navies had overtaken the Italians in the world rankings. By that stage, the Italians could claim 18 battleships in commission or under construction in comparison to just 6 Austria-Hungarian battleships.

With the completion of the final pair of *Regina Elena* class battleships, in 1903, the Italian Navy turned its attention to the construction of a series of large cruisers, rather than any additional battleships. To complicate matters further, a scandal had erupted involving the Terni Steel Works' armour contracts. This was to lead to a Governmental enquiry and that in turn led to the postponement of several projected naval construction programs over the next three years. The combination of these factors would result in the Italian Navy being unable to recommence any construction on additional battleships until 1909 and this 'unplanned holiday' was to provide the Austria-Hungarian Navy with an opportunity to close the numerical difference that lay between the two battle fleets.

By 1903, the Italian lead in the naval race appeared to be an insurmountable obstacle for the Empire. Then in 1906 the rules of the game were to change with the launch in England of *HMS Dreadnought*. The value of the world's existing battleships, (or what history has come to label as the 'Pre-Dreadnought') vanished overnight and the squadrons of battleships within the world's navies were rendered obsolete.

THE TEGETTHOFF CLASS.

This presented the Austria-Hungarian Navy with a unique opportunity to make up for their past neglect in naval matters. In the Spring of 1905, soon after his assumption as Chief of the Navy, Montecuccoli laid out his first proposal for a modern Austrian-Hungarian fleet. He envisaged an armada comprised of 12 battleships, 4 armoured cruisers, 8 scout cruisers, 18 destroyers, 36 high seas torpedo craft and 6 submarines. The plans were ambitious, but they still lacked at that point any ships of the new Dreadnought type. Then the Slovenian politician and prominent lawyer Ivan Šušteršič presented a plan to the Reichsrat in 1905, seeking the (ambitious and unrealistic) construction of nine Dreadnoughts.

Across the waters of the Adriatic, Italy applied for its own admission to the 'Dreadnought Club' with the *Dante Alighieri* ("Dant-ee Al-e-gare-ee"), which had been designed by Rear Admiral Engineer Edoardo Masdea, the Chief Constructor of the Regia Marina and was based on the "All-Big-Gun" ideas of General Vittorio Cuniberti.

The General had proposed a battleship with the main guns all a single calibre and the turrets positioned to provide for maximum broadside fire. Cuniberti has over the succeeding century become best known for an article he wrote for Jane's Fighting Ships in 1903. In the article, he called for a concept known as the "all-big-gun" fighting ship. Until that time the navies of the world had built battleships which combined a mixture of both large and medium calibre guns. There was a constant experimentation to refine the calibre, concept, and layout of each succeeding design. But the ship that Cuniberti had envisaged was to be a "Colossus" of the seas. His main idea was that this ship would carry only one calibre of gun, the biggest available, at the time, the 12-inch (305 mm). The heavily armoured "Colossus" would in addition have sufficient armour to make it impervious to all but the 12-inch guns of the enemy. Cuniberti's article proposed twelve large calibre guns, which would in combination have an overwhelming advantage over the more traditional four guns of the enemy ship. In addition, his ship would be so fast, that she could choose her point of attack. Cuniberti saw this envisioned ship discharging a 12-inch broadside with sufficient weight to enable her to overwhelm one enemy ship, before moving on to the next and destroying an entire enemy fleet in turn. He proposed that the effect of a squadron comprised of six "Colossus" would give a fleet such overwhelming power as to deter all possible opponents, (unless the other side had similar ships!).

Cuniberti proposed a design based on his ideas to the Italian Government, but for budgetary reasons his ideas were declined. But the Italian Admiralty gave the General permission to write the article for Jane's Fighting Ships. The commentary, which had been published before the Battle of Tsushima (27-28 May 1905), had its arguments vindicated in the waters off China. The battle was to see that the real damage to the Russian ships was inflicted by the large calibre guns of the Japanese fleet. The design work on the Italian Dreadnought *Dante Alighieri*, (Motto *"with the soul that wins every battle"*, but she was never to fight a battle!), had put the Austro-Hungarian Navy into a bad position. The Italian ship was as a result due mainly to the leaking of Montecuccoli's Spring 1905 memorandum, while his plans for the construction of the four new Dreadnoughts remained in their planning stages. Making the matter more complex was the collapse of Sándor Wekerle's Government in Budapest, this left the Hungarian Diet, for nearly a year, without a Prime Minister. With no Government in Budapest to pass a budget, the efforts to secure funding and begin the construction of the four ships, came to a halt.

THE TEGETTHOFF CLASS.

In January 1908, the German naval magazine 'Marine Rundschau' was to publish the news that the keel of the first Italian Dreadnought was about to be laid down and this revelation brought an immediate Austro-Hungarian reaction. Five months later, in most likely a response to the German news flash, the Austrian-Hungarian navy on 7th May 1908 first formally met to discuss the idea of Dreadnought construction. The meeting was chaired by Rudolf von Montecuccoli MTK (Marinetechnische Komitee - Naval Technical Committee), Pola/ Vienna. An official design competition for a Dreadnought class was announced on the 24th June 1908 and was made open to all Austro-Hungarian naval architects. The rules of the competition laid down the following guidelines: Displacement was not to exceed 20,000 tons. The main armament was to be comprised of eight 30.5 cm (12-inch) mounted on the centreline. The secondary armament was to be 19 and 10 cm guns. The ships armour belt was to be 230 mm (9.05-inches) at the waterline and a 250 mm (9.84-inches) depth for the barrettes. The Austrian Naval League was to present its own set of proposals for the construction of the new Dreadnought type. The League had in March 1909, petitioned the Naval Section of the War Ministry to authorize the construction of three 19,000 tonnes (18,700 long tons) Dreadnoughts. They argued that the Empire needed a strong navy to protect Austria-Hungary's growing merchant navy, and in addition keeping in mind that Italy's naval spending was twice that of the Empire.

With the completion of what would be the Empire's final Pre-Dreadnought, the three ships of the *Radetzky* class, (*Radetzky, Erzherzog Franz Ferdinand,* and *Zrinyi*) Montecuccoli drafted his first application for Austrian-Hungary's admission into the 'Dreadnought Club'. Making use of the newly established political support for naval expansion that he had raised in both Austria and Hungary, plus Habsburg concerns of a war with

Italy over the Bosnian Crisis during the previous year, Montecuccoli drafted a new plan for the Emperor, Franz Joseph I. In the plan he called for an expansion of the Austro-Hungarian Navy, to include 16 (+4) battleships, 12 (0) cruisers, 24 (+6) destroyers, 72 (+36) seagoing torpedo boats and 12 (+6) submarines. The plan presented to the Emperor what fundamentally was a modified version of Montecuccoli's 1905 scheme. The major difference was the inclusion for the first time of four Dreadnought battleships, each with a displacement of 20,000 tonnes (19,684 long tons) at load. These ships would eventually become the *Tegetthoff* class.

THE TEGETTHOFF CLASS.

Naval strength of Austria-Hungary & Italy in May 1909.		
(Built/building)	ITALY	Austria & Hungary
Battleship	10/2	9/3
Armoured Cruiser	8/2	3/0
Protected Cruisers	6/1	6/0
Torpedo boats	6/0	6/0
Destroyers	17/2	8/4
High seas torpedo boats	8/8	7/17
Coastal Torpedo Boats	29/0	58/14
Submarines	7/5	2/6
Total	121/20	79/34

On 5th November 1908, the Navy asked two of the Empires shipyards to participate in the contest:

1) The Ganz-Danubius Villamossági- and Co, Machine, and Waggon- Shipyard. [1b]
2) S.T.T (Stabilimento Tecnico Triestone), Trieste.

The main criteria for the Dreadnoughts that were now planned, was the installation of four triple turrets with 11-inches (280 mm) of armour and a maximum displacement of 21,000 tonnes.

However, Ganz-Danubius declined to take part in the competition as it had no experience in building vessels of such a huge tonnage size. The result of which was a near automatic acceptance of the STT submission where the Naval Engineer, Siegfried Popper was working. Popper had only recently retired as "Engineering-Admiral" in the Naval Engineering Office and according to rumour the whole competition was 'rigged' for him to be awarded the job of designing the new ships. This was supported by the fact that the ships construction was to begin well before the design contest closing date of 1910.

SIEGFRIED POPPER (1848-1933). THE HARD OF HEARING AND SHORT-SIGHTED DESIGNER, WHO WAS TO BE KILLED BY A TRAM HE DIDN'T SEE OR HEAR COMING.

In February 1909, MTK had presented its first submission, followed in March by a further seven differing versions of Popper's STT's design. There was to be a final total of eight designs (see appendix B) and on the 14th April 1909 the MTK commented on the plans, dividing the submissions into three groups. The designs comprised of five ships armed with ten and two ships with eight guns with the 30.5 cm (12-inch) L/50 calibre weapon.

The gun was to be a product of the Škoda works. But the factory had construction problems with the development of a longer L/50 calibre barrel, resulting in the Trieste shipyard (in the port of Trieste) being forced to redesign the plans of the VI and VII Projects with the L/45 calibre version. The MTK design also had triple expansion engines, while the STT used the modern Parsons steam turbine propulsion units. None of the plans were to bare a close similarity to the finished design.

In March 1909, Popper duly presented his five designs for what would become the *'Tegetthoff'* class. These first drafts were

THE TEGETTHOFF CLASS.

merely enlarged versions of the *Radetzky* class and on 20th April MTK was to ask STT to produce a ninth design, but this time with twelve guns in six turrets. [2] This additional design was completed in under a week, being submitted on the 27th in two versions. Then on the 5th May, at Montecuccoli's request, STT Trieste prepared a tenth design, this time comprised of twelve L/45 calibre guns armed in four triple turrets, and with 11-inches (280 mm) of armour and a maximum displacement of 21,000 tonnes.

This became Project VIII and was to be the first glimpse of what would become the final design. Project VIII was the first to use the triple turret configuration, as it had been learnt that the Italians wanted to equip their new Dreadnought *(Dante Alighieri)* with triple turrets. But even before the competition closing date, on the 20th February Montecuccoli announced, during a meeting of Parliament, the building of a Dreadnought of between 18,000 and 19,000 tonnes. In March of that year, Germany was to launch her first Dreadnought, the *Nassau* and as a result Italy was to postpone the laying of the keel for her Dreadnought, as Cuniberti and his Chief Naval Engineer, Edoardo Masdeo wanted now to rethink their own design.

But the design competition that had been organised by the Austrian Naval Section was to be overshadowed by a series of events during the next six months. In January 1909, Emperor Franz Joseph had approved Montecuccoli's plans, who then circulated it amongst the Empire's Governments in Vienna and Budapest. The Kaiser's permission was received in April and the Austro-Hungarian Frigate Captain Alfred von Koudelka was dispatched to Berlin to research the technical details of the German Dreadnought projects. While Popper was working on his designs, the Austrian Government asked their German ally for information on the particulars of their newest design, the *Kaiser* class. On the evening of 29th April 1909, the secretary of Montecuccoli, Frigate Captain Alfred von Koudelka was received by Grand Admiral Alfred Peter Friedrich von Tirpitz in Germany. The British were by this stage keenly aware of the Austro-Hungarian dreadnought plans and sent a spy to trail the Frigate Captain during his time with Tirpitz. At the start of their meeting, the Grand Admiral, Tirpitz showed Kouldelka from his window the British spy on the other side of the road and asked his guest to wear civilian clothing the next day.

Kouldelka was allowed by the Germans to examine their latest designs, which featured both excellent armour and underwater protection. Tirpitz tried to explain to Koudelka the importance of torpedo protection throughout the entire design process. Tirpitz then elucidated to his Austrian visitor that there needed to be at least two meters distance between both the hulls outer and inner walls, as well as between the inner wall and the torpedo defence wall. The Admiral's knowledge was based on a series of 1:1 scale section experiments. In addition, to help reduce the impact, it was pointed out that coal needed to be stored between the inner wall and the torpedo wall. But in the final design, the distance between the outer hull and the torpedo wall was to be only 68 to 98 inches (1.7 to 2.5 meters) in line with Popper's plans.

Tirpitz stressed that the hull should also be sub-divided into watertight compartments with bulkheads of a strong construction. He advised that the watertight bulkheads should not be weakened with the inclusion of doors, because there was the chance of them accidentally being left open and in addition the bulkheads should be solid with no door, pipe or wires passing through them. Any such fittings would serve to weaken the bulkhead and in the event of an emergency also serve as a means for water to pass between the compartments. During one of Koudelka's meetings with Tirpitz he showed the Grand Admiral the sixth preliminary design. Koudelka re-

THE TEGETTHOFF CLASS.

ceived a muted response from the German naval minister. In the report he wrote following of visit to Berlin, Koudelka wrote:

> "The deployment of ten heavy guns, as well as a large number of auxiliary guns along the sides on the ship of 20,000 tons, forced the designer (i.e. popper) limit yourself to moderate booking on the waterline. The Minister of the Sea [Tirpitz] recommends reducing the number of towers by one, which will save at least 900 tons of load. Elevated towers should be placed along the sides. Reducing the thickness of the upper armour belt from 200 to 150 mm would give further savings, due to which the thickness of the main belt could be increased to 300 mm. Taking into account the fact that even a 28-cm shell pierces 300 mm armour from 4000 meters (with a normal impact), Admiral Tirpitz considers the 230 mm belt to be extremely weak, especially bearing in mind Italian 305 mm guns. Based on the results of artillery and torpedo experiments conducted by the Kaiser fleet, the following suggestions can also be added: the slant of the armoured deck, which closes to the edge of the main side belt, should be taken so as far as possible; the armoured bilge anti-torpedo bulkhead should be tilted inward and the second longitudinal bulkhead outward. The distance of the anti-torpedo bulkhead from the outer side must be increased from 2.5 to 4 m."

Koudelka had brought with him to Germany the plans made by STT and he showed them to Tirpitz, seeking his opinion. Tirpitz having examined the Austrian design advised that the proposed armament of twelve 12-inch (305 mm) guns mounted within twin turrets was too much for the planned 20,000-ton displacement. He proposed reducing the number of turrets by one, thereby reducing the 12 main calibre weapons in number to 10. He also advised the reducing the armour thickness but in turn thickening the armoured belt. In addition, he considered the planned torpedo protection of the ships to be defective, the importance of which he specifically called to Koudelka's attention. The Grand Admiral also advised the Austrian Captain to strengthen the underwater protection and to increase the displacement of the ships to 21,000 tons. A century later, Koudelka's top secret report that he handed to Montecuccoli is still a secret. Its often speculated, how much of the contents Montecuccoli shared with Popper.

On his return to Austria, Koudelka recounted Tirpitz's advice to Siegfried Popper, who chose to simply ignored the information, but the German advice was, despite Popper's efforts at least partly accepted with portions of the armour increased to between 290 and 300 mm. The increased sizes represented the maximum capacity of the Austro-Hungarian shipyards. Popper was to continue to push for his own ideas and went on to threaten his resignation. Unfortunately for the success of the Austrian Dreadnought design and for their crews in 1918, he remained in post.

Having seen the German advice and experience he brought back from Berlin dismissed, Koudelka learnt that two days prior to his meeting with Tirpitz, the basic *Tegetthoff* design had already been passed on the 27th April 1909. In the same month Montecuccoli's memorandum to the Emperor was to find its way into the Italian newspapers, causing a hysteria amongst both the Italian population and their politicians. The Italian Government made use of the leaked report for initiating their own Dreadnought program and for an allocation for the navy of the funds it would require.

Then on the 9th June 1909, the requirement of the Austro-

Hungarian contest was amended with the proposed displacement now increased to 20,500 tons, and the main guns of the 30.5 cm L/45 calibre were altered to the 50 calibre version due to a number of errors in the construction process. The secondary guns were now to be of 15 (5.9-inch) and 7 cm (2.75-inch), with the armour belt increased by 40 mm (1 9/16-inch) to 280 mm (11.23-inch). Four propulsion steam turbines with auxiliary oil-fired boilers next to the coal ones were selected. Popper was to submit a further six proposals a few weeks later with variations in the tripod or pole-mast. Finally, design "F" was to be selected.

Two engineers, Franz Pitzinger and Theodor Novotny were also to present their own drawings in the spring of 1910 when the original deadline was due to expire. But unknown to them, the detailed designs of the Popper Plans had been completed the year prior in November, and a contract had been signed with STT for the construction of two ships. The designs of Pitzinger and Novotny were buried away in the vaults of the archives, but they were to receive cash compensation for their work.

Finally on the 6th June, the Italian Dreadnought 'A' (the future *Dante Alighieri*) was laid down at the naval shipyard in Castellammare di Stabia and as a result the Austrian C-in-C predicted that there would be no difficulty in obtaining the required funds in the 1910 budget (due to be discussed in November 1909). Two of the *Radetzky* class Pre-Dreadnoughts had been launched by this stage, freeing two slips for the Dreadnoughts and STT needed the additional contracts to endure the retention of their force of skilled workers. In August 1909, Montecuccoli suggested that maybe, while the Government struggled to resolve the budgetary issues, STT and Škoda might like to start the construction process at their own expense (and risk). When for political reasons the Dreadnought funds were refused, Montecuccoli embarked on an elaborate campaign of deception to disguise the fact that the ships were to be built without any Parliamentary approval. He claimed, erroneously, that the ship building industry was financing the construction on pure speculation and the shipyards were very uneasy with the situation. It wasn't until Montecuccoli took a 12 million Crown (£12,559,526 at 1914 or £1,377,228,920 at 2017 prices) credit on his own responsibility that the keels of Dreadnought 'IV' and 'V' were laid down on 24th July, (*Viribus Unitis*) and 24th September 1910, (*Tegetthoff*).

Even the selection of names for the Empire's Dreadnoughts was to be anything but simple. The Navy had suggested: *Tegetthoff, Prinz Eugen* and *Don Juan Hunyadi.* But Archduke Franz Ferdinand wanted to name the final ship of the class, the *Laudon.* But opposition from the Hungarians was strong as they had footed part of the exorbitant cost of the ships. The Hungarian Parliament expected that as a reward at least one of the ships would receive a name of Hungarian origin as this was a common practice in the Austro-Hungarian Navy *(Budapest, Zrínyi, Árpád* etc). The debate over the name of the fourth ship saw the proposal of: *Corvin Mátyás* (after Matthias Corvinus). *Szent István* (after St. Stephen, first Christian king of Hungary). *Erzsébet Királyné* (after Empress Elisabeth commonly known as Sisi). But finally, the debate was settled by the Emperor Franz Joseph I who ordered the ships named: *Viribus Unitis Tegetthoff, Prinz Eugen* and *Szent István.*

In the meantime, on the 20th August 1910, Italy had launched the *Dante Alighieri* and had already by then started construction of her second Dreadnought, the *Giulio Cesare* on the 24th June. In addition, France on the 1st September 1910 laid the keel of her first Dreadnought, (the *Courbet*) to match the Central Powers (Austro-Italian) growing Dreadnought superiority in the Mediterranean.

The finalized contracts held a number of penalty causes and in the case of Szent István these were to included:

> *"For each whole tenth node to which the test drive speed should be lower than 19.75 knots, a reduction of the delivery price of 20,000 Crowns court will enter... also excess weight is for each ton over the präliminierte Total weight of the machine complex of 1,056 t, a discount of 800 Kr. access... the warranty period is one year... The occurrence of warlike events: Should warlike events threaten or occur during the construction period, the contractor undertakes to strictly obey all instructions given to accelerate the construction of the ship and the machines from the KUK Kriegsmarine. A separate agreement will be reached on the rights and obligations that ensue, but any late drafting thereof may not affect the implementation of the acceleration referred to therein. Completion date is July 30, 1914.".*

Now that the construction of the first two Dreadnoughts had finally been committed to, Austria-Hungary had to spend around 120 million Krone (very approximately 24 kr=£1), without the approval of either the Austrian Reichsrat or the Diet of Hungary, on a deal that was to be kept secret. Montecuccoli drafted several excuses to justify the Dreadnought construction and the need to keep their existence a secret. These included the navy's urgent need to counter Italy's naval build up and desire to negotiate a lower price with their builders.

THE VIRIBUS UNITIS DURING 1913. THE STOWED BOOMS FOR HER TORPEDO NETS ARE VISIBLE ALONG THE SIDE OF THE HULL.

In April 1910 the agreement was finally leaked to the public by the newspaper of Austria's Social Democratic Party, the 'Arbeiter-Zeitung', but by then the plans had already been completed and construction on the first two Dreadnoughts was about to begin.

As the parliament debated the question of funds for new Dreadnoughts, the delegation from Hungary, (the second full member of the union) demanded that if their country's participation was wanted in the project, incentives would be 'welcome'. Hungary (a land locked country) was no longer content with supplying just food and coal for the fleet, it wanted the prestige of more. In return for agreeing to help find the extra funds now sought for the expensive project, she wanted to have her own Hungarian dreadnought. In 1905 a two and a half mile (4 Km) stretch of coast in Bergudi, (the western suburb of Fiume), was officially transferred to the Budapest company Danubius-Schonihen-Hartmann and formally proclaimed as now sovereign Hungarian territory. The following year, the transformation of the shipyard Howaldt into a major shipbuilding centre was begun. [3]

THE DANUBIUS SHIPYARD IN RIJEKA WAS CONSTRUCTED CIRCA 1909, BUILDING HUSZAR CLASS DESTROYERS AND KAIMAN CLASS TORPEDO BOATS.

To 'win' a contract for the construction of the dreadnought, the Hungarian government in 1910 began a major modernization of the Bergudi complex. This brought the merger of Danubius with a foundry and mechanical plant. With the new shipyard facilities built including a suitable sized boathouse and a commission of the Austrian Military-Technical Committee noted that the company was able now to build a modern capital ship. Even if the estimated construction time was 12 to 15 months longer than that of S.T.T. The sought-after contract was signed on 26th November 1911 but with a special clause. It stipulated the construction of the dreadnought was only to be made from materials of Hungarian production, *"if they are in the right quantity and quality."*

The two Austrian Dreadnoughts, *Viribus Unitis* and *Tegetthoff*, were already into the early stages of construction, when the joint Parliamentary bodies met in March 1911 to discuss that year's budget.[4] In his memoirs, former Austrian Field Marshal and Chief of the General Staff Conrad von Hötzendorf, (the man who, three years later, would push the Emperor to permit Serbia no leeway and ultimately to declare war), wrote that due to his belief in a future war with Italy, construction on the Dreadnoughts should begin as soon as possible. He also worked on a plan to sell the Dreadnought, in his words, to a "reliable ally" (which could only be Germany), should the budget crisis fail to be resolved in short order. But ultimately in 1911, the Austro-Hungarian Parliaments agreed to Montecuccoli's action and even added two more ships to the plan, the future *Prinz Eugen* and *Szent István*.

THE TEGETTHOFF CLASS.

PREVIOUS PAGE: THE EDITION OF THE 'ARBEITER-ZEITUNG' ("THE WORKERS NEWSPAPER) OF 14TH APRIL 1910, WHICH WAS TO BREAK THE STORY OF THE

SECRET FUNDING AGREEMENT FOR THE HAPSBURG DREADNOUGHTS

[1] *Viribus Unitis: meaning With United Forces, was the personal motto of Emperor Franz Joseph I. Tegetthoff: Wilhelm von Tegetthoff (23rd December 1827 to 7th April 1871) was an Austrian Admiral who had commanded the fleet of the North Sea during the Second Schleswig War of 1864 and the Australasian War of 1866. He is regarded as one of the better naval officers of the 19th century, due to his tactical inventiveness, ability to command and an inspirational leadership. Prinz Eugen: Prince Eugene of Savoy (18th October 1663 to 21st April 1736) was a general of the Imperial Army and statesman of the Holy Roman Empire and the Archduchy of Austria and one of the most successful military commanders in modern European history, rising to the highest offices of state at the Imperial court in Vienna. Szent István: Stephen I, also known as King Saint Stephen, was the last Grand Prince of the Hungarians between 997 and 1000 or 1001 and the first King of Hungary from 1000 or 1001 until his death in 1038.*

[1a] "Fiume in that times was part of Hungary, and not Croatia, as a „

"Separatum Corpus" attached directly to the Hungarian Crown, created by Empress Maria Theresia in 1779. Half of the inhabitants were ethnic Italians, the other half Croatians. Fiume between 1924-1945 was part of Italy. In 1945 the Italian inhabitants of the city were expelled or killed by the Yugoslav partisans. Before 1918 de jure Fiume was a Hungarian port". (Krámli Mihály)

THE TEGETTHOFF CLASS.

[1b] Until 1911 the shipyard's name was Danubius Hajó- és Gépgyár Rt. After the fusion with the Ganz Gépgyár, the name was changed to Ganz és Társa, Danubius Gép-, Waggon- és Hajógyár, or shorter in English Ganz and Co., Danubius. The form Ganz-Danubius was the name of the shipyards of Budapest after 1985, but this is a different story.

[2] When the Germans started to design the Bayern class, they considered triple turrets. The Bayern's were to have 4 triple 12-inch guns, but the Germans changed their minds on examining the Austrians Tegetthoff set up. They concluded triple turrets were to vulnerable and to unreliable. One turret lost and you were down three guns. As a result, they reverted to twin turrets.

[3] In chronological order, first the Hungarian government agreed with the navy on the industrial orders, including a dreadnought on 31st January 1911, and after this agreement managed the fusion of the Danubius and the Ganz the main shareholder of the Danubius, the Magyar Általános Hitelbank. It's worth noting, that all the important factories of Fiume were in the hand of the Hitelbank.

[4] "Austrian and Hungarian delegations. In the Dual Monarchy the budgets of the comman army and the navy were voted by the so called delegations, two sixty member bodies elected from the Austrian Reichsrat and the Hungarian Parliament (Országgyűlés)"

CHAPTER 2: CASH AND SCHEMING

The costs to construct the new *Tegetthoff* class Dreadnoughts was by the standards of the Austro-Hungarian Navy, truly staggering! The *Habsburg, Erzherzog Karl* and the *Radetzky* classes of battleships had cost the navy approximately 18, 26 and 40 million Krone per ship. The sum totals for the Empires 1907 and 1908 Naval Budgets had been for the sums 63.4 and 73.4 million Krone, respectively. But each one of the *Tegetthoff* class was singerly to cost over 60 million Krone! Even the pre-Tegetthoff budgets had been over inflated due to the construction of the two *Radetzkys*. Montecuccoli was concerned that the public and both the legislatures in Vienna and Budapest would reject the need for the expensive ships, especially coming on the heels of the political crisis in Budapest. The Dreadnoughts meant that in 1909 the navy would have spent 100.4 million Krone, a huge sum for the time. But the looming construction of four Dreadnought meant the Austro-Hungarian Navy would likely have to ask the Government for a yearly budget much higher than 100 million Krone (£4,166,666).

In order to secure the funds for the ships from the Rothschild family in Austria, (who owned the Witkowitz Ironworks, the Creditanstalt Bank and held a number of assets in both the Škoda Works and the STT), Archduke Franz Ferdinand personally talked to Albert Salomon Anselm von Rothschild to obtain his family's financial support, until the navy could afford to buy the ships. But the funds for the *Tegetthoff* class were to be finally approved after two meetings of the Austrian Reichsrat and the Diet of Hungary in October and November 1910, with opposition having being defeated by the fact that the Italian Navy having laid down another three battleships during the summer,(*Giulio Cesare* on the 24th June, *Leonardo da Vinci* on the 18th July and the *Conti di Cavour* on the 10th August). The retroactive passage of the 1910 budget and the passage of the 1911 budget was finally won between December and March with little opposition.

The politician István Tisza had won Hungary's 1910 election, but instead chose to allow a Government to be formed under Károly Khuen-Héderváry. He then secured the budgets with his large Parliamentary majority once it was agreed that the contract for the Dreadnought that would become the *Szent István*, was to be awarded to the Ganz-Danubius shipyard in Fiume. Tisza's political allies were also secured with incentives such as being appointed to the board of directors of the Gyula Rosenberg (Adria) Shipping Line. Securing the passage of the budgets in the Austrian Reichsrat had been easier as Karel Kramář, leader of the Young Czech Party, had supported the budgets due to a *"certain weakness for the navy."*

The leader of the Slovene bloc, Ivan Šušteršič, gained support by the argument that the Dreadnoughts were in the best interests of the navy and the Slovenian people. In turn Germany's politicians supported the ships construction on the grounds that they would make Austria-Hungary a far more powerful ally for them. The final funds included clauses which ensured that while the armour and guns of the *Tegetthoff* class were to be constructed within Austria, the electrical wiring and equipment aboard each ship was to be assembled in Hungary. Additionally, half of all ammunition and shells for the Dreadnought's guns would be purchased in Austria and half was to be bought in Hungary. The only opposition was to come from the Social Democrats leader, Karl Seitz, who argued that the worsening relations with Italy in fact called for negotiations with Rome to end the Austro-Italian naval arms race. With Austria-Hungary's strained relationship with her nominal Italian ally, the proposal failed with little support outside of Seitz' party. The budgets passed both Parliaments with large majorities, ensuring that the financial questions regarding the construction of the ships were met.

CHAPTER 3: OF RUMOURS AND SPIES.

For a year, prior to the commencement of construction, the Austro-Hungarian Navy strove to keep their Dreadnought plans a state secret. But despite all their efforts, rumours were soon circulating around the Admiralties of Europe concerning two Dreadnoughts being constructed by the Empire. In 1910, the French Naval Attaché in Vienna reported to Paris of an unusually high degree of secrecy within the Austro-Hungarian Navy. In the Pola dockyard and its surrounding area, photography was to be banned once the keels were laid down and a near-constant watch by the Austro-Hungarian police was undertaken. The British Admiralty [1] on learning of the rumours, considered them to be an effort of "concealed addition[s] to the German fleet". Sir Charles Hardinge, the Permanent Under-Secretary at the Foreign Office commented:

> "I cannot help thinking that these new Austrian Dreadnoughts are intended as a thank offering to Germany for her recent support and to force us to place

Dreadnoughts in the Mediterranean and so relieve the strain [for Germany] *in the North Sea".*

Elements in Britain also believed the project to be an Austro-Hungarian method of repaying Germany for the diplomatic support the Kaiser had given them during the Habsburg annexation of Bosnia in 1908. By the Spring and summer of 1909, with the Anglo-German Naval race in full flow, the Royal Navy had come to believe that the Austrian plans were a Machiavellian scheme by the Grand-Admiral von Tirpitz to steal a lead on the British naval construction and not the starting shot in Austria-Hungary's own naval arms race with Italy, which it really was. The British Admiralty was to become so concerned as to the real motivation for the *Tegetthoff* class, that in April 1909 they dispatched their "spy" to Berlin, when Montecuccoli sent von Koudelka to obtain recommendations from Tirpitz, regarding the design and layout of the Dreadnought. In April, the British Ambassador Fairfax Leighton Cartwright asked the Austro-Hungarian Foreign Minister Alois Lexa von Aehrenthal outright about the rumoured Dreadnought. Aehrenthal denied that the project even existed but did admit that plans to construct a new class of Pre-Dreadnought were being considered. To persuade the Ambassador that Austria-Hungary had no plans to construct any ships for the German Navy, Aehrenthal justified that any future naval expansion was required to secure Austria-Hungary's strategic place within the Mediterranean. The British newspapers, politicians and public considered that any Dreadnought construction by Austria-Hungary was the Machiavellian scheming on the part of Germany. On Churchill's appointment as the First Lord of the Admiralty in 1911, he rejected any potential Austria-German collusion regarding the project.

A year after *Szent István's* plans were completed, the newspaper Arbeiter-Zeitung, published the details of the project.

THE TEGETTHOFF CLASS.

The Christian Social Party was a supporter of the construction of four Dreadnoughts and on the advice of the navy, published in its own newspaper, the Reichpost, that the secret project to construct the ship and the related financial agreements to fund it were true. The Reichpost tried to generate public support for the project, using the Austro-Hungarian fears over the Italian Dreadnought then already under construction. When the story finally broke, Archduke Ferdinand and the Austrian Naval League both worked to help build the public support for the construction of the ships.

[1] The Austro-Hungarian navy had no Admiralty. Hermann von Spaun proposed in 1900 to create one, but Franz Joseph rejected the proposal. (Krámli Mihály)

PART TWO: THE SHIPS

*THE PRIDE OF THE AUSTRO-HUNGARIAN FLEET LEAVING HARBOUR.
(IMAGE CREDIT ANDREW WILKIE WWW.VIRIBUSUNITIS.CA)*

CHAPTER 1: THE SZENT ISTVÁN & VIRIBUS UNITIS.
(COPYWRITE ANDREW WILKIE)

THE TEGETTHOFF CLASS.

THE VIRIBUS UNITIS FROM HER PORT-SIDE.

THE VIRIBUS UNITS AT ANCHOR.

A FULL LENGTH VIEW OF THE VIRIBUS UNITIS LOOKING FROM HER PORT BOW TOWARDS THE STERN.

A VIEW ALONG THE SZENTI ISTVÁN'S STARBOARD BEAM TOWARDS HER STERN.

THE TEGETTHOFF CLASS.

THE BOW AND STERN PROFILE

A VIEW FROM THE SZENTI ISTVÁN'S STERN ALONG THE PORT-REAR-QUARTER

PARTIAL SHIP STERN DECK LEVEL FORWARD TURRETS III AND IV

THE TEGETTHOFF CLASS.

PARTIAL SHIP BOW STRAIGHT ON ANCHORS

CHAPTER 2: DESIGN, DIMENSION, DISPLACEMENT & POWER

The creation of the four *Tegetthoff* dreadnoughts was a signal to the world of a dramatic change within the Empire's naval policy, bringing a new generation of warships that were to be capable of more than just their predecessors coastal defence role. Nor where they just to be limited to simply patrolling the Empire's local waters, the Adriatic Sea [1]. They were to be a projection of the Empires 'Super-Power' status and a sign of her embracing of all that was modern and new. As such they were generally well received within the Empire and her Germanic allies. But a ships reputation is built of two elements, a combination of their history and the nuts, bolts and rivets that go together to make the craft.

THE TEGETTHOFF CLASS.

[1] Interestingly they lacked the steaming range to cross the Atlantic from the Austro-Hungarian naval base in Pola and would need to take on coal in a port such as Gibraltar before venturing out into the ocean.

THE HULL

THE AUSTRO-HUNGARIAN NAVAL ENSIGN (1786-1915)

The hulls of the three "Austrian" *Tegetthoff*'s (*Viribus Unitis, Tegetthoff* and *Prinz Eugen*) were 498 ft 8 inches (152 mtrs) in their overall length, with a beam of 91 feet 6 inches (27.90 mtrs) and a draught of 28 ft 7 inches (8.70 mtrs) at deep load. The *Szent István* was 7 inches longer (18 cm) with a length of 499 feet 3 inches (152.18 mtrs), a beam of 91 feet 10 inches (28 mtrs) and a draught of 28 feet 3 inches (8.6 mtrs). The hull was comprised of 216 frames in its overall length.

THE TEGETTHOFF CLASS.

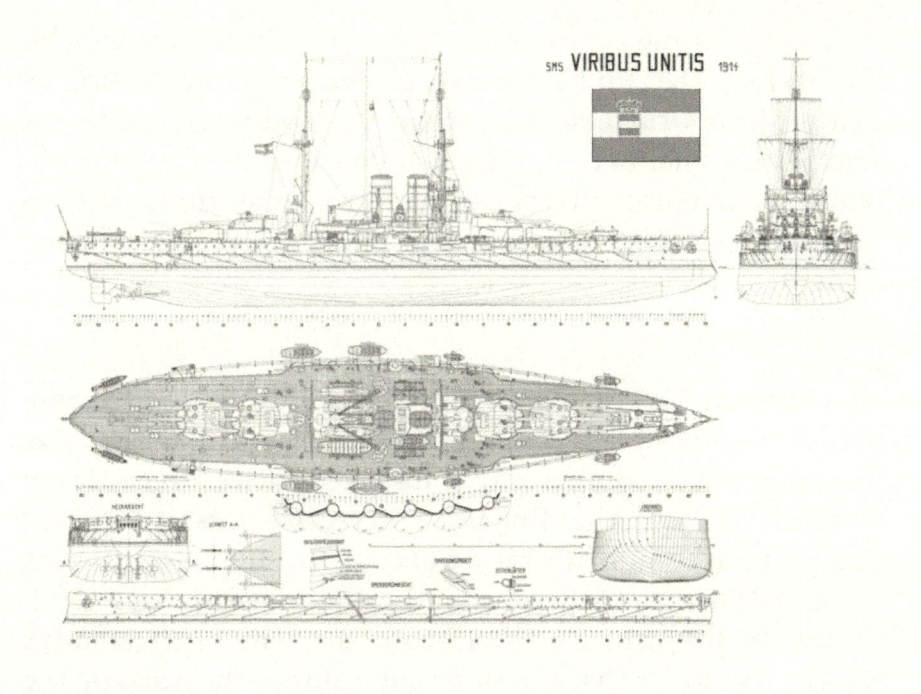

COPYWRITE: FRIEDRICH PRASKY

The three "Austrian" hulls displacements were 19,684 long tons (20,000 tonnes) [1] at standard and 21,346 long tons (21,689 tonnes) at deep load. The seven-inch longer *Szent István* was in turn 19,692 long tons (20,008 tonnes) in standard displacement and 21,346 long tons (21,689 tonnes) at deep load. The ships had three main deck levels (upper, middle, and lower) but with an increase in the thickness of some deck areas, and the upper deck benefited from a teak wood covering. Both measures that were designed to reduce the impact of shells.

The battle to reduce the size and weight within the Tegetthoff's and yet build a powerful class of ship was one to be fought out on the designer's board. During the convoluted design phase, the fire power had been upgraded with the untried

41

concept of triple turrets, to retain a hefty broadside weight, but to keep the ships overall displacement down. Fitting 12 barrels into 4 turrets, rather than 6 two-gun turrets, meant that with a smaller hull, a heavy broadside could still be provided. With triple turrets came fewer over all turret weight, less armour and less supporting machinery, all of which saved weight.

In a further effort to save on tonnage the ships were to be constructed without a raised forecastle deck, which was to give the hulls, (when compared to ships fitted with a forecastle) an extremely poor sea holding capability. Once the ship had been loaded with her full allocation of coal and supplies (totalling about 1,476 tons/1,500 tonnes), the draft increased by an additional 15 3/4 inches (0.4 mtrs) to 28 feet 7 inches (8.70 mtr). On the few times that the ships put out into the Adriatic the draft was to rarely exceed 18.53 feet (5.65 meters). But soon after they commenced their trials, it became apparent that under a full load the bow would drop by about 9 3/4 inches (0.25 meters), which led to it burying itself into the oncoming waves. This in turn forced a reduction in speed to be ordered and all the decks hatches that lay between the conning tower and the bow to be securely battened down. It became almost impossible to make use of the forward turrets and the 2 19/32 inches (66-mm) deck gun under heavy sea conditions. In addition, a ram was built within the bows profile, but the obsolete device was only to serve to reduce their speed further and make steering more difficult. The superstructure was kept small and low to make the ships less visible and harder to hit in combat, their size almost making them a form of coastal-defence dreadnoughts.

THE TEGETTHOFF CLASS.

THE TEGETTHOFF CLASS AT THEIR POLA ANCHORAGES IN 1915.

The German dreadnought designers had chosen to omit watertight doors below the waterline of their dreadnoughts, a concept that they had advised their Austrian allies to adopt. This lack of below waterline doors resulted in the German crew having to use 'ladders' to access the nearest watertight door when moving horizontally through the hull. But despite the sage Germanic advice, watertight doors were fitted beneath the waterline on the Austro-Hungarian ships. To compound matters the bulkhead walls were pierced by numerous pipes and fittings, many with inferior seals, which resulted in watertight compartments being especially not sealed. The ship even included an ash-lift shaft running from the lower deck to just below the upper deck, which would create a convenient route for flood waters to ingress higher decks. It created an open shaft running the depth of the hull with no horizontal deck hatches.

Finally, before we move on to other matters, there was a large degree of post war criticism defining the hulls as being both small and cramped. The critics pointed out that the vessels lacked an adequate range and their lack of stability. The negative voices went on to note the class suffered from bad workmanship [2] and with the *Szent István* was the riveting was described as sub-standard. The poor riveting would be cited was a potential cause for the leakages that doom the ship in 1918.

THE TEGETTHOFF CLASS.

THE VIRIBUS UNITS

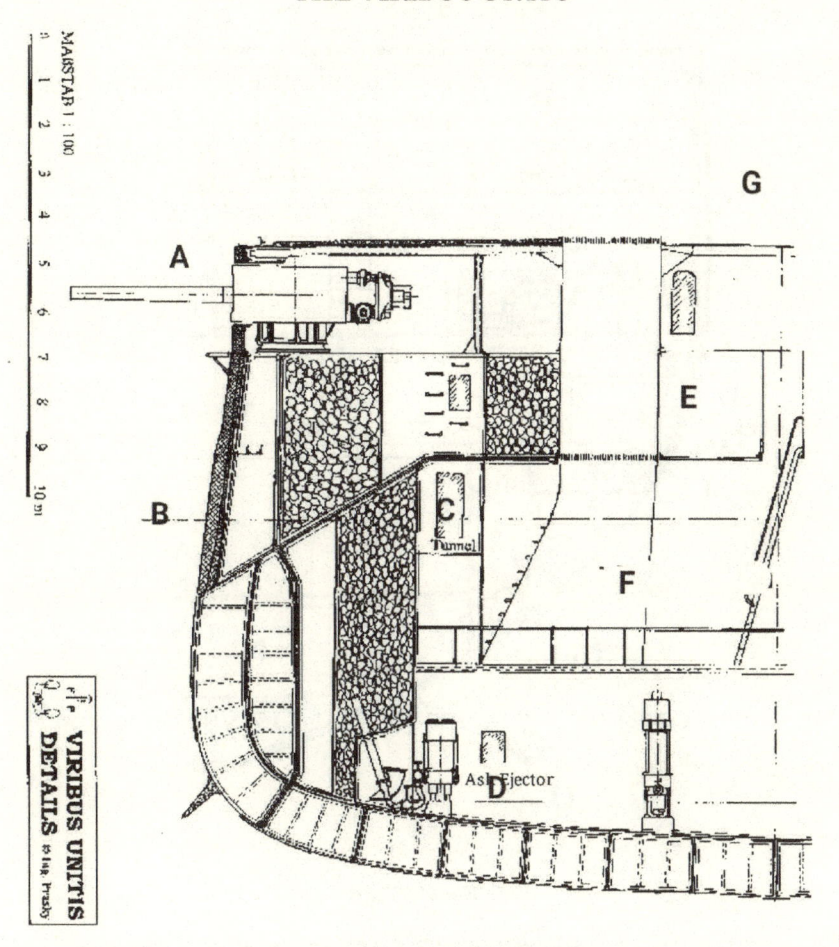

SECTION 28 FORWARD.

A= 15 CM CASEMENT. B= WATERLINE. C= TUNNEL. D= ASH EJECTOR. E= BAKERY. F= FRONT BOILER ROOM. G= 1ST CLASS GIG. H= TOWING. I= QUARTERS J= ADMIRALS SERVING ROOM. K= CABIN. L= STORAGE. M= WATERLINE. N= ADMIRALS STORES. O= TILLER LINK P= 150 MM

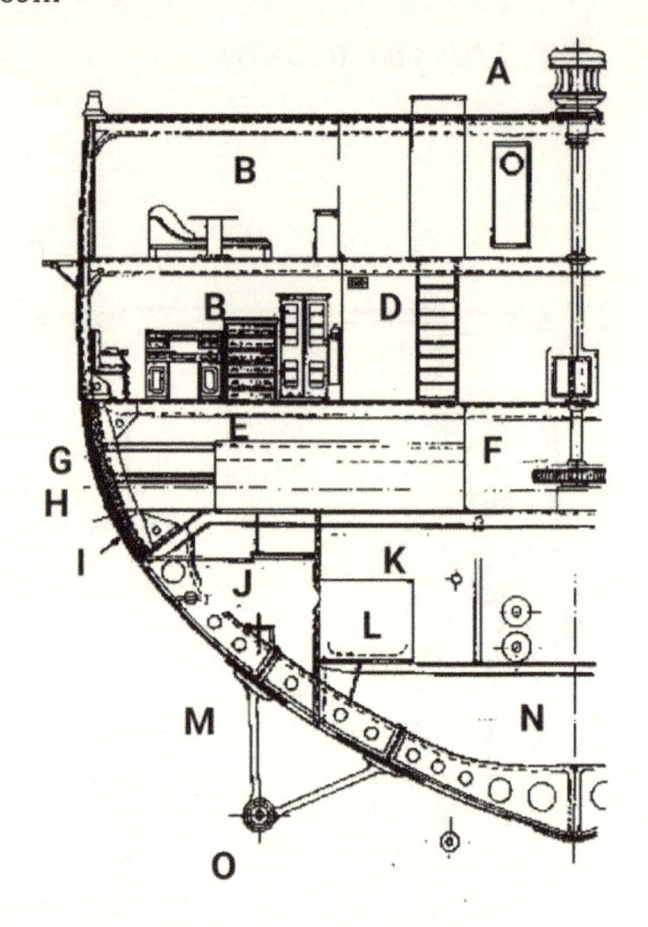

SECTION 89 STERN

A= "STERN SPILL. B= "APARTMENT SENIOR K.U.K YOUR HIGHNESS" (THIS WAS JUST TOO GOOD TO AMEND). C=CHIEF MACHINE OFFICER. D= "CHRONOMETER". E= CAPTAINS STORES. F= "SPILL MACHINERY". G= WATERLINE. H= 150 MM. I= TEAK. J= TORPEDO STORE. K= "PIN & TAIL LANCE" (TORPEDO BODIES?). L= TORPEDO HEADS. M= SHAFT SUPPORT. N= TRIM TANK. O= OUTER SKIN 0.5 INCH (12.5 MM) THICK.

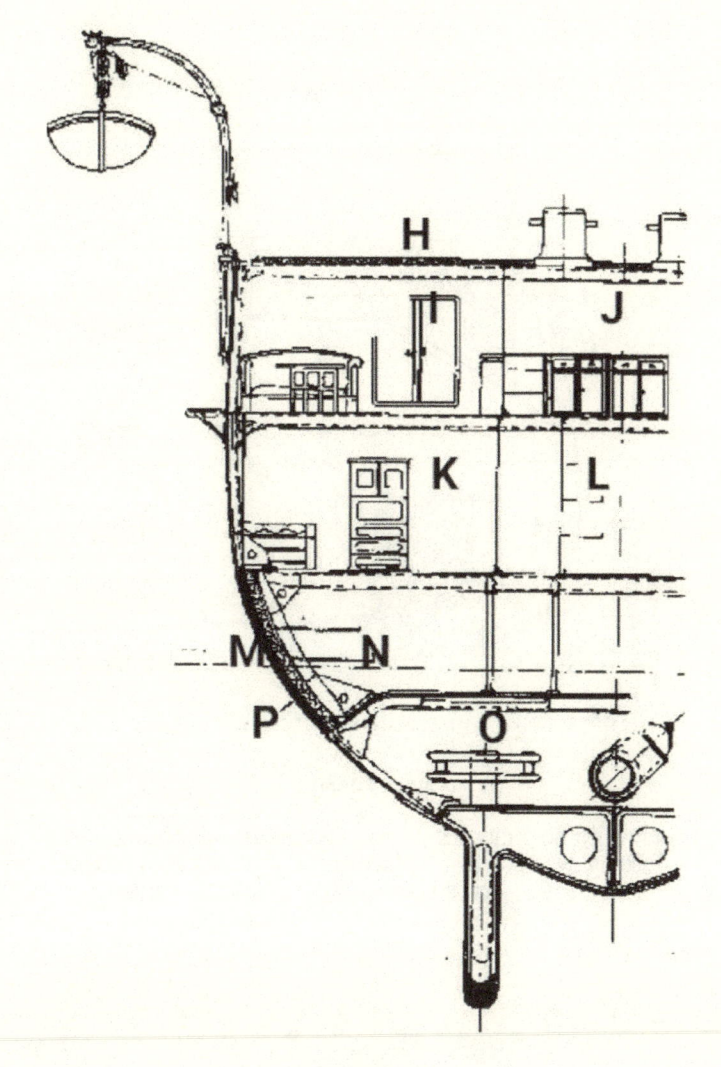

THE TEGETTHOFF CLASS.

SECTION 28.
A= 15 CM CASEMENT. B= WATERLINE. C= TUNNEL. D= ASH EJECTOR. E= BAKERY. F= FRONT BOILER ROOM. G= 1ST CLASS GIG. H= TOWING. I= QUARTERS J= ADMIRALS SERVING ROOM. K= CABIN. L= STORAGE. M= WATERLINE. N= ADMIRALS STORES. O= TILLER LINK P= 150 MM.

ANDY SOUTH

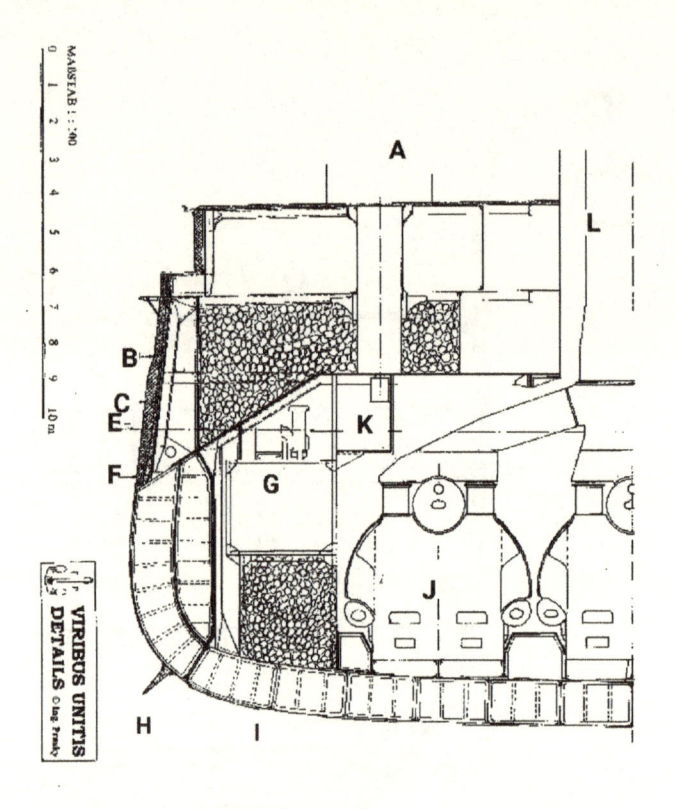

MAIN FRAME

A= 13 TONNE BOAT CRANES. B= 180 C= WATERLINE. D= COAL BUNKERS
E= 280 MM F= 170 MM G= 15 CM MAGAZINE. H= ROLL KEEL. I= OUTER
SKIN 16 MM. J= AFT BOILER ROOM. K= TUNNEL. L= FUNNEL.

THE TEGETTHOFF CLASS.

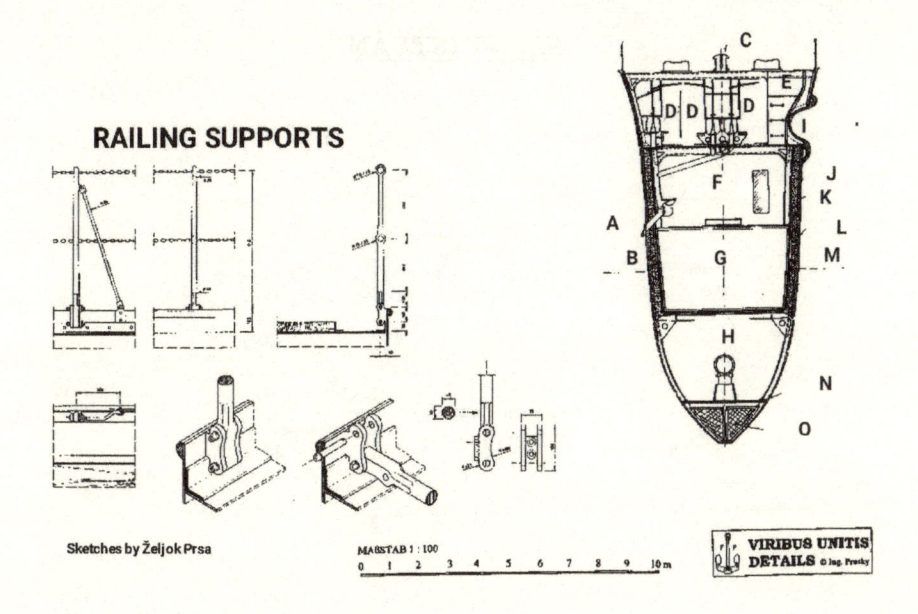

RAILING SUPPORTS

Sketches by Željok Prsa

SECTION 102

KEY A= WC OR TOILET. B= WATER LINE. C= VENTILATION. D=WC. E= STORAGE. F= BATHROOM. G= STORAGE. H= TORPEDO ROOM. I= STEEL GUIDE BLOCKS. J= 110 CM KC. L= TEAK RESERVE. M= 150 MM KC. N= WATER LINE. O= EXERCISE CELL (?)

P= DECK COVERINGS: DECK PLANKS TEAK WOOD 125 MM WIDE, 65 MM DEPTH. IN THE AREA OF THE CHAIN ANCHORS 200 KM WIDE 80 KM DEPTH. UNDER THE CHAIN ANCHORS CHECKER PLATE REINFORCEMENT. DECK AROUND THE BOW: CHECKER PLATE BRIDGES WITH LINOLEUM COVERING IN SIENNA BROWN.

SZENT ISTVÁN

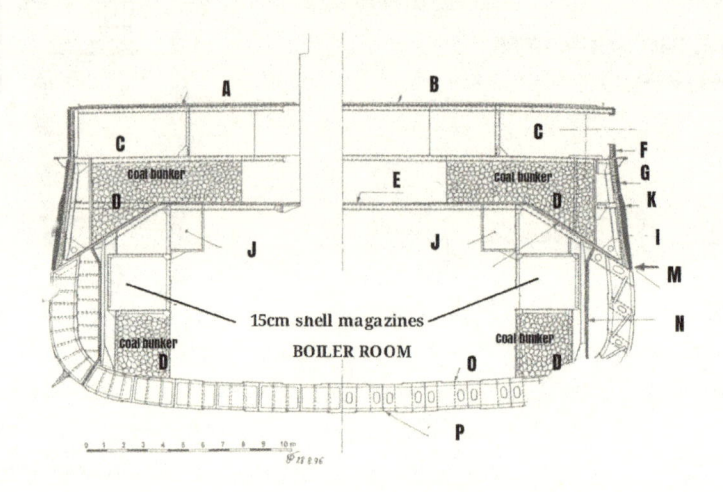

A= 15+15 MM SP. B=89 MM TEAK DECK. C= 15 CM GUN. D= COAL BUNKER. E= 18+18 MM SP. F= 180 MM KC. G= 180 MM KC. I= 180 MM KC. J= PASSAGE. K= 280 MM KC. M=TORPEDO STRIKE (1.5 MTRS DEPTH). N= 25+25 MM S. O=10 MM. P= 16 MM.

[1] A long ton is the imperial (or British) weight and is used in the United Kingdom Interestingly the long ton was the unit set by the Washington Naval Treaty of 1922 as standard for warships, so for example battleships were limited to a displacement of 35,000 long tons (36,000 t; 39,000 short tons). Long ton = 2240 lbs Metric tonne = 2204.62 lbs. Short ton = 2000 lbs.

[2] A claim that was not unique and one that was even levelled against the namesake of the concept, H.M.S Dreadnought the British.

MACHINERY

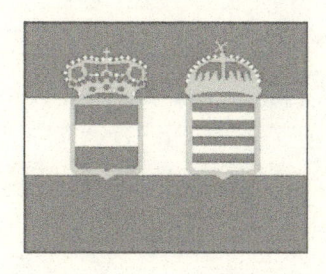

THE AUSTRO-HUNGARIAN NAVAL ENSIGN (1915-1918)

The propulsion units of the first three vessels, (*Viribus Unitis, Tegetthoff* and *Prinz Eugen*), were comprised of four CCT Parsons steam turbines. The turbines were powered from twelve thin tube USA manufactured Babcock & Wilcox double boilers and and all manufactured in the Austrian and the Hungarian shipyards, respectively, under licence. They were designed to produce a total of 25,000 shaft horsepower (20,134 kw). The boilers operated at a steam pressure of 18.5 ATM with a total heating area of 52,784.06 ft2 (4,903.8 mtr2) and were in two groups of six within two boiler rooms.

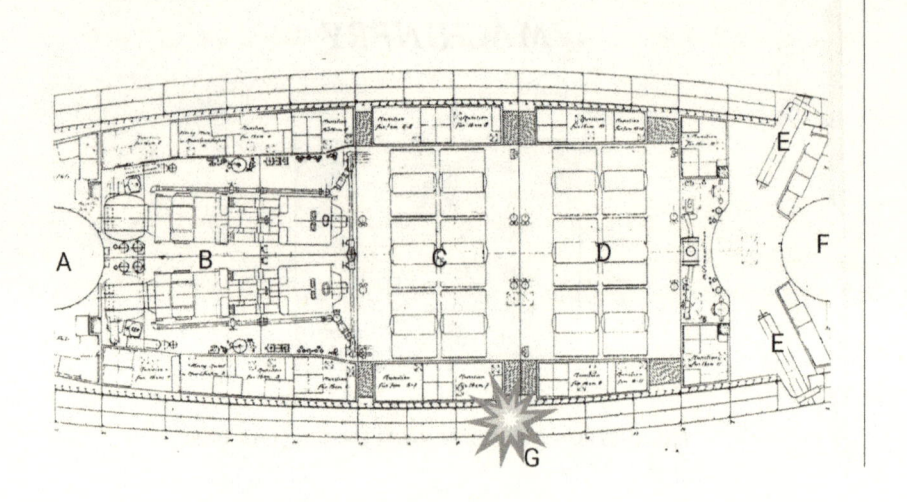

SZENT ISTVÁN
THE BOILER & ADJOINING MACHINERY SPACES.
A= AFT TURRET BARBETTE= TURBINE ROOM. D= BOILER ROOM NO 1. E= BOILER ROOM NO 2. E= TORPEDO TUBES. F= FORWARD TURRET BARBETTE. G= POINT

The turbines of the three ships in turn drove four propellers which was on the design board sufficient for the ships to reach their planned speed of 20.30 knots, In service they had an estimated fuel consumption of 19.93 tons (20.25 tonnes) per hour at full speed.

THE TEGETTHOFF CLASS.

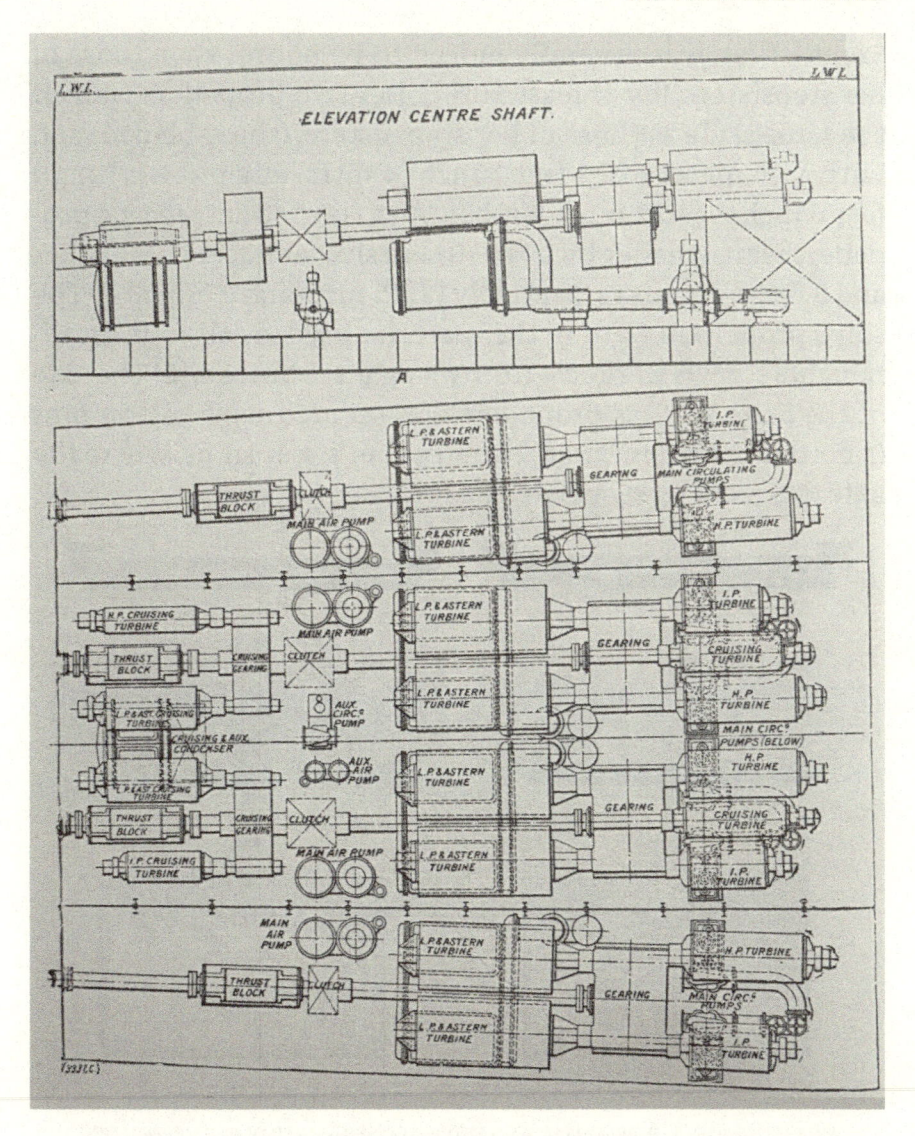

"INSTALLATION OF PARSONS GEARED TURBINES FOR BATTLESHIPS. (REPRODUCED FROM ENGINEERING BY PERMISSION OF THE EDITOR)" SOURCE: BEATYS NAVAL ANNUAL 1913.

The *Szent István* differed from her classmates in having only two steam turbines, two shafts and consequently two propellers (Ø 4.0 mtr). Unfortunately, the performance records for the speed trials were to be lost in the chaos that followed the post-war collapse of the Empire. But the shaft design for the

Szent István was generally judged to be poorer than those of her stepsisters, [by at least 50%?]. Her two propellers were of the same style as those of her step-sisters, (three-bladed) and with a diameter of 13 feet 1 inch (4 mtrs) at a pitch [1] of 10 feet 6 inches (3.22 mtr). But her "Austrian" counterparts' propellers were smaller by over 30% in size, at 9 feet 0.26 inches and 8 feet 6 inches respectively (2.75 mtrs and 2/60 mts). The ships propellers were in the material used, as all four dreadnoughts screws were cast from manganese bronze. [2] The axle of the *Szent István's* propellers was secured with piston pins (a bolted joining method), whereas her sister ships, where the axle was fixed by suspended beams.

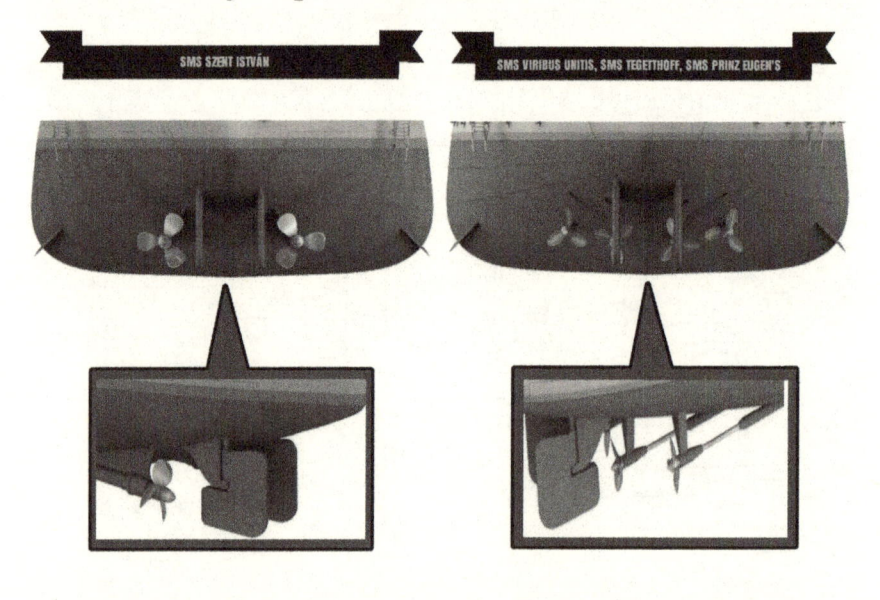

PREVIOUS PAGE. THE PROPELLER AND RUDDER CONFIGURATION. THE DIFFERENCE BETWEEN THE PROPELLER AND RUDDER DESIGN CAN BE CLEARLY SEEN.

After STT had purchased the Parsons Turbine license, Ganz-Danubius were forced to look for another source and finally opted for the German AEG-Curtis Turbines. *Szent István's* turbines were unlike her stepsisters, supplied by 12 Babcock & Wilcox boilers with a total power that was designed to be 25,000 shp, (all four vessels were designed for the same shp).

THE TEGETTHOFF CLASS.

The boiler water capacity was for 168 tons. The *Szent István's* boilers were 47.24 tons (48 tonnes) heavier than the British built Yarrow model built into the "Austrian" *Tegetthoffs*, but they worked more efficiently. The new drive had the advantage of allowing the ships speed to be maintained for an eight-hour period, while in the other units of the class, it was only possible for two hours. The class had two parallel semi-balanced rudders installed on the same line as the two inner shafts, but a few feet nearer the stern. The largest angle of deviation of the rudders from the diametrical plane was 35 degrees on each side. The *Szent István's* rudder placement differed from her stepsister propellers with her rudder and propeller not being in direct line of each other. The placement of her rudders was believed to have compounded the manoeuvrability of the ship, making her a harder vessel to control as compared to her three counterparts. Due to this "shear (transversal) resistance", the rudder could only be turned to an extreme of 15 degrees at her maximum speed if tilting of the ship were to be avoided. As a result, after her sea trials, sudden and more extreme changes of course were to be forbidden. A restriction no captain commanding a fighting warship would ever wish for!

They bunkered 1,844.5 tonnes (1,815.4 long tons) of coal, (or 1519.0 tonnes of Nixon coal briquettes). The Navy had introduced the use of briquettes for coal-fired capital ships since it was *"already of the ideal size of the eyes"* and it didn't require breaking up in the boiler room, before it was introduced to the fire causing less coal dust. [3] In addition 267.2 tonnes (263.0 long tons) of fuel oil was carried. This was sprayed on to the coal to increase its burn rate, a practice that was universal in the world's navies.

FOUR IMAGES OF THE PROPELLERS TAKEN FROM ANDREW WILKIE'S MODEL.
(THE FIGURE IS AN APPROXIMATION)

During the final series of her full power trial runs on the 15th April 1913, the *Tegetthoff*, (with a displacement of 20,280 tons, a shaft power of 24,300 hp and running at 164 revolutions per minute) developed a speed of 20.3 knots, almost reaching her design specifications. All three ships with CTT machines produced similar results with *Viribus Unitis* achieving 20.41 knots at 20,275 tons, (27,200 hp) on the 18th September 1912. The *Prinz Eugen* in turn reached 20.28 knots at 20,373 tons, (26,200 hp). These figures show the class failed in their captains' quest to achieve the sought-after design speed of 20.5 knots while operating with a shaft power of 25,000 HP. In theory this could be explained by a lack of experienced stokers at the time that the ships entered service. But during their few years of commission, the ships were never to realistically achieve their design speed.

The full power trial records for the Szent István's on the 21st November 1915 still exists. The record is a printed document (a form) of a few pages with many text and dotted lines to have been completed with the actual data (power, speed, boiler room temperatures, etc.). The person who filled this form in after the trial (with pencil) oddly enough didn't recorded the speed (average maximum speed) attained during the trial. At the same time the usual table with the speeds attained on different courses in the canale di Fasana, (Fasana channel) is missing.

However, several (unspecified) documents note that the ship was *"constantly lagging behind"* when the class put to sea, which reflects on the operation of her propulsion system. The electric demand on-board was met by four turbo-generators with a capacity of 300 kW and a voltage of 120 V. There was in addition one diesel generator of 75 kW. The ship had a powerful drainage system with a total capacity of 6000 tons per hour.

As previously noted, the classes design speed was a fraction over 20 knots. Due to her more efficient boilers the Szent István could maintain the maximum speed for eight hours. Her sisters could maintain their maximum speed for two hours only. When the fleet was returning from the bombardment of Ancona, the Viribus Unitis couldn't exceed 17.5 knots despite every effort of the stokers.

[1] The pitch of a propeller is defined as "the distance a propeller would move in one revolution if it were moving through a soft solid, like a screw through wood." For example, a 21-pitch propeller would move forward 21 inches in one revolution.

[2] Manganese Bronze. Manganese bronzes are a group of high strength copper-based alloys that include manganese as an alloying agent and high levels of zinc. They are characterized by high strength and hardness. This grade provides tensile strength to 110,000 psi and hardness well over 200 BHN.

[3] The Russian author S. E. Vinogradov cites the bunker capacity as 1148.1 tons of normal coal, which could be replaced by Nixon coal briquettes with a total weight of 1400.4 tons. He adds that with the spare bunkers, the amount of fuel could be increased to 1536 tons of coal or 1871 tons of Nixon briquettes. He quotes 'the official code of the battleship weights for normal cargo', as stating the figure of 1563.3 tons for coal. In addition, he adds the ships received 162.6 tons of oil each (for spraying over a burning layer of coal when moving at full speed).

CHAPTER 3: GUNS, TORPEDOES AND MINES.

30.5 CM MAIN ARMAMENT

ADMIRAL (1894-1915)

The four Austro-Hungarian dreadnoughts had one sole purpose in life, to deliver their main armament to pre-determined locations throughout the Mediterranean and everything onboard was either secondary or supportive to those main weapons.

To fulfil this projection of a 'Great Power' the ships carried twelve 30.5 centimetre (12.008 inch) 45 calibre Škoda K10 guns mounted into four triple super-firing turrets. The K10's calibre was exactly 12.305-mm, but for simplicity, (as with all her armaments) it was rounded up when referred to. Two of the turrets fired forward with the second turret of the pair mounted on a higher level, to permit it to fire over its lower neighbour. This 'super-firing' arrangement (a USA innovation on the *USS Michigan* in 1908) was in turn repeated with the stern turrets. The system gave the Gunnery Officer on each ship 6 guns firing forward, 6 astern and a full broadside of 12 on each beam.

THE TEGETTHOFF CLASS.

THE TWO BOW TURRETS, ONE TRAINED TO PORT AND THE OTHER TO STARBOARD. THE CURVED METAL PLATES TO EITHER SIDE OF THE TURRETS GUN BARREL ARE TO GUIDE THE EMPTY SHELL CASINGS CLEAR OF THE TURRET, AS THE CREW EJECT THEM.

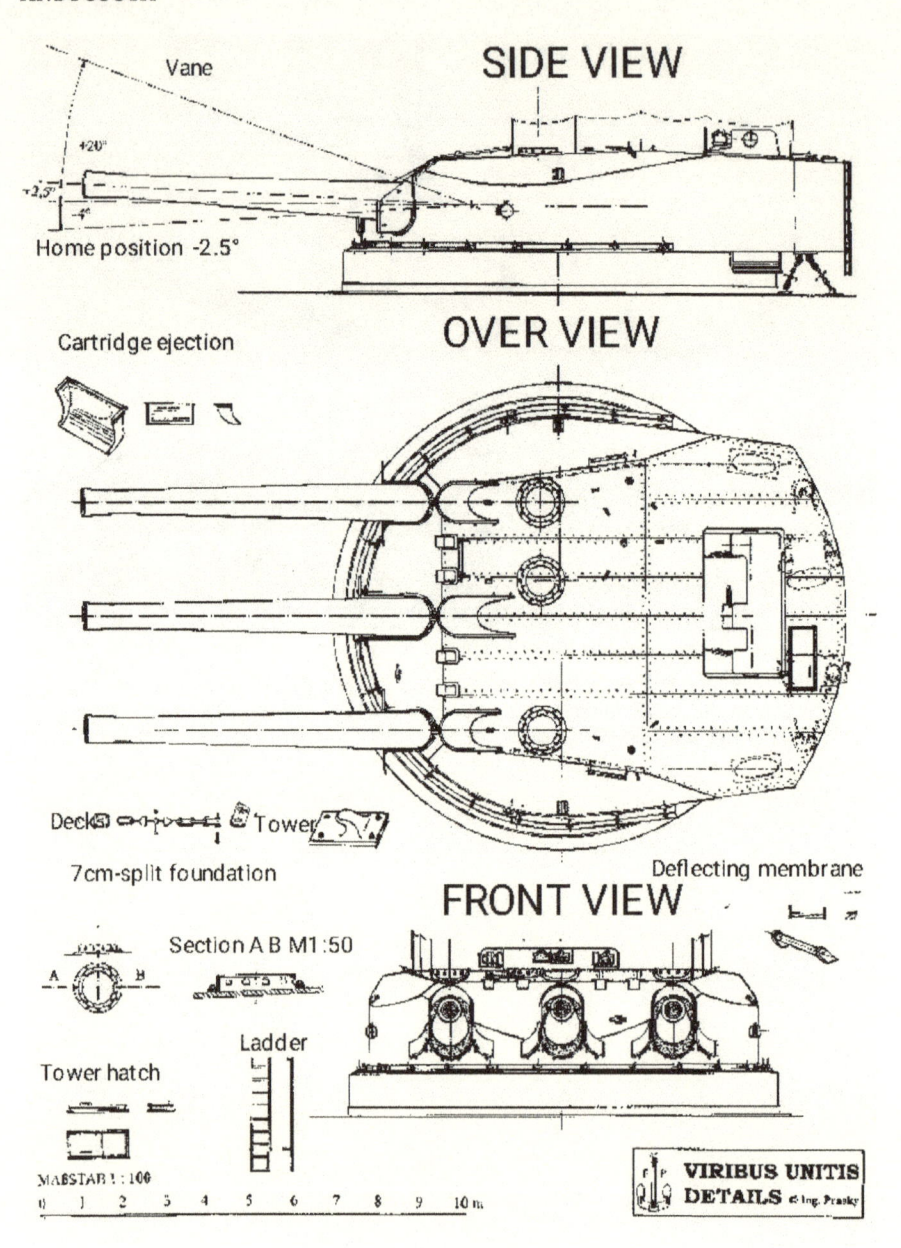

PREVIOUS PAGE TURRETS I & IV

THE TEGETTHOFF CLASS.

THE SZENT ISTVAN CONDUCTING GUNNERY PRACTICE.

The weapons had been manufactured in the Škoda's Works in Pilsen, Bohemia and they were to be the last such weapons to be produced at the plant. Škoda was to produce in total sixty-five of the guns, five of which were retained as spares. Thirteen of the remaining total were destined for the pre-dreadnought *Radetzky* class and the residual fifty-two, (the K10 or 'second series'), were for the *Tegetthoff* class.

OVERVIEW OF TURRETS II & III

"Basic" position 2.5°

Panel cover turrets I to IV (A)

Ladder turrets II & III

Pedestal turrets II & III

Chains turrets II & III

MAßSTAB 1:100
0 1 2 3 4 5 6 7 8 9 10 m

VIRIBUS UNITIS DETAILS © Ing. Prasky

PREVIOUS PAGE TURETS II & III

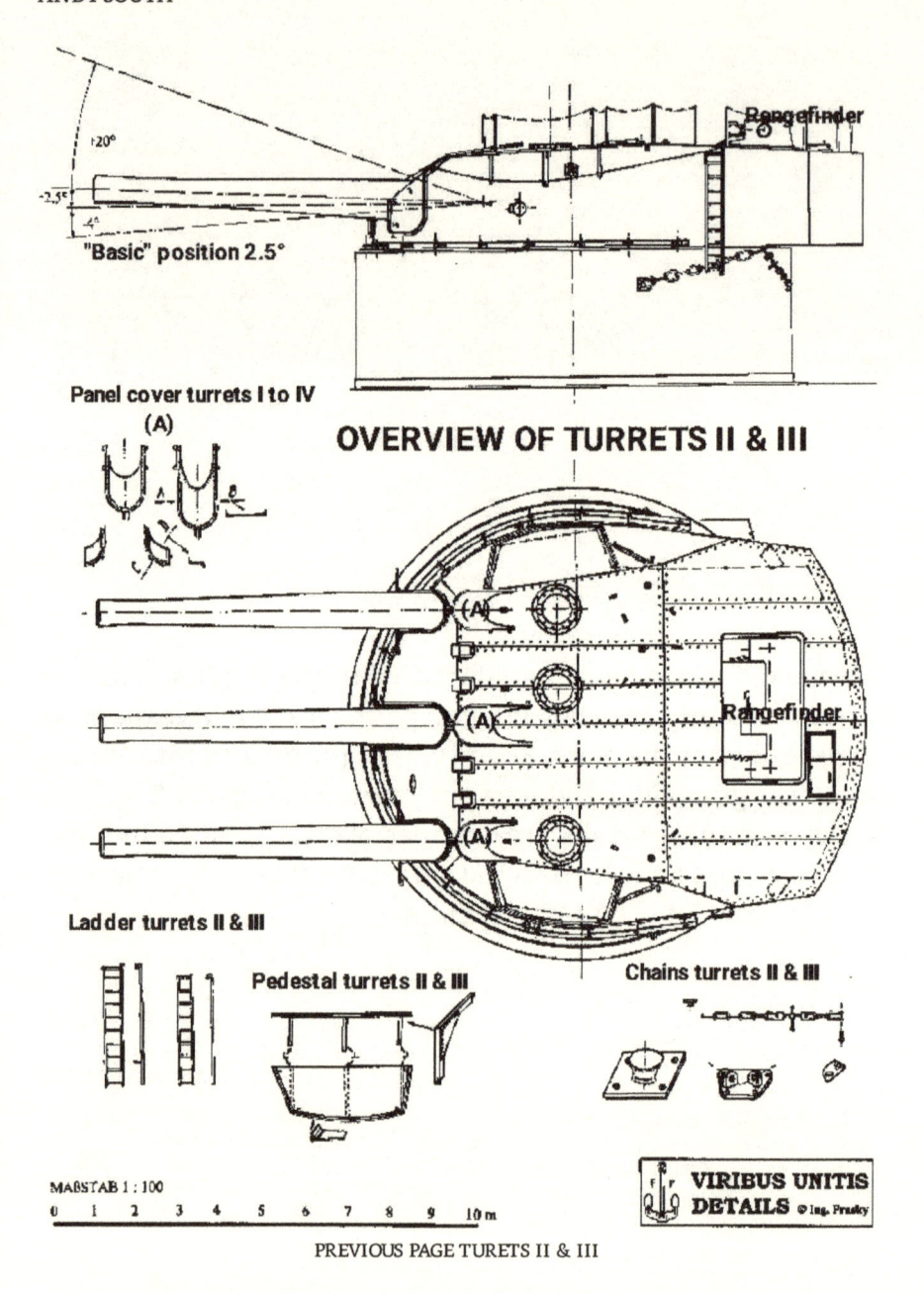

The K10 had been designed in 1908 and was to enter service with the navy two years later. Its weight was 116,070 lbs, (225.89 tons/52,650 kg) and with the breech mechanism that increased to 119,600 lbs (117.71 tons/54,250 kg). The overall length was 45 feet 1 inch (13.750 mtr), the length of the bore was about 42 feet 8 inches (13.000 mtr) and the rifling 34 feet 19 19/32 inches (10.606 mtr).

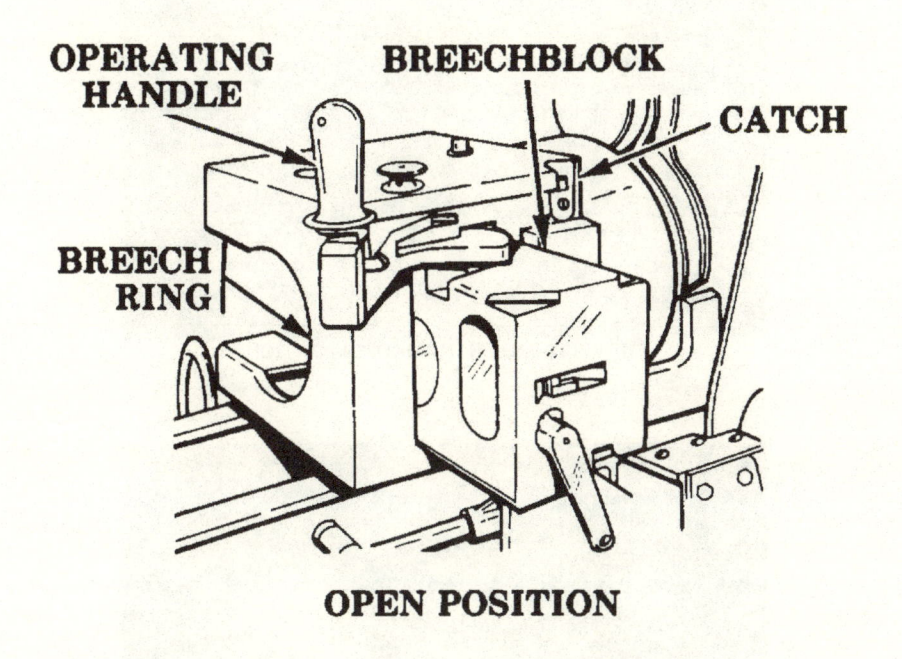

OPERATING HANDLE

BREECHBLOCK

CATCH

BREECH RING

OPEN POSITION

THE KRUPP SLIDING BREECH IN THE OPEN POSTION. THIS FORM OF BREECH WAS UNIVERSAL THROUGHOUT THE CLASS.

THE KRUPP BREECH IN THE OPEN POSITION.

A 30.5CM SHELL BEING LOADED WITH THE KRUPP BREECH FULLY OPEN.

THE TEGETTHOFF CLASS.

30.5 CM L/45 (K10) TURRET

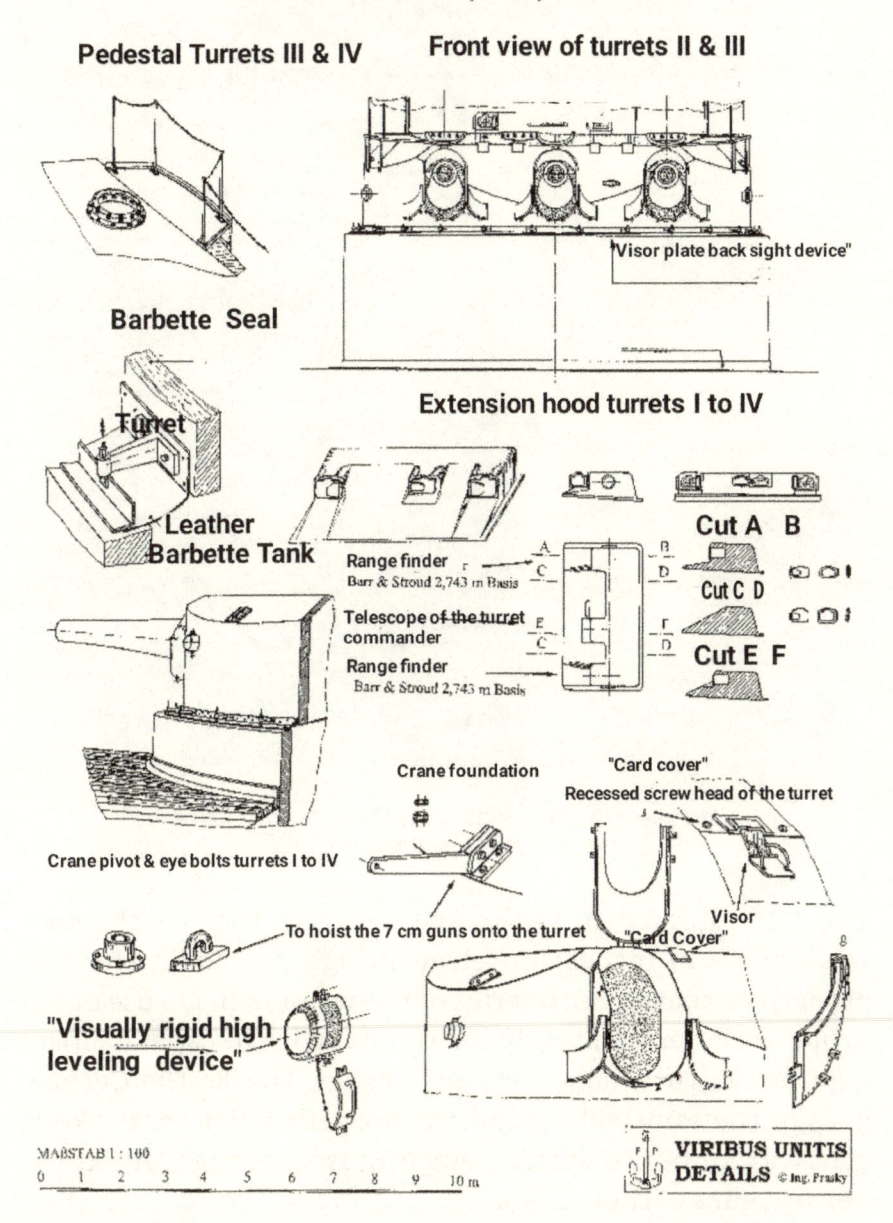

Pedestal Turrets III & IV

Front view of turrets II & III

"Visor plate back sight device"

Barbette Seal

Turret

Leather Barbette Tank

Extension hood turrets I to IV

Range finder
Barr & Stroud 2,743 m Basis

Telescope of the turret commander

Range finder
Barr & Stroud 2,743 m Basis

Cut A B

Cut C D

Cut E F

Crane foundation

"Card cover"
Recessed screw head of the turret

Crane pivot & eye bolts turrets I to IV

To hoist the 7 cm guns onto the turret

Visor

"Card Cover"

"Visually rigid high leveling device"

MA8STAB 1 : 100
0 1 2 3 4 5 6 7 8 9 10 m

VIRIBUS UNITIS DETAILS © Ing. Prasky

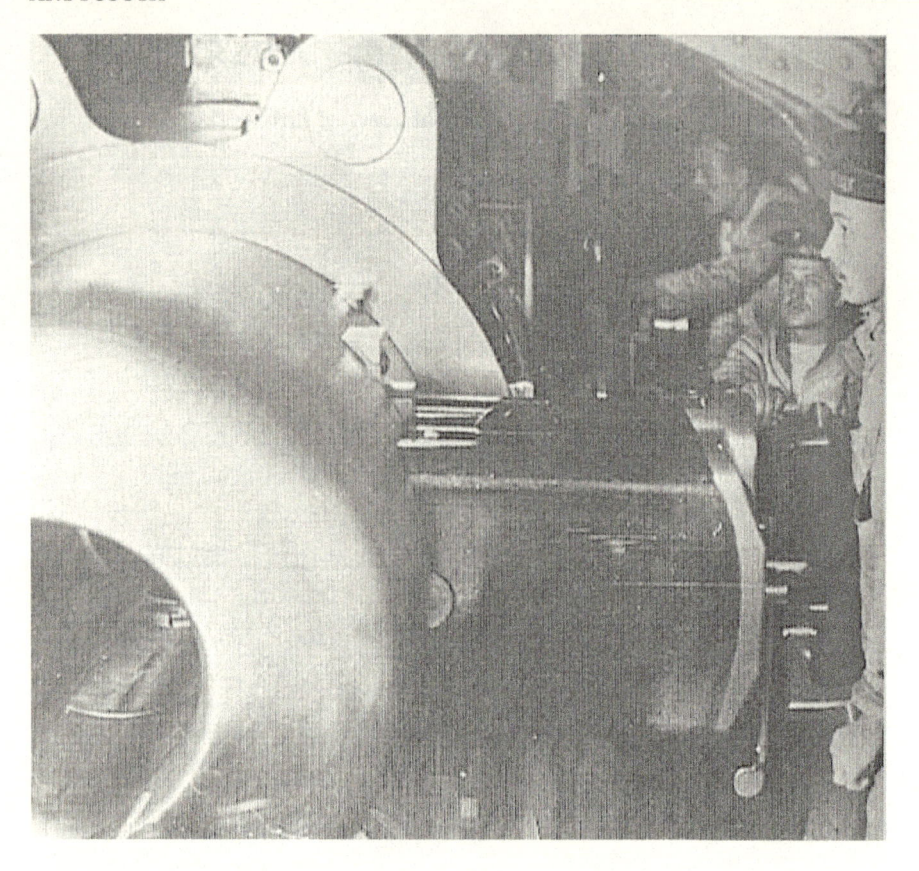

*THE KRUPP BREECH IN ACTION ON BOARD THE PRINZ EUGEN.
THE BREECH IS IN THE OPEN POSITION.*

The 'K10' differed from the first series in that its chamber was 5 cm (1.97 inches) longer, enabling it to handle a heavier propellant charge. Both series of the weapon made use of the Krupp horizontal sliding breech blocks with its separate loading brass cased charges and projectiles. Unlike the German guns of the same calibre, all the propellant for these Škoda guns was contained within a single brass cartridge. Unlike the German guns of this calibre, the K10 had no "fore charge" as all the propellant charge was in a single brass case The K10 had the capacity to fire four types of shell:

THE TEGETTHOFF CLASS.

- AP L/3,1 crh: 992 lbs. (450 kg). Broadside weight 11,904 lb.

- APC L/3,7 4.5crh: about 996 lbs. (452 kg). Broadside weight 11,952 lb.

- APC L/4,3 5crh: about 1001 lbs. (454 kg). Broadside weight 12,012 kg.

- Common L/4,0: 992 lbs. (450 kg). Broadside weight 11,904 lb.

OVER PAGE

AUSTRO-HUNGARIAN 30.5 CM NAVAL AP SHELL. (MUSUEM OF MILITARY, BUDAPEST, HUNGRY)

KEY
(measurements in mm)

A = 563 DIA. B = 278 DIA. C = 97.5 DIA. D = 101 DIA. E = 116.5 DIA. F = 153 DIA. G = 173 DIA. H = 303.5 DIA. I = 318.5 DIA. J =11.5 DIA. K= 18 DIA. L= 310 DIA. M= 9 DIA. N= 41 DIA. O=39 DIA. P= 948 DIA.

SKETCH BY KIND PERMISSION OF ANDRAS HATALA AND COPYWRITE TO HIM.

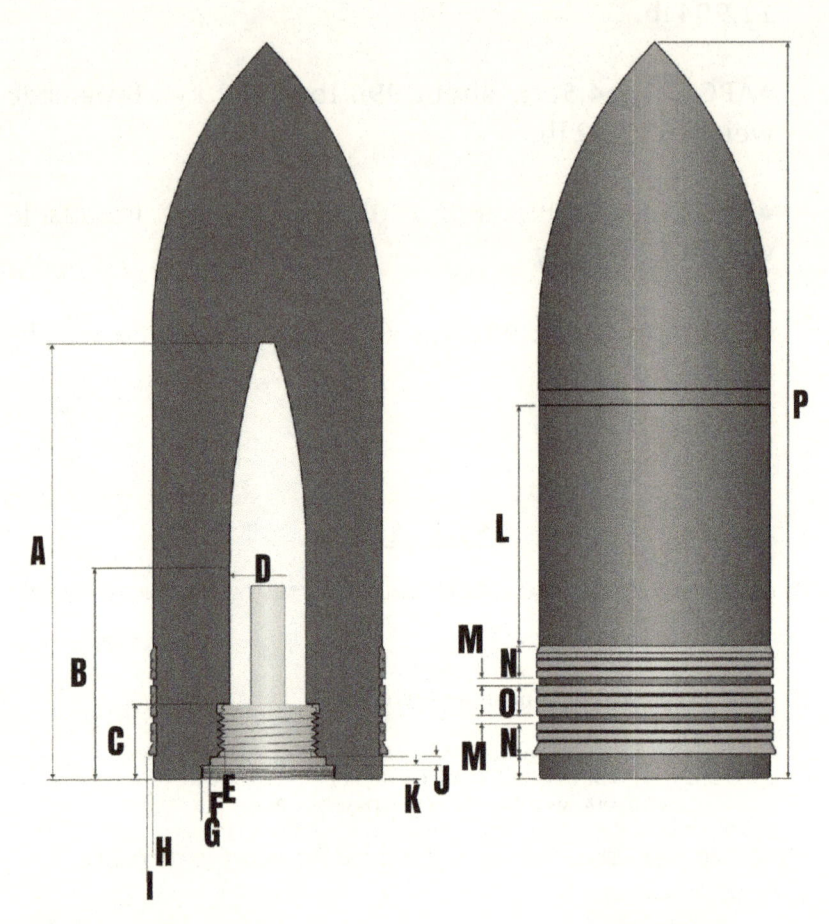

SECTION BASE PLATE.
(Fuse & charge are unknown)

SIDE VIEW

THE TEGETTHOFF CLASS.

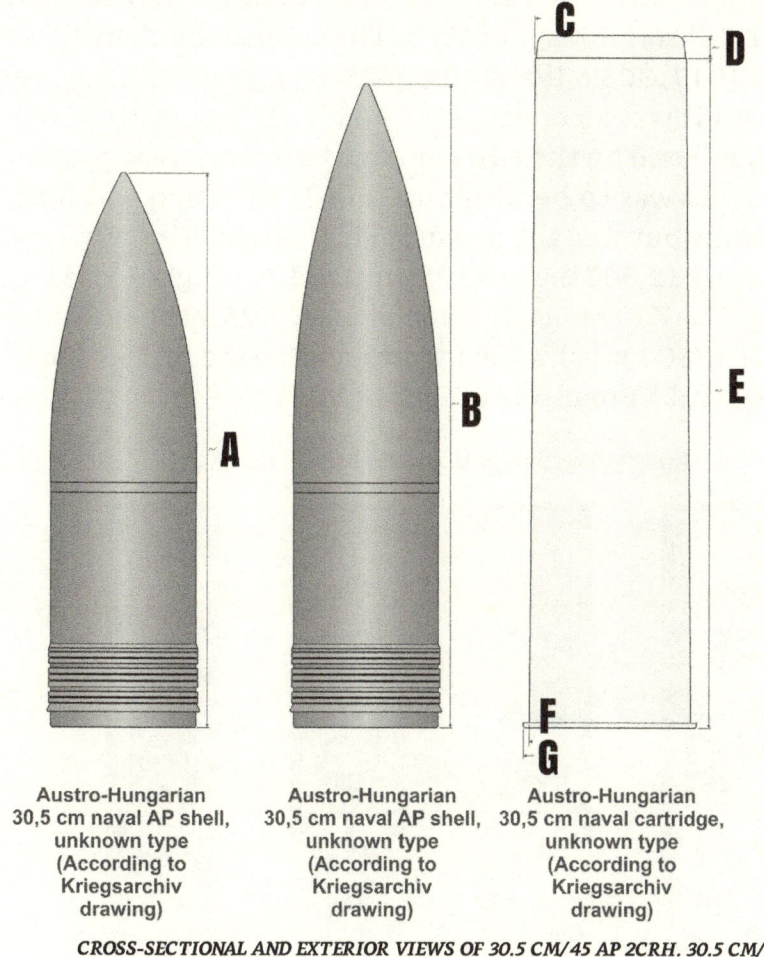

Austro-Hungarian
30,5 cm naval AP shell,
unknown type
(According to
Kriegsarchiv
drawing)

Austro-Hungarian
30,5 cm naval AP shell,
unknown type
(According to
Kriegsarchiv
drawing)

Austro-Hungarian
30,5 cm naval cartridge,
unknown type
(According to
Kriegsarchiv
drawing)

CROSS-SECTIONAL AND EXTERIOR VIEWS OF 30.5 CM/45 AP 2CRH. 30.5 CM/45 APC 4.5CRH. 30.5 CM/45 APC 5CRH. 30.5 CM/45 CARTRIDGE.
KEY
A =1136 MM. B = 1319 MM. C = 317 MM DIA. D = 46 MM.
E = 1372 MM. F = 338 MM DIA. G = 326 MM DIA.

SKETCH BY KIND PERMISSION OF ANDRAS HATALA AND COPYWRITE TO HIM.
(CONT OVER PAGE)

PREVIOUS PAGE. SKODA BASE USE USED ON THE 30.5 CM/45 CAL AP AND APC PROJECTILES. NOTE HOW THE BALL BEARINGS KEEP THE FUSE FROM DETONATING AFTER THE PROJECTILE LEAVES THE BARREL (SOFT BORE). SKETCH BY KIND PERMISSION OF ANDRAS HATALA AND COPYWRITE TO HIM.

The shells bursting charge for the APC (Armoured Piercing

shell) comprised of 8.8 lbs (4.0 kg) of TNT and for the common shell, 58.9 lbs. (26.7 kg) of TNT. The propellant charge was prior to 1913, 308.6 lbs. (140 kg) 25/660 mm M97 f.R.P. 6)). After 1913 it was amended to 313.05 lb (142 kg (estimated), which was based on the K10's enlarged breech. A new propellant formula was to be introduced in 1914 which was both cooler while burning and produced less smoke. The cartridge case size was 12.007 inches (305 mm) and its weight 153.4 lbs. (69.6 kg). The K10's muzzle velocity was 2,625 feet per second (2.35 Mach/800 mps) with a working pressure of 18.4 tons/ (2,900 kg/cm2). Broadside weight 11,904 lb.

Function of Skoda B.Z. M/9. base fuse

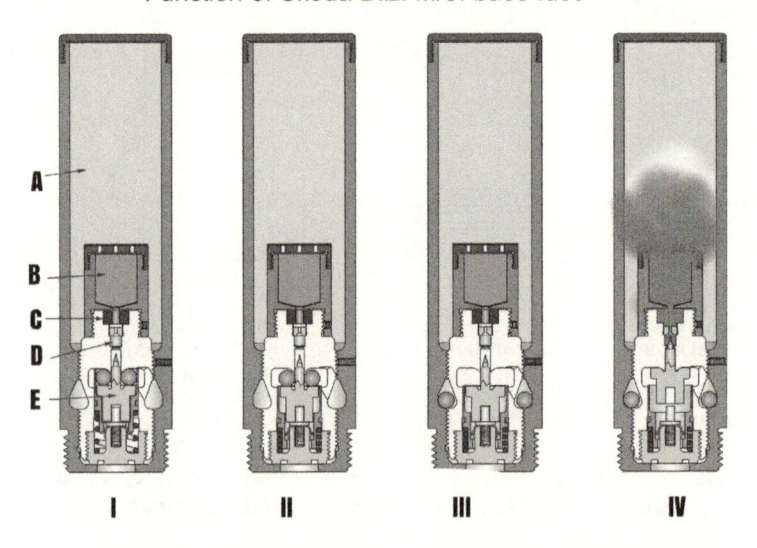

SKODA BASE USE USED ON THE 30.5 CM/45 CAL AP AND APC PROJECTILES. NOTE HOW THE BALL BEARINGS KEEP THE FUSE FROM DETONATING AFTER THE PROJECTILE LEAVES THE BARREL (SOFT BORE).

FROM LEFT TO RIGHT: A CROSS-SECTIONAL AND EXTERIOR VIEWS OF THE 30.5 CM/45 CAl AP 2 crh. 30.5 CM/45 crh. 30.5 CM/45 CARTRIDGE.

KEY
A = DETONATOR. B = BOOSTER POWDER. C = DELAY POWDER. D = PRIMER. E = STRIKING PIN.

I. BEFORE FIRING
II. FIRING (IN THE BARREL)
III. DURING FLIGHT (ON THE TRAJECTORY)
IV. IMPACT.

SKETCH BY KIND PERMISSION OF ANDRAS HATALA AND COPYWRITED TO HIM.

The armour piercing shell used by the K10 had a length of 41 inches (104 cm) and a weight of 990 lb (450 kg). The Common Pointed shell used was seven inches longer at 48 inches (122 cm) but was ultimately the same weight as the armoured piercing shell. For each of the 30.5 cm breeches there was a supply of shells held ready in the turret's racks and deep within the ship's magazines. In total the magazines held 912 shells available for the gun crews use. The shell allocation per gun for the *Tegetthoff* class was 38 AP and 38 Common held in the ships magazines plus another six rounds per gun (18 per turret) [1] in the rear of each gun-house, which also served to helped balance the turret. There was in fact space in the turret for additional shells, but the turrets never carried the full capacity. The breeches could be reloaded at an angle of +2.5 degrees. Another unverified source claims the weapon could be loaded at "any" angle?

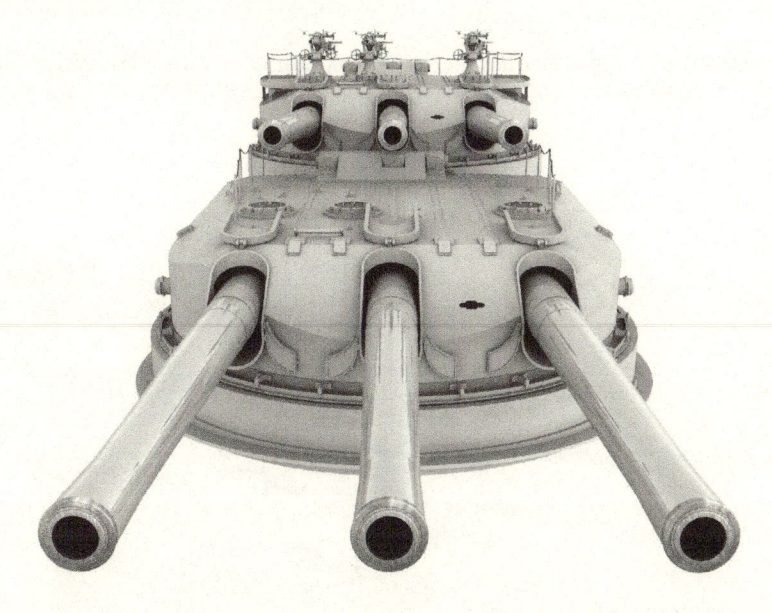

TWO OF THE 30.5 CAL TURRETS, WITH THE TRIPLE 7 CM GUNS ON THE REAR MOST. THE THREE 'U' SHAPED ITEMS ON THE FORWARD EDGE OF THE TURRET ARE 'SHARP SHEETS. THEIR ROLE WAS TO PREVENT ANY WATER BREAKING OVER THE DECK FROM ENTERING THE TURRET. LATER

ANDY SOUTH

IN THEIR CAREERS, THE SHEETS WERE REMOVED AND REPLACED WITH CANVAS SUBSTITUTE.

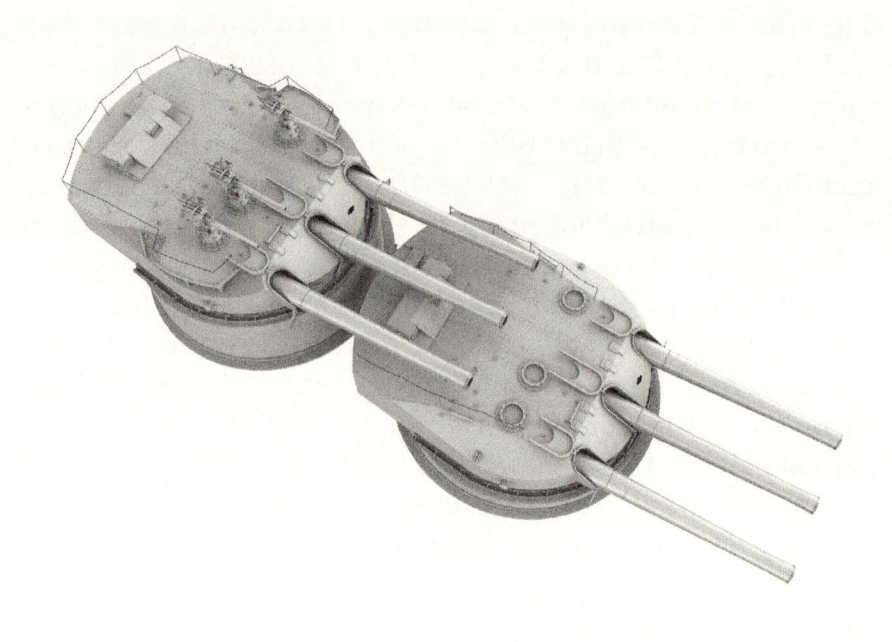

AN OVERVIEW OF THE TURRETS. CLEARLY VISIBLE ARE THE BARR & STROUD RANGEFINDERS, WHICH WERE FOR LOCAL CONTROL SHOULD CENTRAL DIRECTIONS BE LOST.

THE TEGETTHOFF CLASS.

*TWO 30.5 CM TURRETS WITH ONE TRAINED TO PORT (LEFT)
AND THE OTHER TO STARBOARD (RIGHT).*

*A REAR VIEW OF THE 30.5 TURRETS. THE LADDER ACCESS TO THE ROOF AND
THE SAFEY RAIL ARE VISIBLE, AS ARE THE 7CM AND RANGEFINDER.*

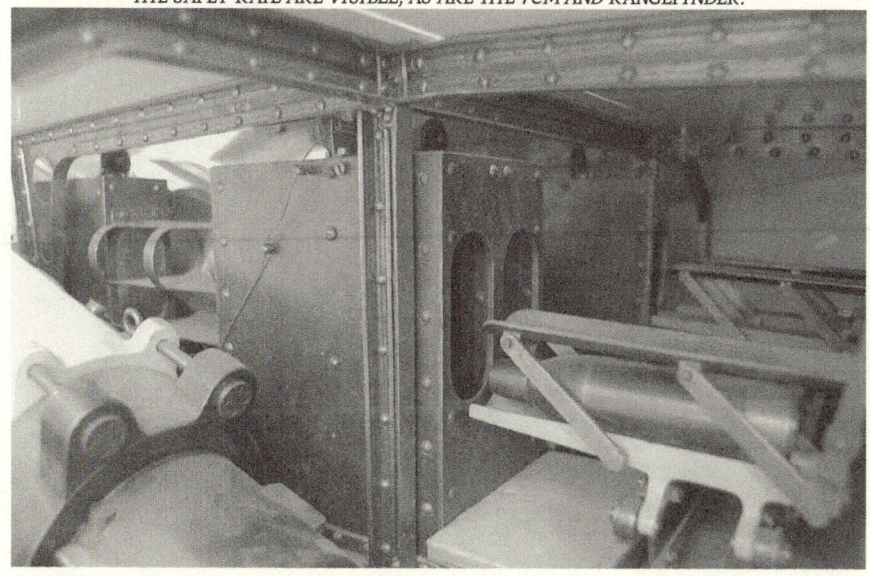

A MODEL OF THE SHELL CRADLE AND LIFT FROM A MODEL OF A 30.5 CM TURRET IN A VIENNA MUSEUM TODAY. THE SHELL IS LIFTED FROM THE MAGAZINE BY THE HOIST WITHIN THE SQUARE BOX BEFORE THE SHELLS CAP AND PUSHED OUT ONTO THE CRADLE. IT IS THEN TIPPED SIDEWAYS BY THE CRADLE SO IT LAYS BEFORE THE BREECH OF THE 30.5 GUN VISIBLE TO THE LEFT OF THE PHOTO.

As has been mentioned prior, the 30.5 cm used separate loading ammunition with charges contained within a brass cartridge case to provide for obturation [2]. The cartridge case had a weight of 153 lb (69.6 kg) in combination with a charge of between 304 and 309 lbs (138 kg-140 kg). With an elevation of 3.3 degrees, (firing an APC shell), the gun could range out to 6,560 yards (6,000 mtr), but with a 6 degrees incline on the barrel, the range increased to 10,930 yards (10,000 mtr). At 16 degrees that became 20,890 yards (19,100 mtr) and at the maximum elevation of 20 degrees the range was approximately 20,890 yards (19,100 mtr). Firing a 992 lbs. AP 2crh shell, with a 16 degrees elevation, the range was 17,830 yards (16,300 mtr) and on 20 degrees about 24,000 yards (22,000 mtr).

A 30.5 CM CARTRIDGE BEING RAMMED INTO THE BREECH. THE PHOTOGRAPH IS OF THE INTERIOR OF A RADETZKY CLASS PRE-DREADNOUGHT. BUT THE WEAPON TYPE WAS IDENTICAL TO THE TEGETTHOFF'S. (THE REAR OF THE IMAGE SHOWS A SHELL IN THE AUXILIARY HOIST, BUT THIS TYPE OF HOIST WAS ONLY USED IN THE TWIN GUNNED TURRET).

With a turret crew that had passed a combat training course, an estimated rate of one round every 30 seconds was achievable. In the first sixty second using the shells held within the turrets, three salvos were easily managed. But once the crews were dependent on shells supplied from the magazine, this number fell to 40-50 seconds. With the ammunition held within the ship and the average rate of fire, the magazines [3] stocks would diminish from full to empty in 36 minutes and 30 seconds. The approximate barrel life was for 200 firings.

THE PRINZ EUGEN AT SEA. (NOTE THE METALLIC SHARP SHEETS HAVING BEEN REPLACED). THE CREW MEN ON DECK APPEAR TO BE WEARING UNIFORMS THAT ARE NOT AUSTRO-HUNGARIAN (WHITE) SO THE IMAGE MAY BE POST WAR.

Having travelled the relevant distance and arrived on target, the AP shell at 6,560 yards (6,000 mtr) would penetrate to a depth of 5.3 inches (136 mm) when impacting against KC (Krupp Cement) side armour. At 19,900 yards (18,200 mtrs) that diminished to 4.2 inches (106 mm). Firing an APC shell over a range of 6,560 yards (6,000 mtr) 18.7 inches (475 mm) of KC side armour was penetrated. At 20,890 yards (19,100 mtr) that dropped dramatically 6.8 inches (173 mm).

THE PRINZ EUGEN'S FORWARD 30.5 CM TURRETS. PHOTOGRAPHED BY COMMANDER H.L. PENCE USN AT POLA SOON AFTER THE WARS END. SOURCE: NAVAL HISTORY AND HERITAGE COMMAND. THE DARK CANVAS REPLACEMENTS FOR THE SHARP SHEETS ARE VISIBLE IN THIS IMAGE.

The four turrets had in theory a weight of between 669 and 679 tons (680-690 tonnes) each and the superimposed turrets were heavier than the lower turrets. The weights of each of the turrets was to differ slightly, for example, turret III on *Prinz Eugen* was 687 tons.[5] There are some references that quote the *Tegetthoff* class having turret weights of between 616 and 619 tons (626-629 tonne). But these figures are taken from the Škoda plans dated October 1909 which used 9.84-inch (25 cm) turret armour. The turrets sat 29.25 feet (8.91 mtr) above the waterline but that increased to 45 feet (13.71 mtr) for the two super firing turrets. The superimposed turrets heavy weight was to cause hull distortions, requiring stiffening of the longitudinal frames.

ANDY SOUTH

PRINZ EUGEN'S BOW 12-INCH TURRETS, PHOTOGRAPHED BY COMMANDER H.L. PENCE, USN, AT POLA SOON AFTER THE END OF WORLD WAR I. NOTE ALSO 12-POUNDER GUNS, ANCHOR CHAIN AND WINDLASS. COPYRIGHT OWNER: NAVAL HISTORY AND HERITAGE COMMAND

THE TEGETTHOFF CLASS.

THE TEGETTHOFF'S 7CM OVERSHADOWED BY HER 30.5 CM TURRETS. THE RELAXED ATMOSPHERE WOULD INDICATE THIS IS A PRACTICE SHOOT.

The elevation range for the *Tegetthoff's* guns was between -4 and +20 degrees, with an increase rate of 2.5 degrees per second. That allowed the barrel to be raised from 0 degrees to its maximum elevation in 8 seconds. The turret could rotate between +140 & -140 degrees, at 3 degrees a second, meaning it could rotate through its full arc in 93.3 seconds, or from facing directly over the stern or bow to its maximum broadside position in 46.6 seconds. The *Viribus Unitis* alone could elevate all her guns to 20 degrees either individually or in unison. The other ships in the Tegetthoff class were able to elevate all guns individually to between the -4 and +20 degrees range, but when the guns were lifted together, the elevation range for the centre gun was -3 to +15.5 degrees and the outer guns were limited to between -4 and +16 degrees. The loading angle was +2 degrees. [5]

Each turret had a crew comprised of 91 men:

- 1 Officer (The Turret Commander),

- 38 Artillery men (Gunners, Sight-Setters, Signalmen, etc.),

- 50 crew below decks, as well as several support crew in other parts of the ship.

Before we move on to the secondary armament, we need to review a 'folk-lore' tale the turrets suffered from poor ventilation. Many sources claim that under the conditions of battle, the propellant gasses would be sucked in and after 15 minutes the gun house would become uninhabitable.

However recent research by Mihály Krámli cast doubts on this 'fact' and states that the oxygen supply was probably adequate. [6]

THE TEGETTHOFF CLASS.

A SHELL FROM THE VIRIBUS UNITIS ON DISPLAY TODAY AT THE VICTORY LIGHTHOUSE IN TRIESTE.

THE VIRIBUS UNITIS WITH HER GUNS TRAINED TO STARBOARD, RATHER as HER SISTER SHIP SZENT UNITS HAD LOOKED ON THE DAY OF HER LOSS.

LOOKING DOWN PAST THE SEARCHLIGHT STATION, BRIDGE AND CONNING TOWER TO THE VIRIBUS UNITIS'S FORWARD TURRETS.

THE TEGETTHOFF CLASS.

THE TEGETTHOFF'S FORWARD GUNS TRAINED TO STARBOARD. THE UPPER BRIDGE NOW HAS A CANVAS SCREEN AS OPPOSED TO THE OPEN RAILING OF THE EARLIER YEARS.

PREVIOUS PAGE: THE RESTOCKING OF THE PRINZ EUGEN'S 30.5 CM MAGAZINES. FROM EARLY IN HER CAREER. TO THE REAR OF THE CREW IS A SMALL FOUR-WHEEL TROLLEY THEY HAVE USED TO TRANSPORT THE SHELL TO THE HOIST AND HATCH

THE FULL BROADSIDE. OF THE PRINZ EUGEN IN 1915. GIVEN SHE NEVER ENGAGED THE ENEMY THIS WOULD BE A PRACTICE SHOOT.

THE TEGETTHOFF CLASS.

THE BEAUTY AND THE AWE INSPIRING SHAPE OF THE PRINZ EUGEN'S DEMONSTRATED BY THE AUSTRO-HUNGARIAN NAVY.

THE FIRST TURRET FOR THE VIRIBUS UNITIS BEING MANUFACTURED.

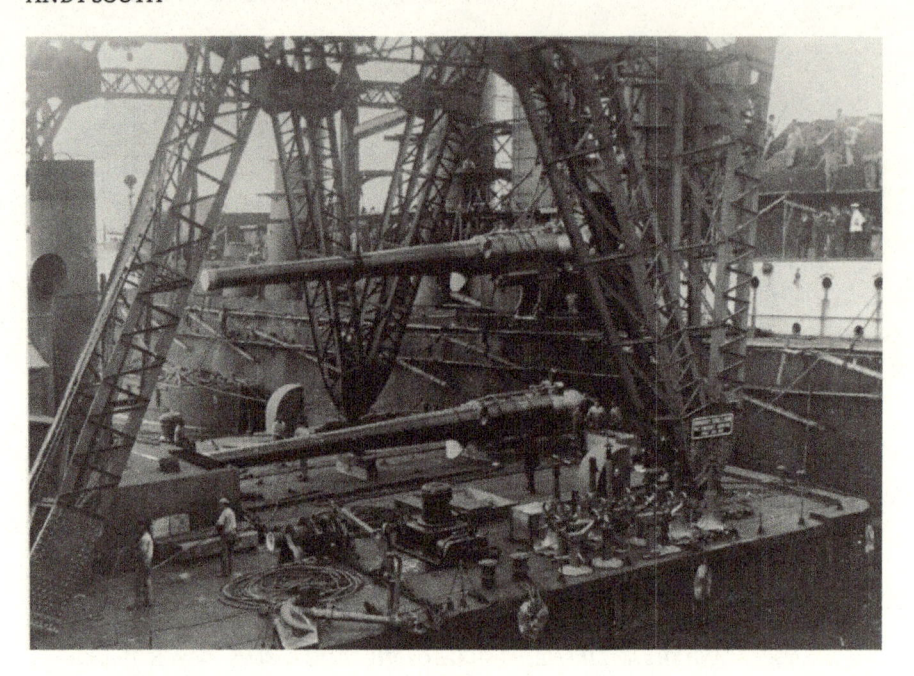

THE INSTALLATION OF 'B' TURRET ON THE PRINZ EUGEN AS SHE FITS OUT IN POLA IN 1913. SOURCE: NAVAL HISTORY AND HERITAGE COMMAND.

THE TEGETTHOFF CLASS.

THE INSTALLATION OF THE VIRIBUS UNITIS 30.5 CM GUNS. SOURCE: NAVAL HISTORY AND HERITAGE COMMAND.

POST WAR, IN LA SPEZIA, THE TEGETTHOFF WITH HER 30.5 GUNS REMOVED, AS THE WASHINGTON TREATY SEALS HER FATE

IT HAD BEEN THE PRACTICE IN THE PRE-DREADNOUGHTS TO ERECT A CANVAS THREE-SIDED TENT OVER THE SMALL CALIBER GUNs CARRIED ON THE TURRETS ROOFS. THE PRACTICE WAS CONTINUED WITH THE NEW CLASS, AND THE FORE TURRETS IN THIS IMAGE HAVE JUST SUCH A TENT IN SITU.

THE PRIOR MENTIONED TENT ON THE RADJEZKY CLASS.

THE TEGETTHOFF CLASS.

THE GUN ON THE LEFT IS A 30.5 CM/45 CAL WHICH EXPLODED ON THE 21ST AUGUST 1913, KILLING IN THE PROCESS VICE ADMIRAL LANJUS VON WELLENBURG. PHOTO COURTESY OF MIHALY KRAMLI.

THE BREECH OF THE EXPLODED 30.5 CM WHICH HAD EXPLODED AT THE SACCIORGANA

TEST GROUNDS NEAR POLA. PHOTO COURTESY OF MIHALY KRAMLI..

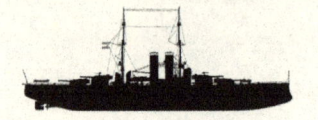

[1] Obturate: "to close (a hole or cavity) so as to prevent a flow of gas through it, especially the escape of explosive gas from a gun tube during firing" (Dictionary.Com).

[2] The sums total to 960, which conflicts to a few dozen in number with other sources magazine content totals.

[3] The Russian author S. E. Vinogradov claims that the# stern turret had reported arc of fire of 300 degrees and the turret looming over it 320 degrees. The 30 seconds rate of fire– only in the case of the so called "rapid fire", when the guns were fed from the Umladestation (working chamber) directly under the gunhouse. After the bitter German experiences at Dogger Bank, this method was abandoned in 1915. The realistic rate of fire was one round per 40-60 seconds.

[4] The Russian triple turret mounted onto the Gangut class weighed 757 to 767 tons. In turn the Dante Alighieri's triple turret weighed 645 to 670 tons. This made the Russian turrets rank as the heaviest and the Italians the lightest.

[5] The magazines were cooled, which was controlled from the "central station".

[6] SEE APPENDIX A

SECONDAY ARMAMENT

VICE-ADMIRALS FLAG (1894-1915)

The secondary armament of the *Tegetthoff's* (or of any dreadnought) was defensive in its nature. While the main guns pounded targets out nearer the skyline, the smaller calibres defended the ship closer in. They were there to fend off torpedo boat attacks and to engage any hostile forces that dared to draw to close to the ships position.

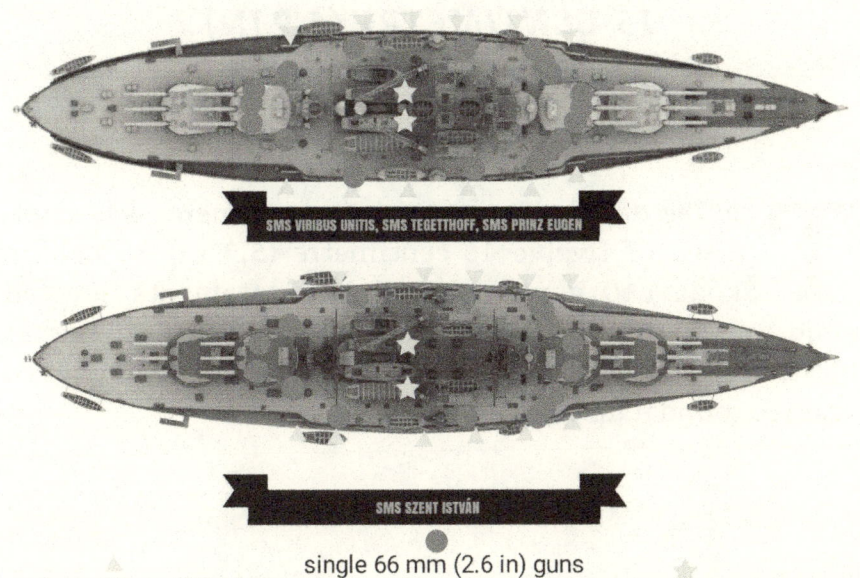

THE TEGETTHOFF CLASS.

SMS VIRIBUS UNITIS, SMS TEGETTHOFF, SMS PRINZ EUGEN

SMS SZENT ISTVÁN

single 66 mm (2.6 in) guns
single 15 cm (5.9 in) guns
single 66 mm AA guns

THE PLACEMENTS OF THE SECONDARY ARMAMENTS COMPARED BETWEEN
THE AUSTRIAN AND HUNGARIAN DREADNOUGHTS.

15-CENTIMETRE (5.9 IN) 50 CAL ŠKODA L10

The *Tegetthoff* class secondary armament was comprised of twelve 15-centimetre (5.9 in) 50 calibre Škoda L10 guns mounted into casements, located amidships on the port and starboard sides. The true diameter of the bore was 14.91 cm (5.97 inch) but it was simpler once again to round it up to 15 cm.

THE MIDSHIPS PORTION OF THE HULL, HOLDING THE CASEMENT GUNS AND THE SMALL 7 CM BATTERIES. ALSO, VISIBLE (MARKED WITH THE RED SQUARE) IS ONE OF THE BAR AND STROUD DECK LEVEL RANGEFINDERS.

THE TEGETTHOFF CLASS.

ANDREW WILKIE'S EXCELLENT MODEL SHOWING CLEARLY THE CASEMENT GUNS, THE RANGEFINDER ON THE DECK ABOVE THEM AND THE TORPEDO NET SECURED UNDERNEATH THE CASEMENTS. NOTE THE PAIR OF EMPTY DAVITS.

The *Tegetthoff* class secondary armament was comprised of twelve 15-centimetre (5.9 in) 50 calibre Škoda L10 guns mounted into casements, located amidships on the port and starboard sides. The true diameter of the bore was 14.91 cm (5.97 inch) but it was simpler once again to round it up to 15 cm. The weapon had been designed in 1910 and as with the 30.5 cm K10, it too entered service two years later. Overall, the weapon was 24 feet 7 inches (7.50 mtr) in its length and with the casement insulation of the *Tegetthoff* class, the manually operated weapon had an elevation range of between -6 and +15 degrees. They could also be trained (manually) from -60 to +60 degrees (approximately). As with the turret's 30.5 cm, the 15 cm was fitted with the horizontal sliding-block breech.

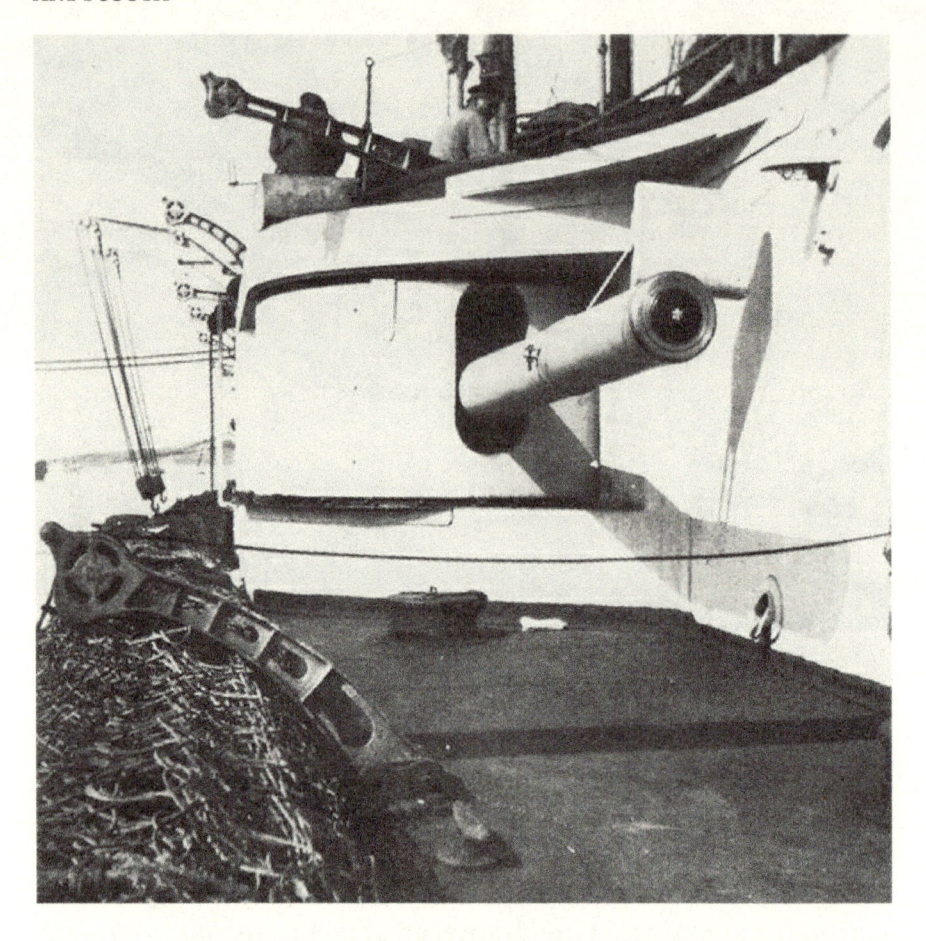

THE TEGETTHOFFS 15 CM IN ITS CASEMENT. WE CAN ALSO SEE THE MECHANICS FOR DEPLOYING THE NETS, AS WELL AS THE NETS THEMSELVES. WITH SO MANY OF DAVITS EMPTY THE SHIP IS MOST LIKELY IN PORT

The weapon had two types of shell available for its use, the High Explosive 100 lbs (45.5 kg) and an Armour Piercing 100 lbs shell. While available records omit the weapons bursting charge and the projectile length, we are told the propellant charge was 37 lbs. (16.85 kg). As with many navies of the period, one of the reasons the calibre was selected for use was the thinking that its shell was the maximum in weight a crewman could manhandle. The muzzle velocity was 2,887 feet per second (2.588 mach/880 mps) and the working pressure 17.4 tons/in2 (2,745 kg/cm2).

THE TEGETTHOFF CLASS.

The records also tell us the barrel life was for 180 firings and the book Naval Weapons of World War One by Norman Friedman claims 180 AP shells were carried for the weapons. Firing a 100 lb (45.5 kg) shell, the gun could range out to 16,404 yards (15 km/9.3 mi) at +15-degree barrel elevation. The volume "A Szent István Csatahajó" records that at a range of 1,100 yards (1,000 mtrs), striking KC armour, the shell could penetrate to a depth of 5.7 inches (145 mm). With a well-trained and proficient crew, it was possible to fire six shells in the space of 60 seconds, which is one round every 10 seconds.

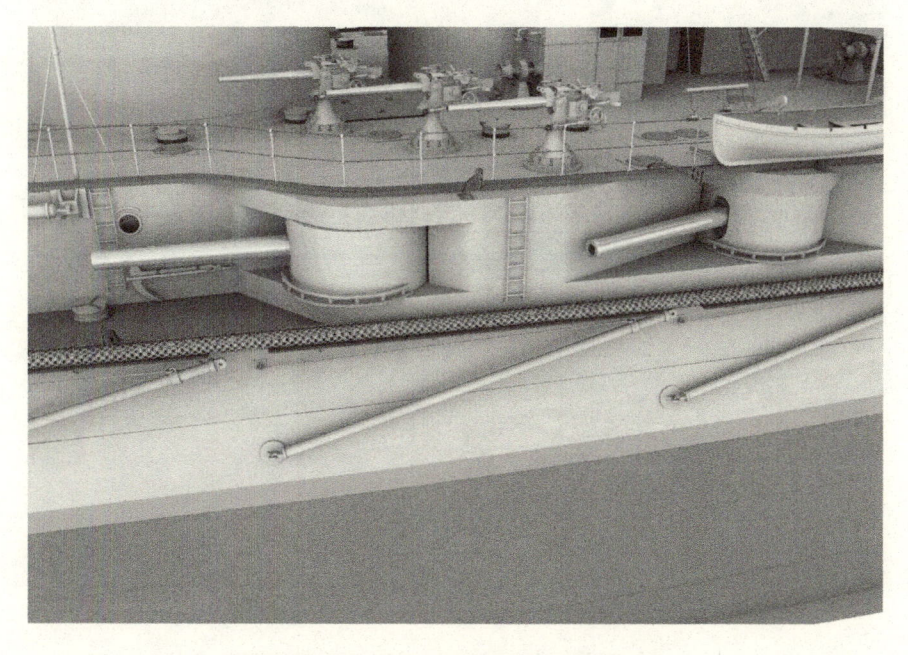

THE THREE MAIN CALIBRES OF THE CLASS ARE ILLUSTRATED HERE. THE 30.5 CM TURRET IS VISIBLE IN THE TOP HALF OF THE IMAGE, A BATTERY OF THREE 7CM GUNS SITS ON THE DECK ABOVE THE CASEMATE 15CM BATTERY.

The six casement mounts on each beam of the dreadnoughts were generally deemed to have been poorly designed, as they lacked for ventilation. It is claimed that if smoke penetrated into the casements interiors, the gun crews were rendered unable to function.

ONE OF THE FINEST IMAGES OF THE CASEMENT GUNS, FRAMED OVERHEAD BY THE 30.5 CM GUNS. THE TURRET APPEARS TO HAVE EITHER A CANVAS CAMOUFLAGE ON ITS ROOF, OR THE FABRIC OF A THREE SIDED SHELTER FOR THE 7 CM GUN CREWS. SOURCE: NAVAL HISTORY & HERITAGE COMMAND.

THE TEGETTHOFF CLASS.

PREVIOUS PAGE.REAR VIEW OF THE 7CM/45 CAL. OPENING IN CASEMATE APPEARS TO HAVE BEEN ENLARGED, ALLOWING HIGHER ELEVATIONS. NOTE SLIDING BREECHBLOCK, TYPICAL OF KRUPP AND SKODA WEAPONS OF THIS PERIOD. PHOTOGRAPH COPYRIGHTED BY CASPAR VERMEULEN AND USED HERE BY HIS KIND PERMISSION.

15 CM/50 SKODA GUN AT BATTERIE MADONNA ON THE ISLAND OF VELI BRIONI NEAR PULA, CROATIA. THIS IS ONLY REMAINING COMPLETE GUN OF THE FOUR-GUN BATTERY. THE ENGRAVINGS ON THIS GUN HAVE BEEN OBSCURED BY RUST, BUT IT APPEARS THAT THIS IS GUN SERIAL NUMBER 15 AND WAS MANUFACTURED IN 1912. PHOTOGRAPH COPYRIGHTED BY CASPAR VERMEULEN AND USED HERE BY HIS KIND PERMISSION.

NEXT PAGE. A PLAN OF THE 15CM CASEMENTS.

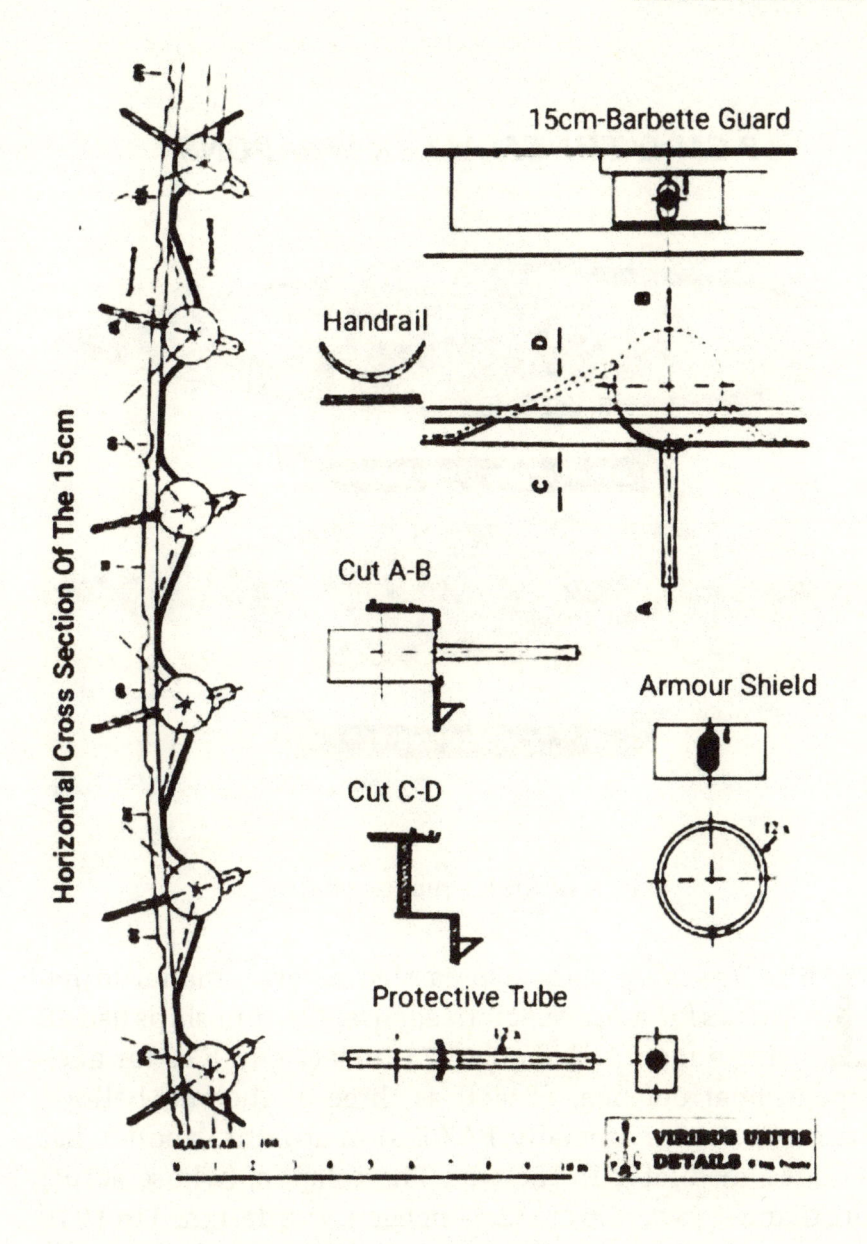

THE TEGETTHOFF CLASS.

Horizontal Cross Section Of The 15cm

15cm-Barbette Guard

Handrail

Cut A-B

Armour Shield

Cut C-D

Protective Tube

VIRIBUS UNITIS DETAILS

7 CM & THE SMALLER WEAPONS.

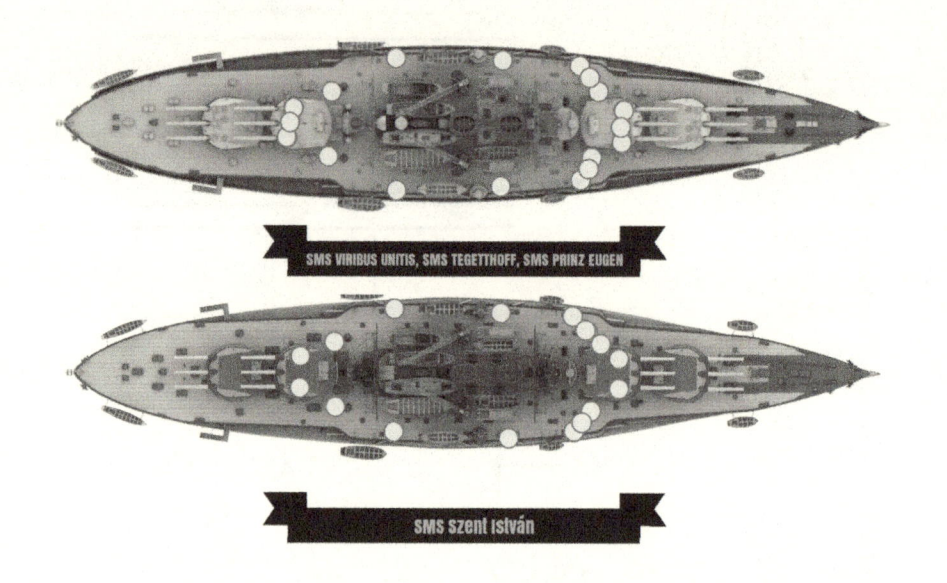

SMS VIRIBUS UNITIS, SMS TEGETTHOFF, SMS PRINZ EUGEN

SMS Szent István

THE PLACEMENTS FOR THE 7 CM WEAPONS.

The *Tegetthoff* class also carried several smaller armaments for more 'specialized' use. The four ships had 18 single mounted Škoda 2.75 inch (7 cm) K10 for anti-torpedo boat defence, as well as three of the anti-balloon version ("B.A.R" or officially, BAK Ballon-abwehr Kanone) that were designed later in the war. The weapon, (whose actual bore diameter was 6.6 cm (2.6-inches)), was designed in 1910 at the Škoda Pilsen complex and entered service in 1912. Each of the class carried twelve K10 guns on open pivot mountings located on the upper deck above the casements and on the turrets roof. They were dual purpose weapons, but initially on the *Tegetthoff's*, they were for anti-torpedo boat defence.

THE TEGETTHOFF CLASS.

Their location on the upper deck brought suffocation for the 6.6 cm gun crews by muzzle gases from when the main armament was fired. They were also vulnerable to being rendered out of action after the first heavy shell burst nearby having no armour shielding and an unprotected gun crew. Their value as a weapon that could repel the attacks of enemy destroyers during a fleet action was highly questionable. They were also deemed to be portable, but this was more theoretical than practical. As the war years passed the number of the weapon carried on all four dreadnought was constantly reduced.

PREVIOUS PAGE. THE FORWARD PORT TRIPLE BATTERY OF 7 CM SHROUDED IN SMOKE AS THE NEIGHBOURS THE 30.5 TURRETS FIRE OVER THE BOWS QUARTER.

In 1915 the six 6.6 cm mounted on the roofs of 'B' and 'X' turrets were replaced by two of the 66cm anti-airship version, the L45. They in turn were replaced in 1917 with four of an even newer version. In this location the weapons could elevate between -6.5 and +20 degrees.

PREVIOUS PAGE. A GOOD VIEWS OF THE 7CM POSITIONS ON THE TURRETS.

The roof turret mounted weapons had their vertical guidance drives connected to the corresponding mechanisms of the 30.5 cm heavy guns in the respective turrets. This allowed for a simultaneous vertical elevation of both calibres. According to the original concept, the idea was to assist in the training of the 30.5 cm gunners, while reducing the consumption of the expensive larger shells and lessening the wear to the heavy gun barrels.

THE TEGETTHOFF CLASS.

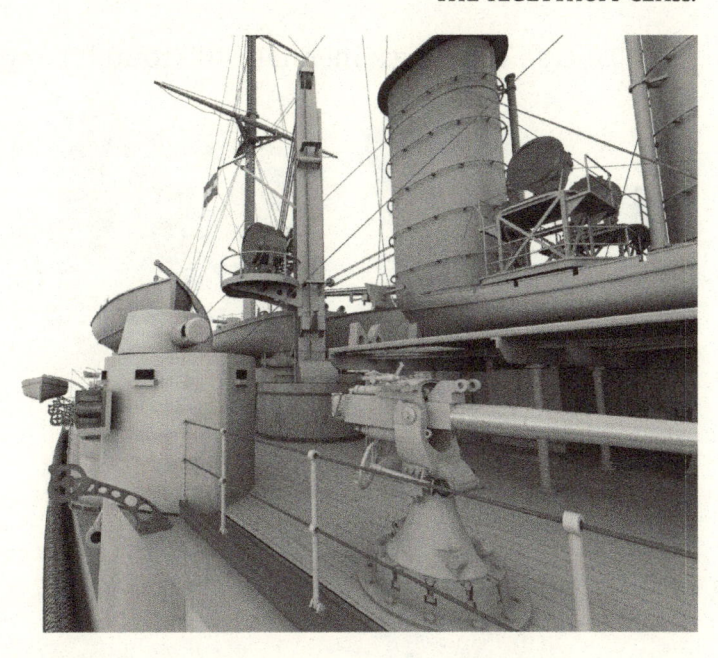

AN AMIDSHIP 7CM WITH A RANGEFINDER POSITION TO THE REAR OF IT

Only the *Viribus Unitis* was to enter service with a complete set of the 7 cm guns. Her three sisters joined the fleet without these guns, having them installed post-commissioning. The weapons barrel was made of steel and as with the main armament, had a horizontal sliding breech block. The weight, (without the breech), was 1,146 lb (520 kg) and the overall length was about 11 feet 6 inches (3.500 mtrs). The weapon used a high explosive 9.9 lbs. (4.5 kg) shell with a bursting charge and a propellant charge of 3.5 lbs. (1.6 kg) each. The muzzle velocity was 2,887 feet per seconds (880 mps) and the working pressure was 18.4 tons/in2 (2,900 kg/cm2). In an Anti-torpedo boat version, the gun could elevate between -10 and +20 degrees, but in the Anti-balloon version this was -5 to +90 degrees. The weapon could train through a full 360 degrees. A good crew could achieve between 15 and 20 rounds per minute and with a 9.9 lb shell and 20-degree elevation the weapon could reach to 8,750 yards (8,000 mtrs). In its anti-balloon configuration, the achievable ceiling was 16,400 feet

(5,000 mtrs). The magazines help 400 rounds per gun.

*PREVIOUS PAGE. THE 7CM. NOTE WHEELS FOR SUPPOSED EASY MOBILITY?
THE SIDE VIEW OF THE 7CM.*

The class had a number of other weapons which included:

- 2 x 66-mm / 18 (2.59 inch), landing guns,

- 2 x 47-mm / 44 (1.85 inch) salute guns,

- 2 x 8-mm Schwarzlose machine guns,

6.6 CM ŠKODA G. L/18

- 392 x 8-mm M95 rifles for use by landing parties

- 133 x 8-mm M07 pistols for use by landing parties.

The two 8-millimetre (0.31 in) Schwarzlose M.07/12 anti-aircraft machine guns which were mounted, (during the war years) on top of the armoured cupolas of each ship's rangefinders. With a 250 round cloth belt feed, they could fire between 400 and 580 rounds per minute. This gave each belt a life of approximately 30 seconds.

THE VIRIBUS UNITS A/A CREW SPORTING GAS MASKS.

The two 6.6 cm Škoda G. L/18 weapons were for use with landing parties and most likely had a wheeled gun carriage for use ashore. They had a rate of fire of around twenty 4.4 kg (28lbs) rounds per minute.

Finally, the vessels had two 47-millimetre (1.9-inch) Škoda SFK L/44 S guns for use against small and fast vessels such as torpedo boats and submarines. These also served as Saluting guns when the occasion required courtesies to be rendered. These were also capable of being mounted onto the bow of the Admiral barge.

THE TEGETTHOFF CLASS.

TORPEDO TUBES

VICE-ADMIRAL (1894-1915)

As with most, if not all dreadnoughts, the Austro-Hungarian ships were equipped with several torpedo tubes. The warships had four torpedo tubes of the 533 mm calibre (20.98 inch), carried beneath their waterline. One torpedo tube was installed within the bow and another in the stern. The remaining two were between the fore and the aft mast, two more were in a large compartment immediately behind the second 30.5 cm turret. The tubes had a 63-degree rotation movement on their axes, from the diametrical plane. Each ship had a supply of 14 torpedoes [1], (3.36 m long) of which 12 were combat and 2 training models. The new 533-mm long torpedo tubes for the dreadnoughts could use the older 450-mm torpedoes (total weight 662 kg, charge 110 kg). The total weight of the torpedo's (including compressors, pipes, various equipment, etc.) was 56.13 tons.

THE TEGETTHOFF CLASS.

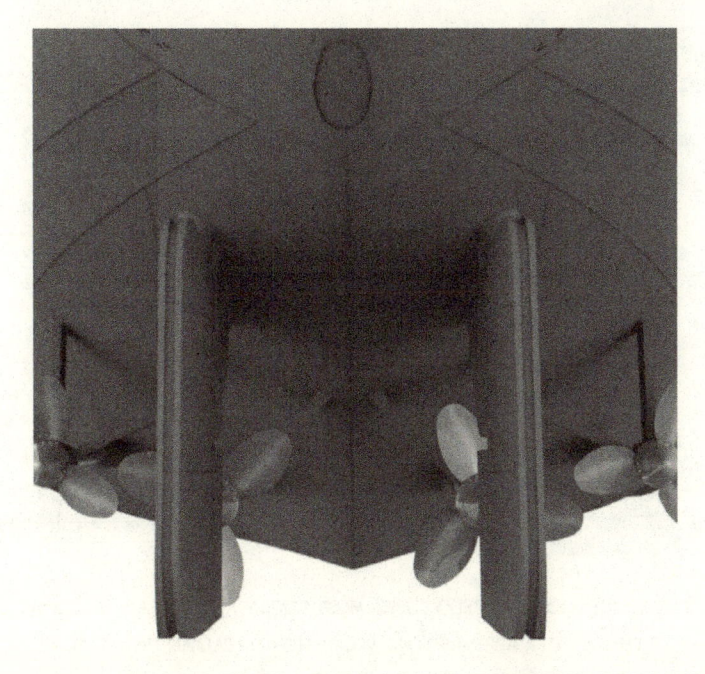

THE VIRIBUS UNTIS REAR TORPEDO HATCH CAN JUST BE MADE OUT IN THIS IMAGE.

ONE OF THE CLASS TAKING ON TORPEDOES.

ANDY SOUTH

THE TEGETTHOFF TORPEDO TUBES, MOST LIKELY A POST WAR IMAGES AS THE OFFICER APPEARS TO BE WEARING AN ITALIAN UNIFORM.

[1] The torpedoes were of the Whitehead type made by Fiume.

MINES

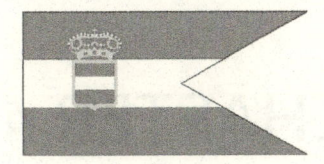

COMMODORE (1894-1915)

The ships also could carry 20 anchor mines that were designed to protect the vessel whilst at anchor. The mines total weight was 2.32 tons (2360 kg) and the total weight of both the mines and their support machinery was 5.5 tons.

CHAPTER 4: ARMOUR AND MINE PROTECTION

As with many armoured ships at the time of their construction, the *Tegetthoff's* used Krupp's cemented armour plates, theirs being manufactured by the Rothschild owned company. The armour scheme for the *Tegetthoff's* was all but a carbon copy of the preceding class, the pre-dreadnought *Radetzkys*. The only major difference was to be a slight increase in the thickness of a small number of individual pieces of armour.

ARMOURED BELTS

FLEET-ADMIRAL (1915-1918)

The *Tegetthoff's* main belt was 280-mm (11.02 inches) in its thickness and it ran along the hull's waterline level. It stretched in this depth from between the centre point of the foremost and stern turrets, covering in the process 55% of the length of the ship. At its forward extremities it thinned from 280-mm to 150-mm (11.02-5.90 inches). Then a secondary belt ran on towards the bow and stern with a depth of 130-mm (5.11 inches) belt. Finally, as it reached the ship's bow and stern, it diminished to its final thickness of 110-mm (4.33 inches).

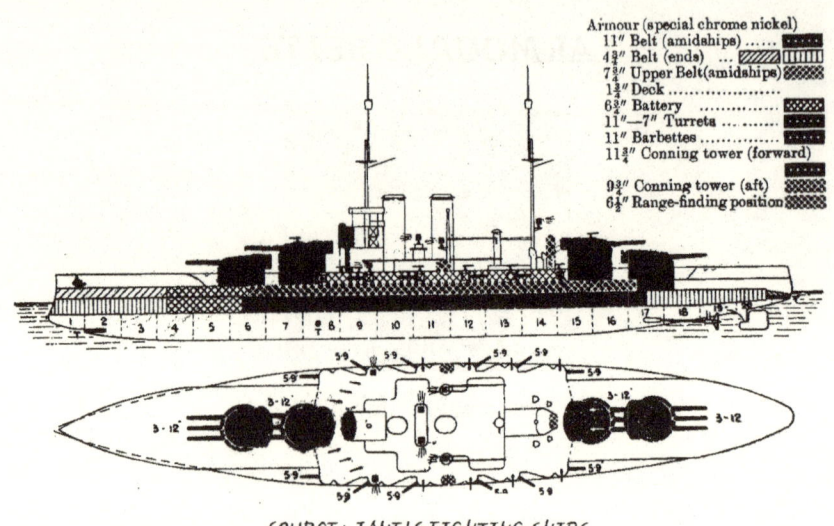

SOURCE: JANE'S FIGHTING SHIPS

THE ARMOUR CONFIGURATION AS DETAILED IN THE 1919 EDITION OF JANES FIGHTING SHIPS.

Running parallel but sitting above the main belt was a secondary layer of armour which was 180 mm (7.08 inches) in its depth. The upper edge of this 'secondary belt' reached up to the level of the middle deck and ran in its length out to the bow. By the stage that it reached the ships prow, it had diminished in its thickness to a depth of 110 mm (4.33 inches).

In the stern portion of the hull, behind the fourth turret, the secondary belt had a thickness of 150 mm (5.90 inches). It reached up to the 102nd frame, where the width of the hull was blocked from side to side by a transverse bulkhead 130 mm (5.11 inches) in thickness. At the stern itself the upper belt was non-existent. Internally the vertical armour scheme was supplemented by both transverse and inclined armour, which contributed to the ships armoured citadel. In both the bow and stern the 280 mm (11.02 inches) belt was supported by 160 mm (6.29 inches)) traverses. In turn the 180 mm (7.08

inches) belt was met by 120 mm (4.72 inches) traverses in the bow and 180 mm (7.08 inches) in the stern.

The class benefited from a near completely protected waterline by the height of their armoured belt in the bow. But with a thickness of 110 mm (4.33 inches) the upper belt here could easily have been reduced to a minimum of 80 mm (3.15 inches) without suffering any loss and saving at least 30 tons of weight. This would have improved the trim on the bow and maybe would have made them less wet before the conning tower?

All armour with a thickness of more than 75 mm (2.95 inches) was surface hardened or "Krupp cemented".

TURRETS.

ADMIRAL (1915-1918)

In general, the four turrets benefited from a good level of protection. But being the *Tegetthoff's* they were to be let down in some areas of their design.

The dreadnought's turrets had armour of 11 11/32 inches (28 cm), but in general the turrets are considered to have been poorly protected with thin armour. There was an unprotected slot between the gun-house and the barbettes, plus the cupolas for the rangefinders on the turret roofs were overly large. A hit on one of these could easily have destroyed a turret roof. The final weight of the turrets armour and internal fittings was to exceed the "guaranteed" design weight, adding 1.5 inches (3.81 cm) to the hulls final draft.

Both the barbettes and the sides of the turrets benefited from armour 280 mm (11.02 inches) in its depth. The roof of the turrets was 200 mm (7.87 inches), while the sloping section of the roof was 150 mm (5.90 inches) and the flat 60 mm (2.36 inches).

CASEMATES & DECKS.

VICE-ADMIRAL (1915-1918)

The 150-mm casement battery on the middle deck was protected by a series of 180-mm (7.08 inches) steel plates (from both port, starboard and from the traverse directions). The 180-mm plates were covered from above by a deck comprised by two thicknesses of high-resistance steel, both of 15-mm (0.59 inches).

The middle deck ran from the bow to the casement battery and then in turn from the stern to the fourth turret which was comprised of two layers, both were 15 mm (0.59 inches). The lower deck within the armoured citadel, was comprised likewise of two steel sheets, but in that instance, both were 18 mm (0.70 inches) on the horizontal level, rising to 18 + 30 mm (0.70-1.18 inches)) on the bevelled sides. Outside the citadel the lower deck had also a protective layer of two high resistance steel sheets.

Forward of the citadel it was 18 and 25 mm (0.70 & 0.98 inches) and aft it was 18 + 30 mm (0.70-1.18 inches).

THE INSULATION OF THE SHIPS ARMOURED DECK. THE SLOPED SIDE IS TO LESSEN THE IMPACT OF ANY SHELL THAT DETONATES AGAINST IT.

CONNING TOWER

THE TEGETTHOFF CLASS.

REAR- ADMIRAL (1915-1918)

The conning tower was protected by between 250 and 280 mm (9.84-11.02 inches) armour on the sides, while the flat roof was protected by two steel sheets of 30 mm (1.18 inches) each.

The bridge even benefited from 25 mm (0.98 inches) armour plates. The A/A rangefinder positions for the secondary artillery was armoured with 180-mm (7.08 inches) plates from the sides and covered with a 40-mm (1.57 inches) roof. The rangefinders cupola on the conning tower and the aft A/A position were protected by 30 mm (1.18 inches) cast Krupp steel.

Another question mark was the absence of any anti-splinter protection for the funnel. A shell impact in the area could cause a drop in the funnels draw and a consequential decrease in the already low speed, as well as inflict smoke on the nearby gun and rangefinder posts. The armoured grates on the upper and middle decks would only prevent large fragments from getting directly into the boilers.

"MINENPANZER"

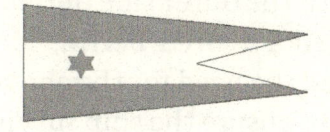

COMMODORE (19151918)

The Achilles Heel of the classes 'Protection-scheme' was the 'Mine Protection', or "Minenpanzer" that had been conceived and designed by Popper. In 1906, while he was working on the *Radetzky* class, the Austro-Hungarian navy conducted two sets of experimental explosions against the hull of the former battleship, *Kaiser Max* (1875-1941). Based on the results of these underwater tests, (which were largely conditional as they had been conducted against compartments based on a scale of 1:10 of the *Tegetthoff* design), Popper developed his underwater protection design, which he called "Minenpanzer" (mine protection). Despite the grand title it was in fact merely an ordinary double bottom with a depth of 4 feet 11 1/16 (1.5 mtrs) [1] and with a reinforced inner lining comprised of two layers at 0.98 inches (25 mm) each.

All three of the *Radetzkys*, as well as the four dreadnoughts that followed, were to be equipped with what was effectively a useless design. At the same time Germany conducted a series of trials on a full-scale compartment. As a result of these experiments, it was concluded in Berlin that in order to provide an effective counter from the threat of flooding to vital parts of the ship, the anti-mine bulkhead protecting them should be located at a distance of at least 13 feet 1 to 14 feet 9 inches (4–4.5 mtrs) from the outside, the depth of the double bottom should be at least 6 feet 6 inches (2 mtrs). Any less in the space between the anti-torpedo bulkheads or the second bottom were prone to damage.

Also, for a better level of stability the Germans concluded that the bulkhead impacted by the explosion should not be vertical or parallel to the outer side but have incline inwards. In 1909 while Kudelka visited Berlin, Tirpitz, the German minister emphasized the need for the above dimensions to be the minimum used to ensure the ship survived. But in the final

THE TEGETTHOFF CLASS.

design of the *Viribus Unitis*, the advice of Tirpitz was not considered, and no changes were made to the draft design.

THE "MINENPANZER"

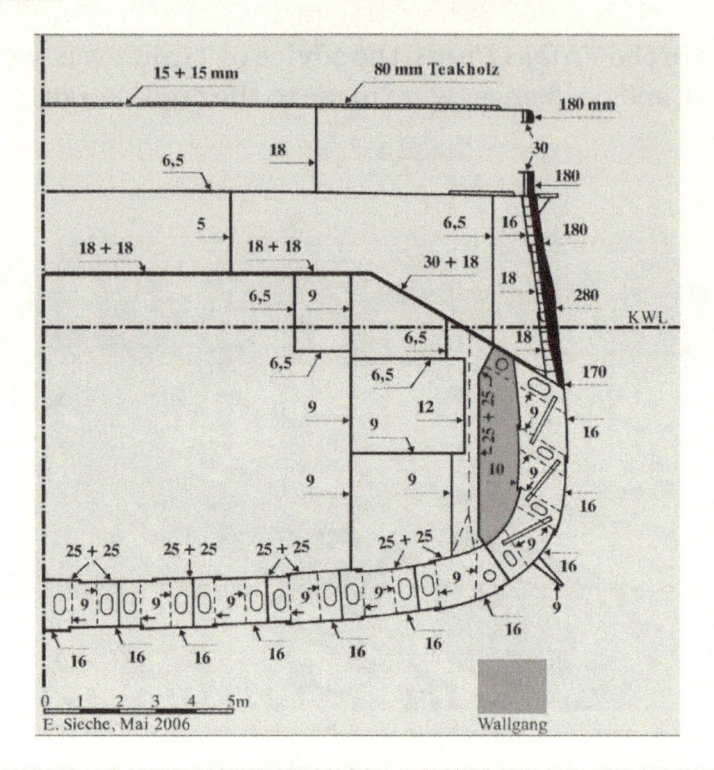

MAIN FRAME OF THE TEGETTHOFF SOURCE: E. SIECHE, MAY 2006 THE GERMAN EXPLOSIVE TESTS HAD SHOWN THAT THE WALLGANG [PLATE] (SHOWN HERE IN GREEN) HAD TO BE AT LEAST 4 M WIDE TO OFFER SUFFICIENT EXPANSION SPACE FOR EXPLOSION GASES. OTHERWISE THE INTERNAL TORPEDO BULKHEAD (25+ STRONG) WOULD BE PUNCTURED. POPPER APPARENTLY IGNORED THIS SCIENTIFIC KNOWLEDGE, WHICH ULTIMATELY ENDED BOTH SZENT ISTVÁN AND UNITIS. THE ARMOURED "MINE FLOOR" (25 + 25 MM THICK) INTRODUCED BY POPPER EXTENDS TO THE SIDE FLANK OF THE FUSELAGE, WHERE THE THICKNESS OF THE INNER FLOOR IS ONLY 9 MM.

[1] *Other sources record the gap as being 1.220 meters.*

CHAPTER 5: THE SHIPS CONNING TOWER, BRIDGE & FIRE CONTROL.

THE CONNING TOWERS

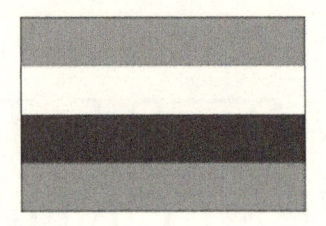

YUGOSLAVIA NAVAL ESIGN (1918-1922)

The four *Tegetthoffs* were served by two conning towers. The main and 'traditional' one was just before the bridge. But aft just forward of the rear turrets was a less well protected second one.

The forward one served as the control center for the ships when in combat, allowing officers (whilst protected by thick armour), to observe everything unfolding around the ship and to direct the crew.

THE TEGETTHOFF CLASS.

PREVIOUS PAGE. THE TWO STORIES TOWER WITH THE BRIDGE ABOVE AND BEHIND IT.

The conning towers were simple armoured cylinders with a series of vision slits within its outer wall. But they needed to be heavily armoured to afford a higher level of protection to the 'Command' crew and to be positioned to allow a good view of the surrounding seas. This meant the *Tegetthoff's* towers were built below the bridge but of sufficient height to provide this better view. The inside of a conning tower was never a pleasant post as conditions were cramped and the walls thickness was unpleasantly 'claustrophobic'.

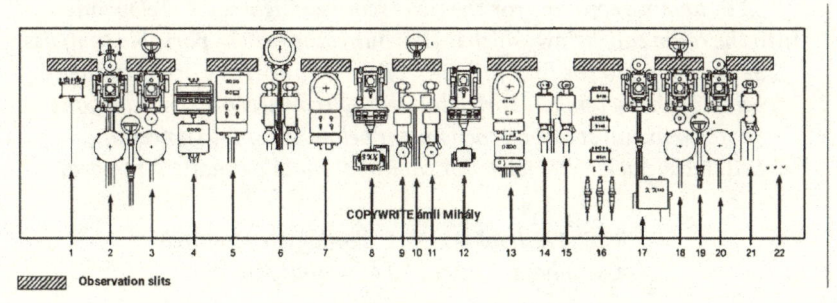

THE INTERNAL LAYOUT OF THE REAR CONNING TOWER OF THE VIRIBUS UNITIS.

Since it was to serve as both a Fire Control Centre and an auxiliary Command Bridge, the F.C.C. included both the fire control and a reserve navigation station. The instruments for these operations were mounted along an inner wall that was comprised of 4 cm (1 19/16 inches) of armour, to protect the equipment (and the personnel) from the shell fire received during an engagement.

<u>KEY</u>

L. Semi-enclosed lamps illuminating downwards. 1. Heavy Artillery

129

Fire Trigger Gong Buton. 2. Telephone into the first command tower and underneath the tachometer (propeller). 3. Telephone to the fire control centre on the upper level of the first conning tower. Beneath it is a tachometer and a connector for a portable telegraph. 4. Fire readiness indicator for 30.5 cm cannons. Below it are ammunition indicators for the 15 cm cannons. 5. Distance and deflection transmitter for 30.5 cm cannons. 6. Rear Artillery Monitoring Station Transmitter Receiver. Below it is a mouthpiece and bell in the right battery command position and in the rear crow's nest. 7. Target and projectile type, method and start of firing, etc. 8. The artillery call centre. 9. Nozzle and bell to the aft, under-armour fire control centre. 10. Torpedo launcher command signalling device. 11. Mouthpiece and bell in the torpedo launch room in the tat. 12. Crow nest telephone exchange. 13. The type of target and projectile in the first fire control centre, the method of firing, etc. receiver of the selector's transmitter. Underneath are ammunition for 15 cm cannons. 14. Nozzle and bell in the rear dynamo. 15. Mouthpiece and bell to left battery command position. 16. Remote controls for the three rear headlights. 17. Telephone into the radio cab, below which is the connector for the portable compass. 18. Telephone to the first fire control centre under the armoured deck, below tachometer. 19. Portable telegraph connector. 20. Telephone for manual steering, tachometer below. 21. Mouthpiece and bell in the back. 22. Hooks for cables for mobile headlight remotes.

SOURCE: *The book Az Osztrák-Magyar Monarchia Csatahajói 1904-1914 by ámli Mihály.*

Translation from the original Hungarian by Google.

THE TEGETTHOFF CLASS.

ACCESS TO THE CONNING TOWER WAS BY A HATCH IN THE REAR WALL INTO THE TOWERS LOWER LEVEL LOCATED BELOW THE BRIDGE STRUCTURE. THE HATCH NEEDED TO BE NEAR THE COMMAND BRIDGE TO PERMIT QUICK ACCESS IN THE EVENT OF SUDDEN COMBAT.

ANDY SOUTH

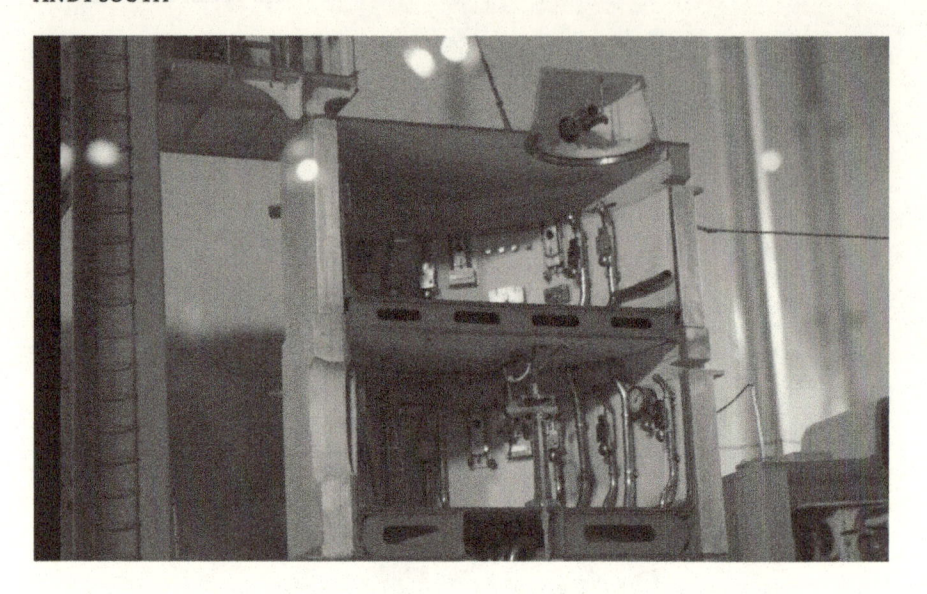

THE VENICE MODEL SHOWING THE CONNING TOWERS INTERIOR. THE TOWER WAS COMPRISED OF TWO LEVELS, ACCESSED BY A REAR WALL LADDER. THERE WERE TWO EXITS, ONE VIA THE HATCH IN THE REAR WALL AND THE OTHER VIA A LADDERED TUBE DOWN INTO THE SHIPS DEPTHS, THE LADDER TO THE REAR OF THE IMAGE IS THE INTERNAL ACCESS TO THE SHIPS MASTS UPPER LEVELS. CUT INTO THE ROOF OF THE TOWER IS ONE OF THE SHIPS MAIN RANGEFINDERS.

THE TEGETTHOFF CLASS.

THE REAR CONNING TOWER OR ANTI-AIRCRAFT CONTROL FOR THE SHIPS SECONDARY

THE RANGEFINDERS

GRAND ADMIRAL

T he conning tower was surmounted by the ships main Barr and Stroud rangefinder, encased as we have seen in an armoured hood.

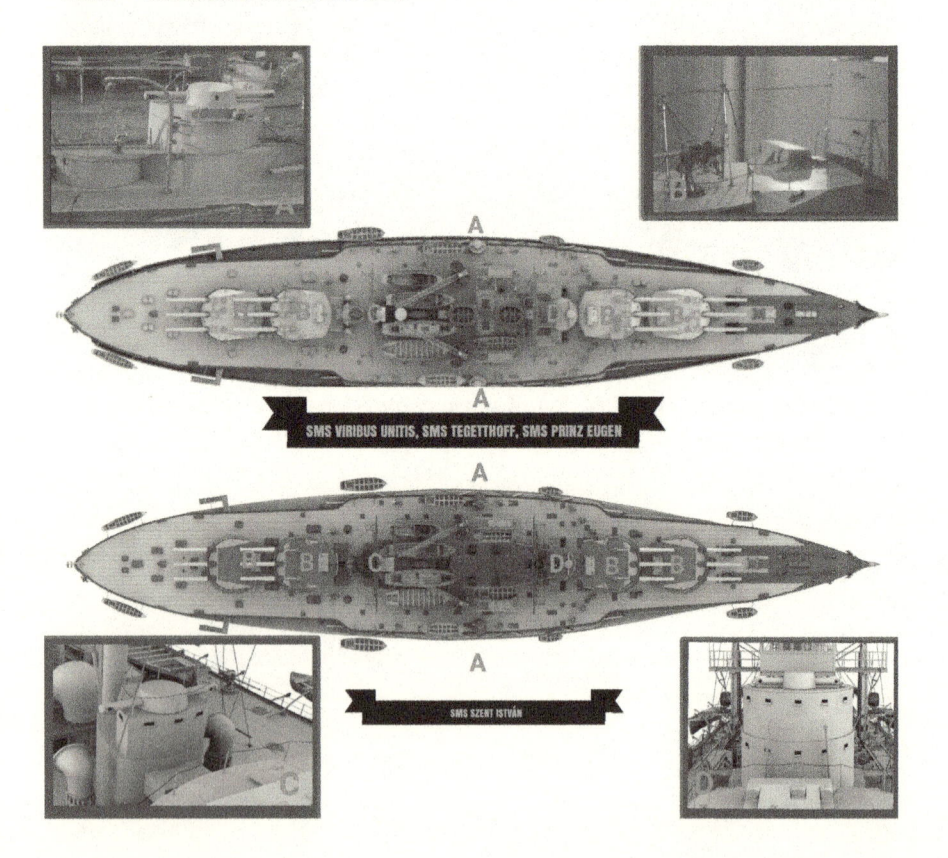

SMS VIRIBUS UNITIS, SMS TEGETTHOFF, SMS PRINZ EUGEN

SMS SZENT ISTVÁN

THE TEGETTHOFF CLASS.

A= 15 CM RANGE FINDER
B= 30.5 CM ROOF TURRET RANGEFINDER
C= AFT CONNING TOWER RANGEFINDER
D= FWD CONNING TOWER RANGEFINDER.

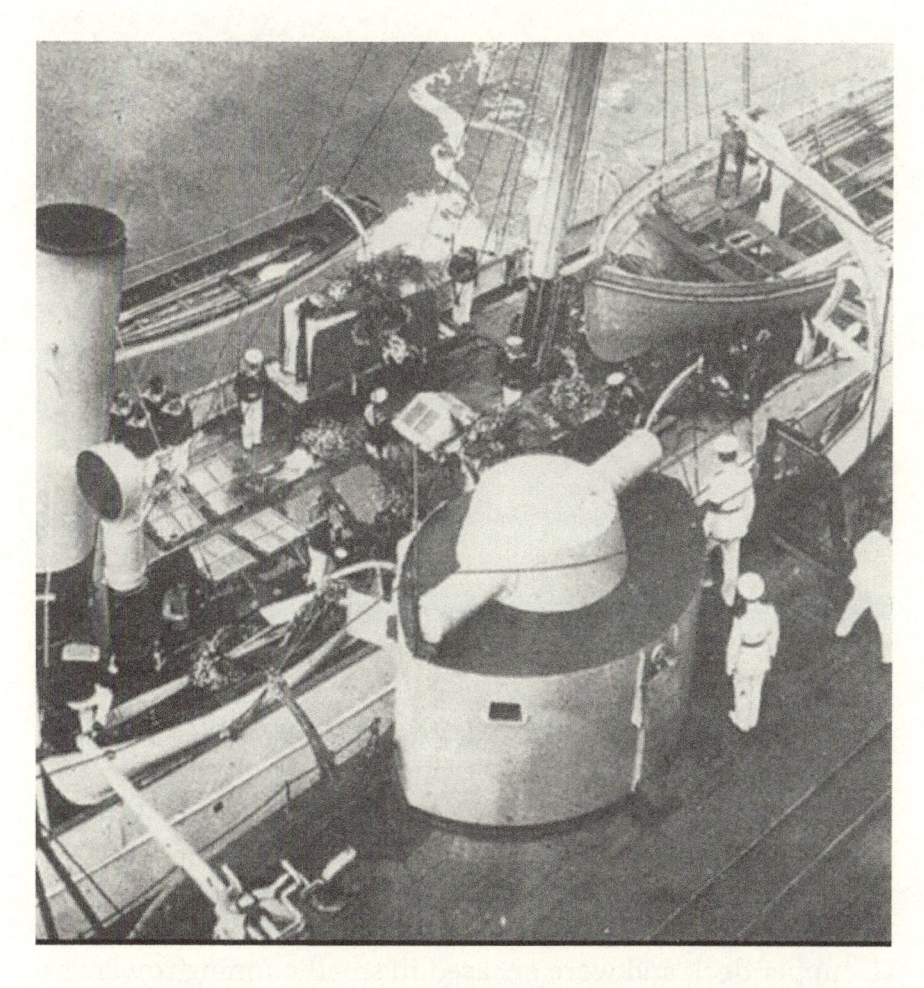

PREVIOUS PAGE. THE 15CM DECK LEVEL RANGE FINDERS, THE BOAT ALONGSIDE HOLDS THE COFFINS OF THE ARCHDUKE FERDINAND AND HIS WIFE IN JUNE 1914.

The 'science' of control was carried out in the same way as on all other dreadnoughts within the worlds fleets, the lookouts on the fore-mast noted the fall of the shells and transmitted the information by telephone to allow the necessary adjustments to be made to the shooting calculation data. Then the adjustments required were transmitted to the turrets and casements.

A DECK LEVEL VIEW OF THE 15CM RANGEFINDER. THE METAL PILLAR TO THE RIGHT IS ONE OF THE SUPPORTS FOR THE SMALL BOAT STRUCTURE.

The records show that the *Radetzkys* and the *Tegetthoffs* used British manufactured Barr & Stroud optical rangefinders. The two main rangefinders had a 12-foot (3.65 m) base and were located on the conning towers [C & D]. Then there were six 107.29/32-inch (2.74 mtrs) range finders which were there to support the 15 cm gun crews. Four were carried located on the upper deck and were encased in small conning towers or cupolas [A]. These rangefinders were protected by a 25 mm of armoured and reportedly housed the 0.310-inch (8-mm) Schwarzlose M.07/12 anti-aircraft machine gun. There was in addition four rangefinders [B] were within the turret's roofs, for local gunnery control.

.

THE TEGETTHOFF CLASS.

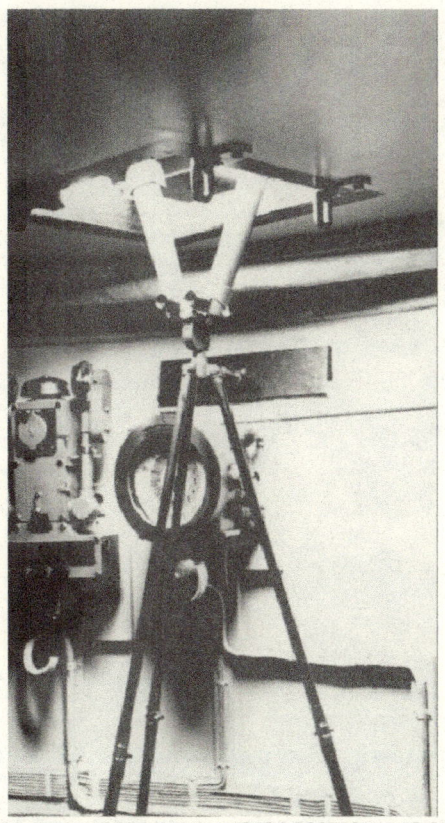

PREVIOUS PAGE. THE TURRET COMMANDERS POSTION AND RANGEFINDER
FROM WITHIN ONE OF THE VIRIBUS UNITIS FOUR TURRETS

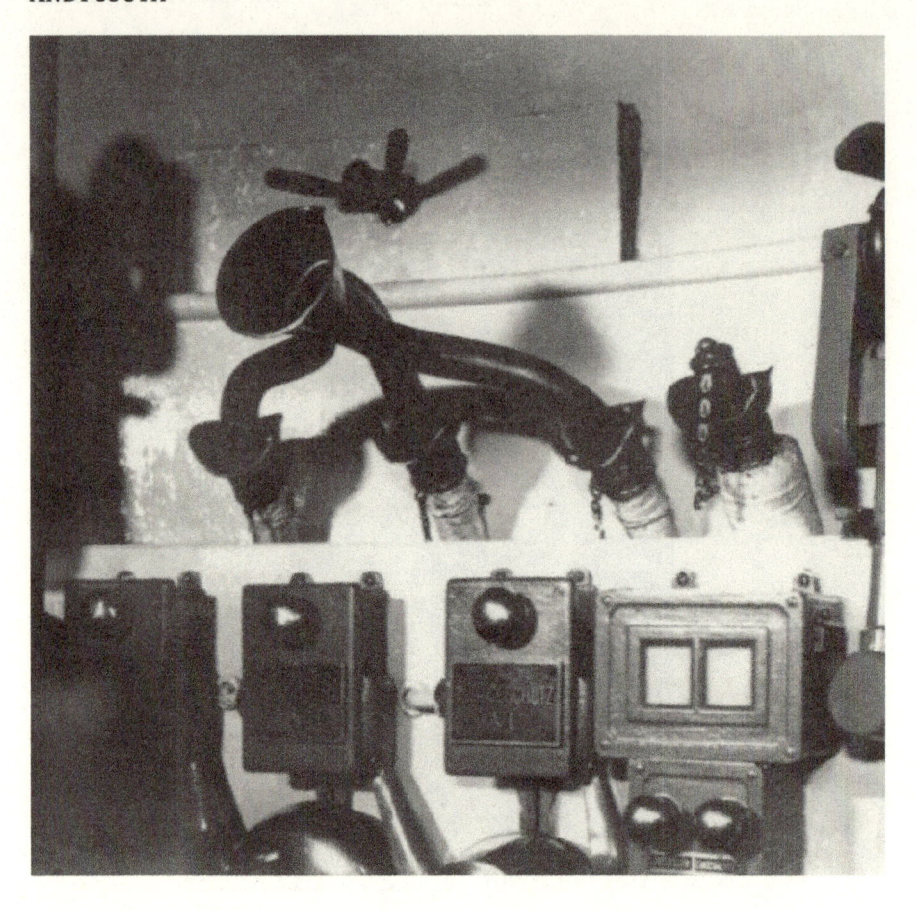

ANDY SOUTH

THE TURRET COMMANDERS EQUIPMENT BANK FROM WITHIN A TURRET ONBOARD THE VIRIBUS UNITIS.

THE BRIDGE STRUCTURE.

THE TEGETTHOFF CLASS.

ADMIRAL

The bridge was not armoured in any significant form but was larger and far more spacious. It was for this reason, the ships command post when not in combat was from this latter position.

*THE SHIPS COMMAND BRIDGE. UNLIKE OTHER NATIONS, THE FLEET FLAGSHIP LACKED A SEPARATE ADMIRALS BRIDGE. THE BRIDGE STRUCTURE WAS SIMPLE IN ITS DESIGN AND THE OPEN BRIDGE WAS ACCESSED BY ...
.....TWO LADDERS TO THE REAR OF THE ENCLOSED STRUCTURE. GIVEN THE PROXIMITY OF THE TWO LARGE SEARCHLIGHTS, I QUESTION THE VALIDITY OF THE COMMAND CREW'S NIGHT VISION WITH THEM ILLUMINATED?*

Given the warmer climate of the Mediterranean, the Tegetthoff's bridge was less all-encompassing than her Anglo or

Germanic rivals. Plans and photographs imply it even lacked doors, just being a windowed rectangle with two doorways. With the weather on the after quarter, the bridge interior would have been a cold, wet and windy place.

The bridge held the usual ships wheel, compass, telegraph, and communication tubes. But a number of these were replicated on the roof, creating an open bridge for those milder 'Mediterranean' days.

PREVIOUS PAGE. THE CONNING TOWER AND BRIDGE. ACCESS TO THE BRIDGE WAS SOMEWHAT EXPOSED TO THE WEATHER.

THE TEGETTHOFF CLASS.

THE REAR OF THE TWO STRUCTURES. IT CLEARLY SHOWS THE LACK OF 'COMPLEXITY WITHIN THE BRIDGE STRUCTURE. THERE APPEARS TO BE LITTLE STRUCTURAL SUPPORT TO THE BRIDGE ASIDE FROM TWO SET OF 'STRUT' LEGS? THE SQUARE PLATE TO THE REAR OF THE UPPER LEVEL IS A SMOKE SHIELD, TO PROTECT THE BRIDGE CREW FROM FUNNEL EMISSIONS

AN OVERVIEW OF THE COMPLEX. LATER IN THEIR SHORT SERVICE LIFE'S

ANDY SOUTH

THE UPPER BRIDGES RAILINGS WERE TO BE CANVAS CLAD, WHICH MUST HAVE MADE THE CREW FEEL LESS BATTERED BY THE WEATHER.

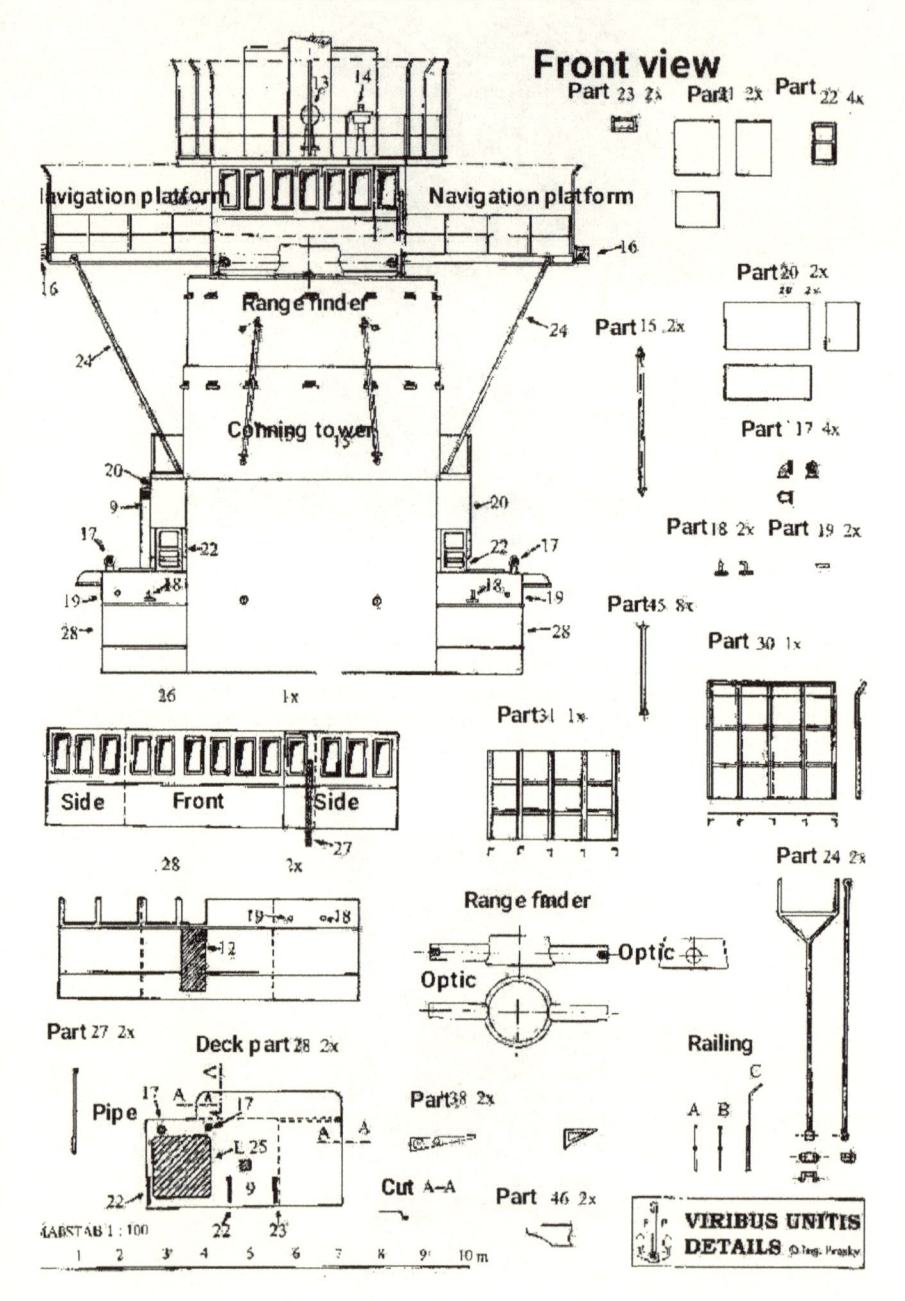

142

THE TEGETTHOFF CLASS.

PREVIOUS PAGE. FRONT PLANS OF THE BRIDGE STRUCTURE.

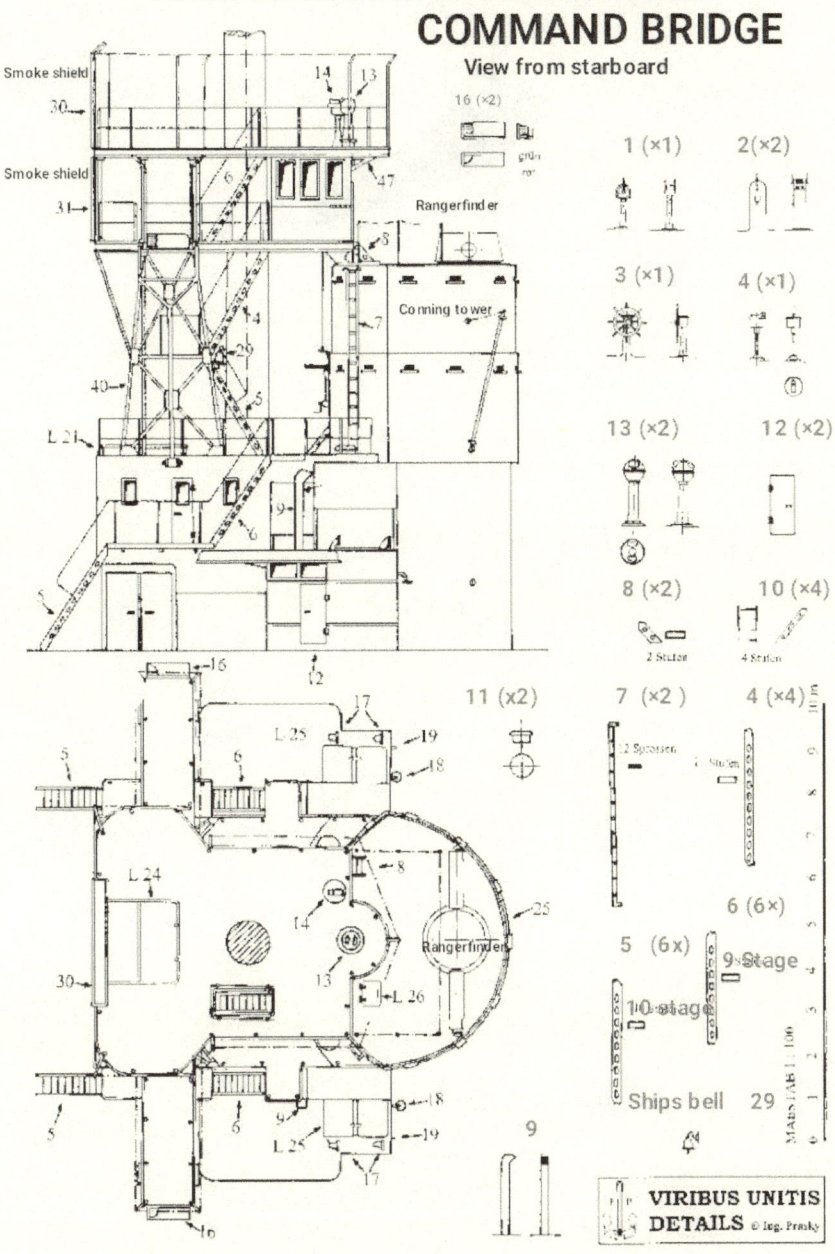

COMMAND BRIDGE
View from starboard

PREVIOUS PAGE. SIDE PLANS OF THE BRIDGE STRUCTURE

143

ANDY SOUTH

CHAPTER 6: SHIP COLOURS.

Between the turn of the century and 1914 the Austro-Hungarian navy employed an olive-green paint scheme to their ships. But a change to the more universal grey was in the main to be completed by the outbreak of the war in 1914.

Photos from the year prior to the war seem to imply the *Viribus Unitis* and *Tegetthoff* sported the olive-green scheme. But a photo dated May 1914 of the *Tegetthoff* hints that by that date she was in the new grey. Similarly, photos of the Viribus Unitis bearing the Archduke's body home in August also hint that she too had adopted the grey livery. In the years between 1899 and 1914, the ships hulls, superstructures, all exterior visible parts such as vents, masts, cranes, boats etc... bore a dark green colour. The scheme was nicknamed 'Montecucolin' after the then current C-in-C. The Waterline was a pink and the submerged hull a "green poison colour".

THE 'MONTECUCOLIN' COLOUR SCHEME

The first ship to apply this vivid colour scheme was the cruiser *Leopard* in the September 1899. Then from 1st June 1901, all the navy's newly commissioned warships were to receive the 'green/pink' scheme. In 1906, this was to be taken up officially by the remainder of the fleet apart from the torpedo-boats, which were painted overall black in colour and the yachts, which were painted white.

By February 1914, it had been assumed by the Admirals in Vienna that as the fleet would most likely fight on the open seas, the dark green colour that was designed, to camouflage the ships operating under the coast would no longer serve its purpose. A new "bluish light gray" colour scheme was ordered and was to be first applied on the pre-dreadnought *Radetzky* and the *Saida*, following her launch. On 23rd December 1913, the colour scheme was adopted for the fleet and nicknamed 'Hausian' after the then C-in-C. In 1915 the pink waterline, which had a too bigger contrast to the hull was changed to a dark grey waterline.

THE TEGETTHOFF CLASS.

BATTLESHIP PAINT COLOUR HAUSIAN, USED ABOVE THE WATERLINE. (RGB: 182,200,204. CMYK: 12,0,3,20 HEX: B6C8CC) Source: http://www.viribusunitis.ca/viribus-unitis-class

BATTLESHIP PAINT COLOUR ROSA, USED AT THE WATERLINE. (RGB: 221,121,176. CMYK: 9,65,0,0. HEX: dd79b0) Source: http://www.viribusunitis.ca/viribus-unitis-class

ANDY SOUTH

BATTLESHIP PAINT COLOUR ANTI-FOULING GREEN, USED BELOW THE WATERLINE. (RGB:0,105,85 CMYK:90,0,60,50 HEX: 006955) source: http://www.viribusunitis.ca/viribus-unitis-class

CHAPTER 7: FIXTURES AND FITTINGS.

ANCHORS

VICE-ADMIRAL

The class carried three Taizak stockless anchors [1], two on the port side of the bow weighing 8.28 tonnes (8.14 ton) and the third at 8.22 tonnes (8.10 ton) as a spare on the bows starboard side. The chain these were connected too was of 70-mm (2.57 inches) in its calibre and ran along the bows decking, before dropping down several decks into a storage compartment. A Taizak anchor of 3.04 tonnes (2.99 ton) was carried on the stern hull on the starboard side with a 47 mm (1.85 inch) gauge link chain. Two small Admiralty anchors (with a stock) of 1.50 tonnes (1,47 tons) and 0.75 tonnes (0.73 tons) were secured to the port side. The total weight of all the anchors together with chains was 9.92 tonnes (9.76 tons). The anchor spiers, stoppers, locks, and other anchor equipment weighed 35.56 tonne (35 tons).

THE TEGETTHOFF CLASS.

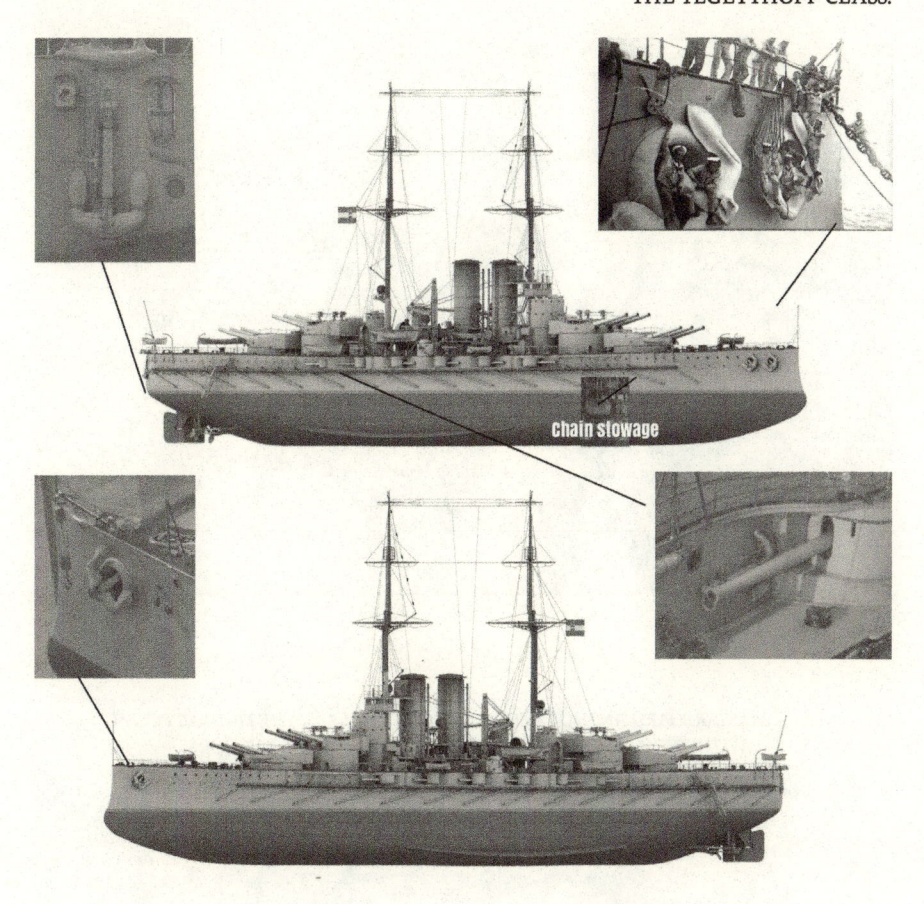

chain stowage

THE TWO STARBOARD ANCHORS FROM ONE OF THE CLASS. THE FIGURES POSING WITH THEM GIVES A GOOD SENSE OF SCALE TO THE ANCHORS.

THE TEGETTHOFF CLASS.

THE VIRIBUS UNITIS AND TEGETTHOFF ANCHORS TODAY AS DOOR GUARDIANS TO THE (ITALIAN) NAVAL HISTORY MUSEUM IN VENICE.

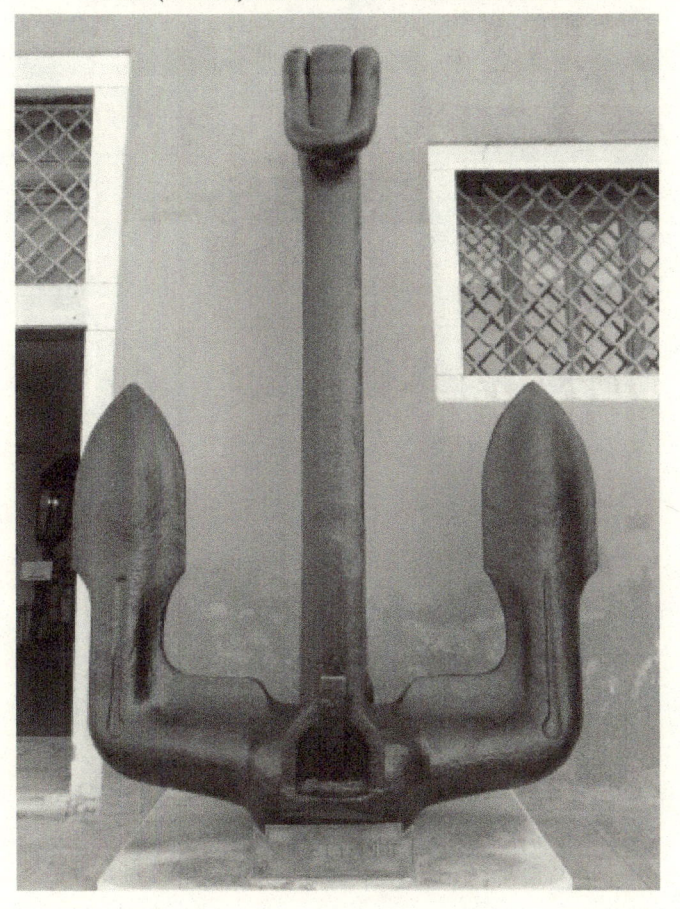

THE TEGETTHOFF's ANCHOR

ANDY SOUTH

THE VIRIBUS UNITIS" ANCHOR

THE TEGETTHOFF CLASS.

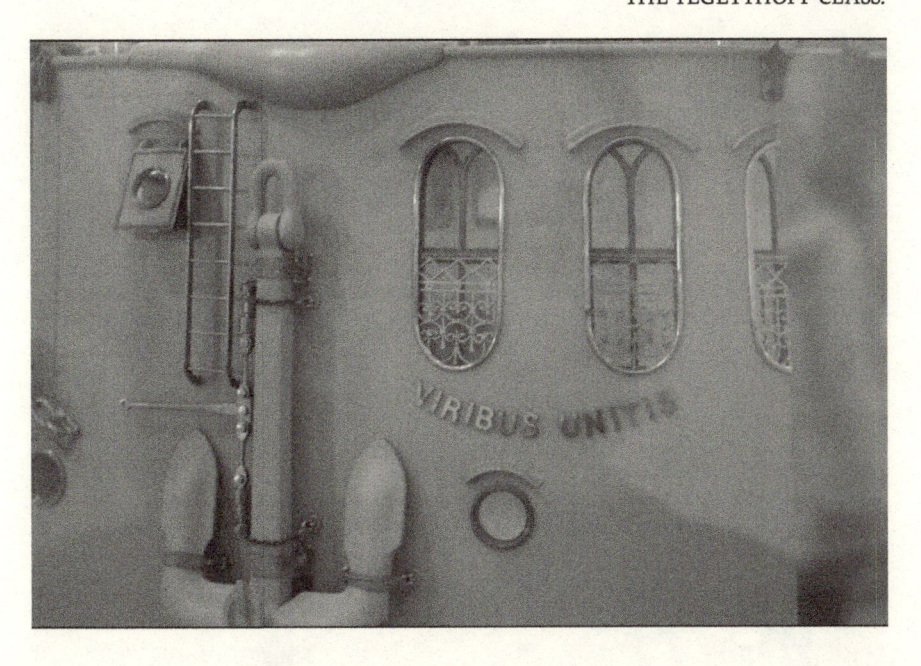

ONE OF THE STOCKLESS STERN ANCHORS, 1500 KG (1.6 TONS).

PREVIOUS PAGE: THE PRINZ EUGEN A FEW DAYS PRIOR TO HER LAUNCH. THE IMAGE SHOWS FULL SCALE ANCHORS. HOWEVER HER BOIW ANCHORS WERE STOCKLESS AND THESE BOTH BEAR THE CROSS BAR.

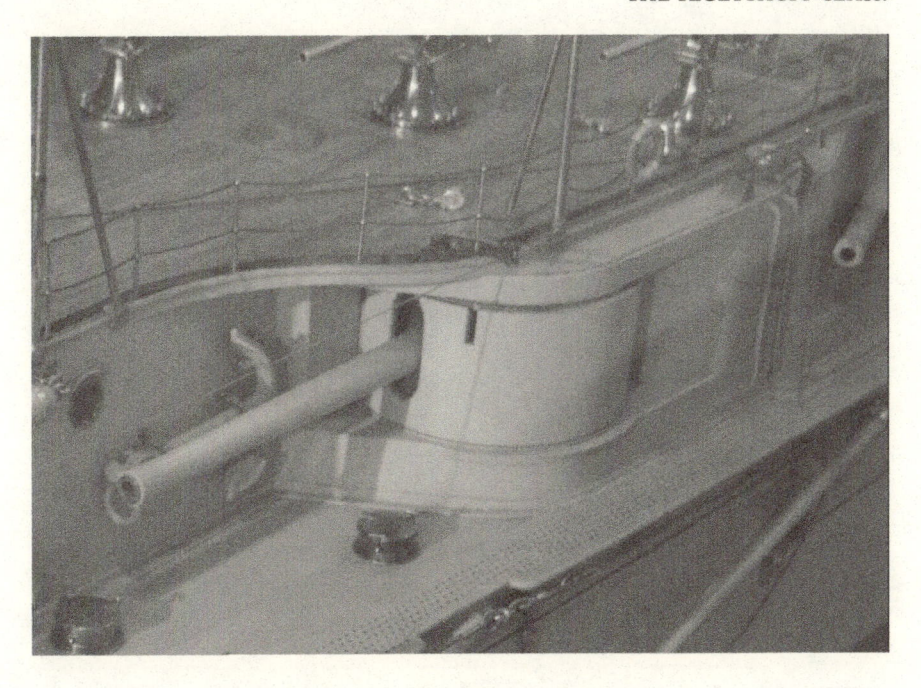

BARELY NOTICEABLE AND ONLY ON THE ONE SIDE OF THE HULL WAS A SMALLER ANCHOR NESTLED IN AGAINST THE FORWARD CASEMENT. 750 KG (0.673 TONS)

[1] A Taizak anchor was the invention of a Scotsman called George Taizak. It was to become common through out the world's Navies. It omitted the traditional horizontal bar at the head of the stock that had been common place until then.

COMMUNICATIONS

REAR ADMIRAL

Each ship was equipped with a long-range 500-watt Telefunken (German) radio station as well as two Morse telegraphs, for which the ships masts bore one large and one small antenna. There was also an improved model of the Austrian companies Sellner system of night communication, which permitted signaling at night through the use of coloured lights. [1] The navigation aids included three Anshütz (German) gyrocompass.

THE TEGETTHOFF CLASS.

W= Turn lights
D= Distinction lights
M= Machine lights
K= Machine cone
W1= Pennant starboard
W2= Pennant port

Oyster-basket type antenna
Bamboo ring
Lightning rod
Top lantern crane
Umbrella & egg isolators
Sellner system (night signal apparatus)
Crows nest
Connecting stays
Sellner gaf
Flags gaf
Leading cables
Conducting cable
White
Red
Blue
Red forward
White
Red
Blue
White
Red
Gaff vang
Navigation lights
Red backwards
Conductor cable
Jackstay
Shrouds

VIRIBUS UNITIS DETAILS © Ing. Prasky

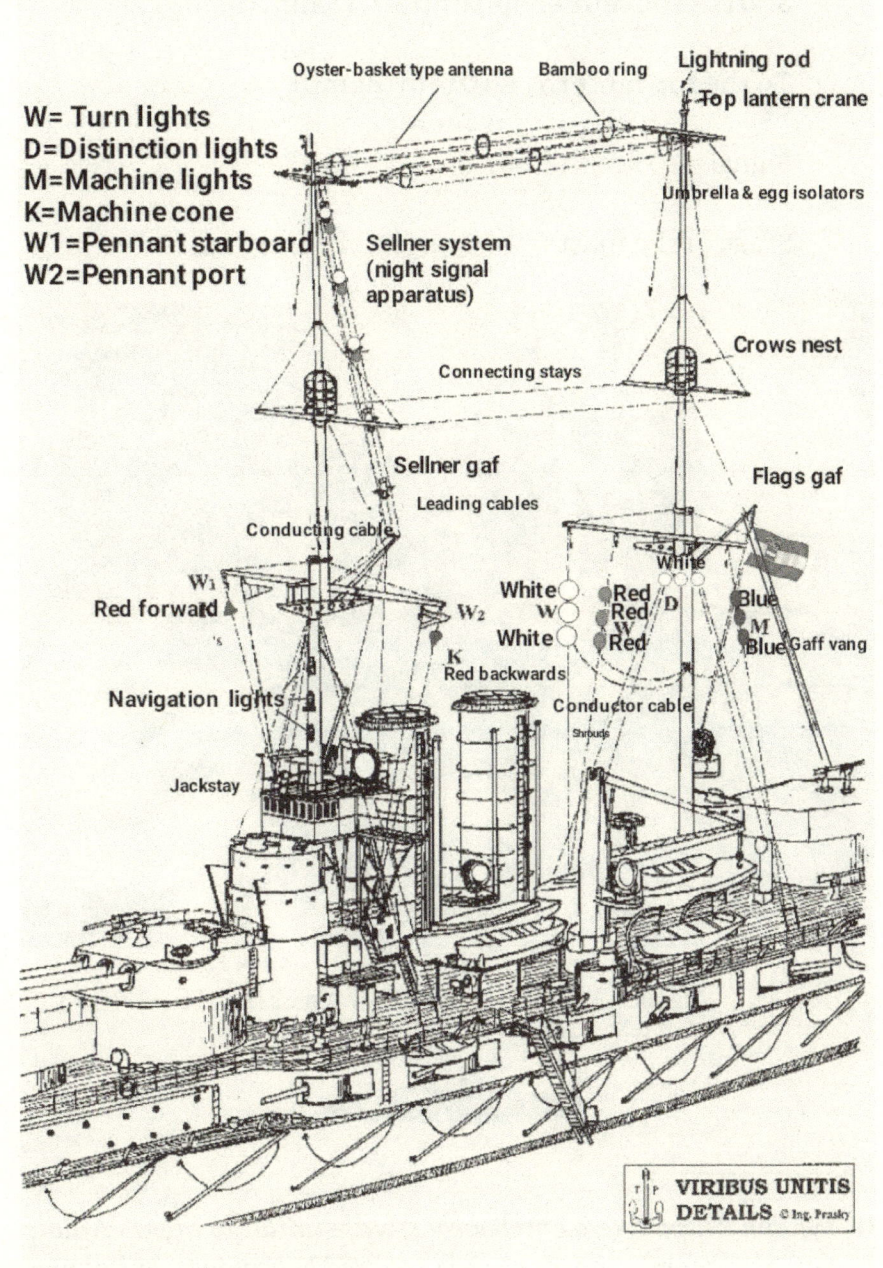

The masts wire gauges were:

Shrouds of the jib and coarse mast = 32 mm steel (wire)

Start of the sellner apparatus = 15 mm (hemp)

To the top lanterns = 10 mm (hemp)

Signal = 10 km (hemp)

Stage of the masts= 16 mm (steel wire)

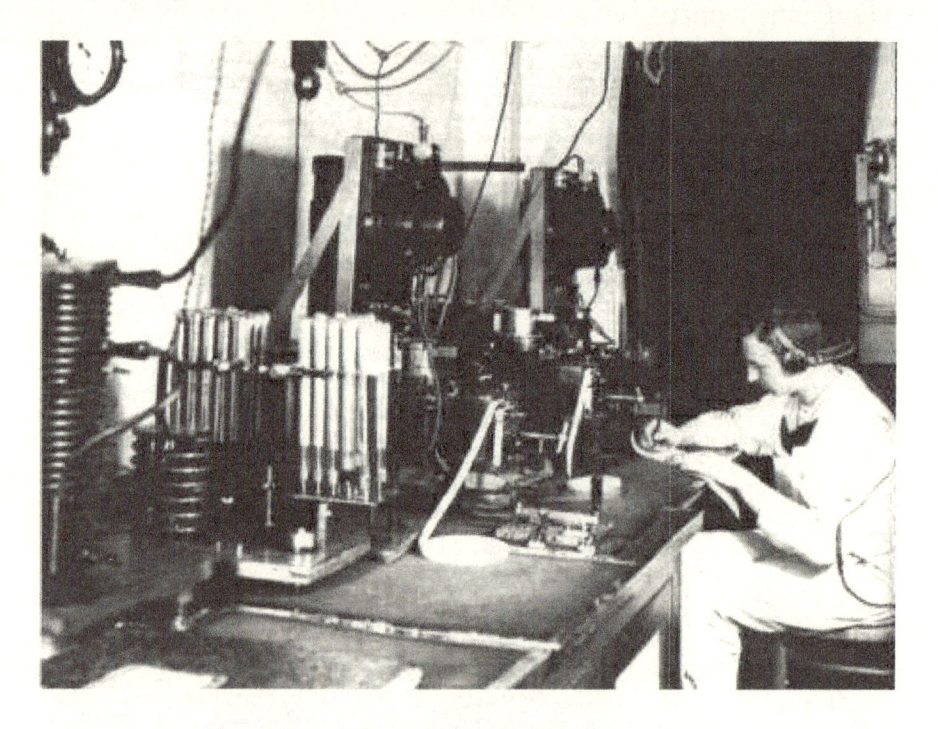

PREVIOUS PAGE.THE VIRIBUS UNITIS WIRELESS ROOM.

[1] Lyndon Redpath (c/o Facebook) "It was similar to the US Ardois system of transmitting Morse by Coloured light where a Dot was indicated by a Red light and a dash was indicated by a white light (A=Red ,White, B=White Red Red Red and so on.) In 1891-1892 , the US navy did comparison studies on the Ardois and Sellner sys-

tems, and although the Sellner system was cheaper to produce, the Ardois was better made and thus more reliable".

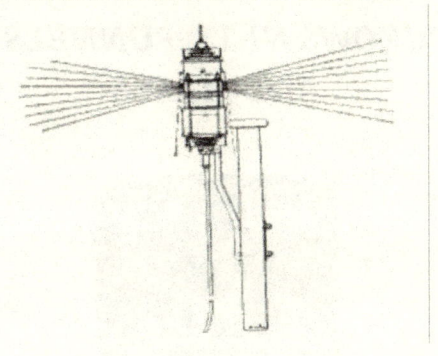

CROWS NETS, FUNNELS AND MASTS

BATTLESHIP CAPTAIN

The class had two masts, both fitted with crows' nests, which due to the better visibility found in the Mediterranean, were installed higher than on the battleships of the other navies. Access to these lofty perches was by a ladder contained within the masts steel casing.

The two funnels that the crow's nest overlooked were 44.25 feet (13.5 metres) in height and were later to be covered with wire nets, (*Prinz Eugen* excepted), due to a perceived danger of enemy planes dropping their bombs into the funnels. During the war years, the port of Pola and its ships would be subjected to over eighty air raids by the newly formed Italian Air Force, but scoring no notable success, neither down the funnels or otherwise.

THE TEGETTHOFF CLASS.

THE COMPLEXITY OF THE SHIPS 'RIGGING', A LARGE PERCENTAGE OF WHICH WAS 'COMMUNICATION' IN ITS FUNCTION. THE TWO CROWS' NESTS ARE VISIBLE, ODDLY REMINISCENT OF A BY GONE SAIL BOUND AGE. THE TORPEDO NETS ARE JUST VISIBLE ALONG THE RIGHT EDGE OF THE IMAGE.

The masts rigging gauges were:

Shrouds of the jib and coarse mast = 32 mm steel (wire)

Start of the sellner apparatus = 15 mm (hemp)

To the top lanterns = 10 mm (hemp)   Signal = 10 km (hemp)

Stage of the masts = 16 mm (steel wire)

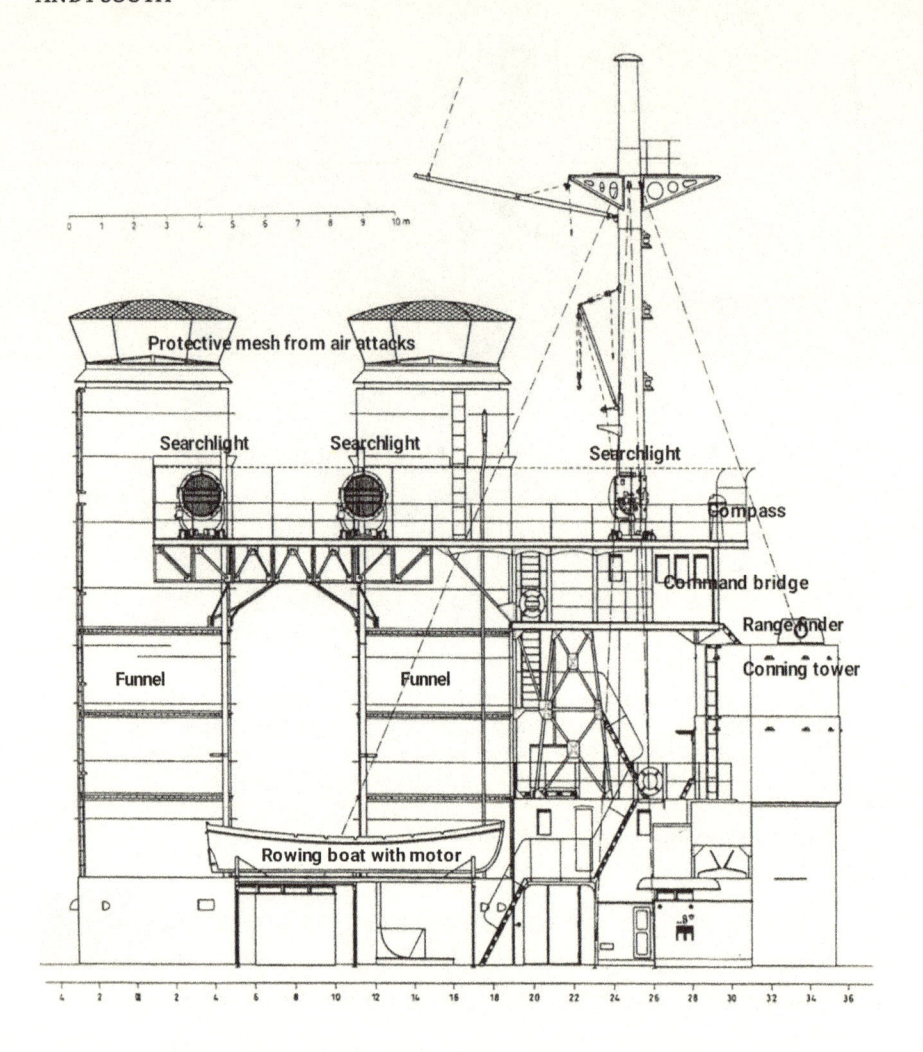

THE LOWER PORTION OF THE MAST WITH ITS SURROUNDING STRUCTURES.

THE TEGETTHOFF CLASS.

BARELY VISIBLE WITHIN THE FUNNELS GLOOM ARE TWO HATCHES WHICH SEALED THE UNIT SHUT. THEIR USE IS UNCLEAR, BUT I WOULD SPECULATE THEY SERVED SOME FORM OF SPLINTER PROTECTION. THE RIGHT 'DOOR' BEARS A SMALL CIRCULAR HOLE FOR OMISSIONS. THE DOORS ARE CENTRE HINGED AND WHEN OPENED HUNG VERTICALLY DOWN THE FUNNELS CENTRE.

SEARCHLIGHTS

FRIGATE CAPTAIN COMMANDER)

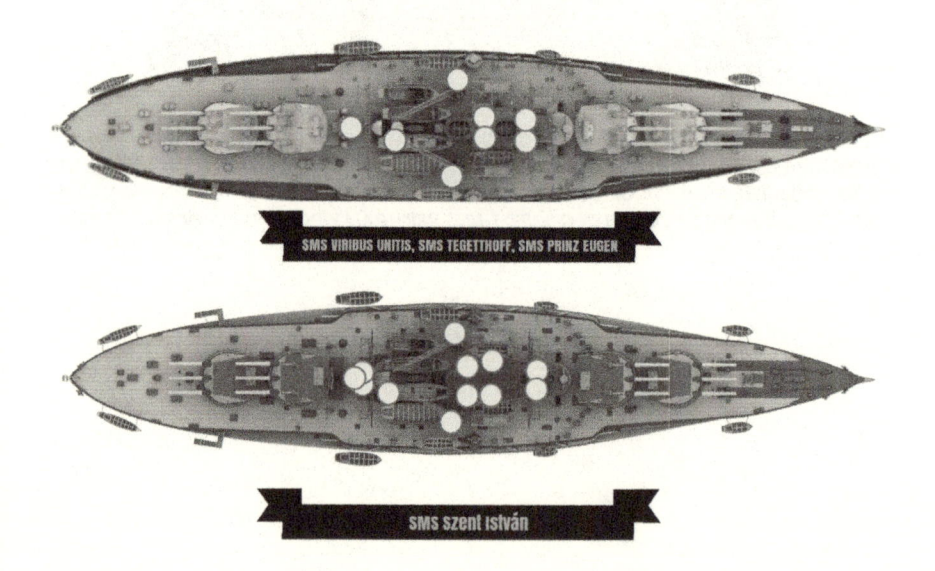

SMS VIRIBUS UNITIS, SMS TEGETTHOFF, SMS PRINZ EUGEN

SMS Szent István

THE SEARCHLIGHT STATIONS.

The most strikingly obvious visual difference between the *Szent István* and her stepsisters was the platform built around the fore funnel of the former. It ran from the bridge to the aft funnel and on it were mounted several

THE TEGETTHOFF CLASS.

of the ship's searchlights. These formed the ship's night combat system which was comprised of eleven searchlights with a mirror diameter of 43.30 inches (110 cm).

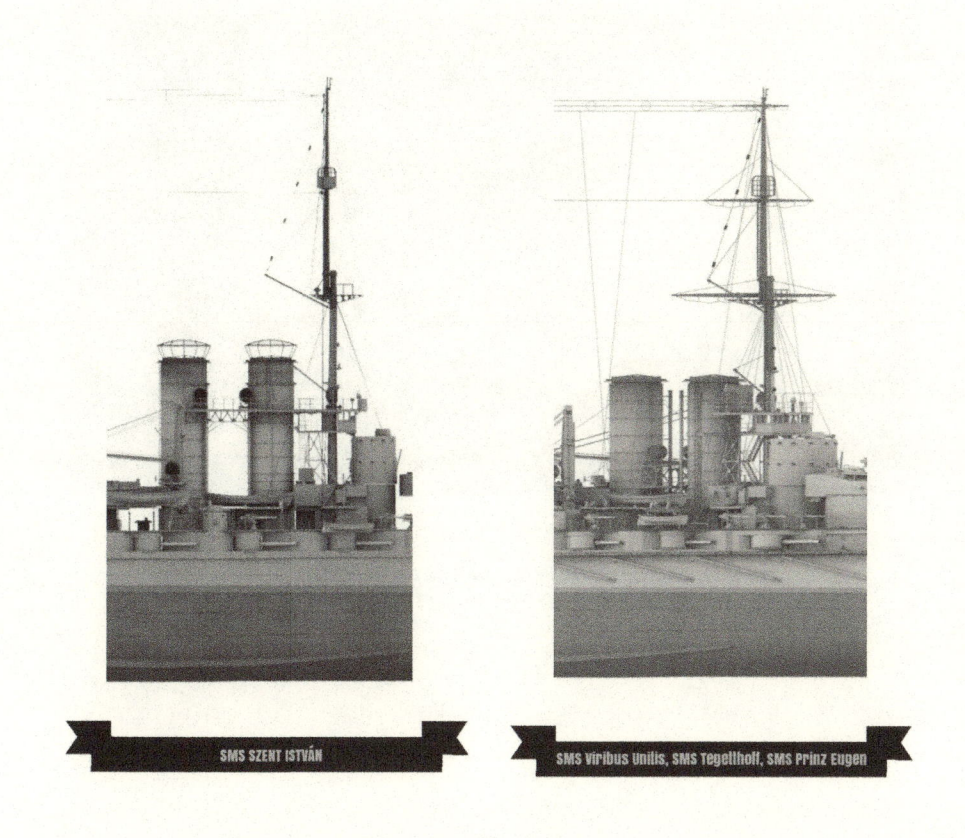

SMS SZENT ISTVÁN

SMS Viribus Unitis, SMS Tegetthoff, SMS Prinz Eugen

PREVIOUS PAGE. THE MAJOR DIFFERENCE BETWEEN THE AUSTRIAN AND HUNGARIAN DREADNOUGHTS WAS THE AMID SHIPS STRUCTURE.

They were located on platforms around both masts, on platforms between the funnels and behind the second funnel, as well as on the side of the boat cranes. The searchlights were designed primarily for operations at night and were equipped with a remote-control system (one vertical and three horizontal guidance speeds), so that they could be activated without leaving the conning tower. The three 'Austrian' ships carried seven of these pieces of equipment and the *Szent István* eleven. In addition, a smaller version was mounted on the 10-13 tonne motorboat.

THE BASE OF ONE OF THE PRINZ EUGENS 36 INCH SEARCHLIGHTS. SOURCE: NAVAL HISTORY & HERITAGE COMMAND.

THE TEGETTHOFF CLASS.

SEARCH LIGHT PLATFORMS AND UPPER WORKS OF THE PRINZ EUGEN, PHOTOGRAPHED POST WAR AT POLA. SOURCE: NAVAL HISTORY & HERITAGE COMMAND.

THE VIRIBUS UNITIS (IN A HAND COLOURED IMAGE) USING HER SEARCHLIGHTS.

ANDY SOUTH

SOURCE:MILIATRY IMAGES.COM

A CLOSE UP OF ONE OF THE VIRIBUS UNITIS MAIN SEARCHLIGHTS.

TORPEDO NETS

CORVETTE CAPTAIN (LIEUTENANT COMMANDER)

In the period prior to and during the first years of the war, torpedo nets had become a common part of a warship's life while in port or at anchor. They would be hung out from the stationary ships beam by a series of horizontal booms which ran in a line just below the casement level. The free ends of the booms would be swung out with the net hung on the opposite ends, suspending the net at a distance from the ship's hull.

The idea was that with this in place any torpedoes aimed at the ship would impact with the nets mesh and become ensnared or explode at a sufficient distance from the hull, in order to prevent serious damage being inflicted to the structure. But by 1915 with the British and French navies losing three battleships while their nets were deployed, most navies accepted the torpedo net was not an effective deterrent or safeguard. A lesson even their enemies noted. The three "Austrian" dreadnoughts used the British made Bullivant nets, but the *Szent István* was never to have her nets installed, as the outbreak of the war meant the English manufacturer was unable to ship them out [1]. However, her three stepsisters retained their nets until June 1917.

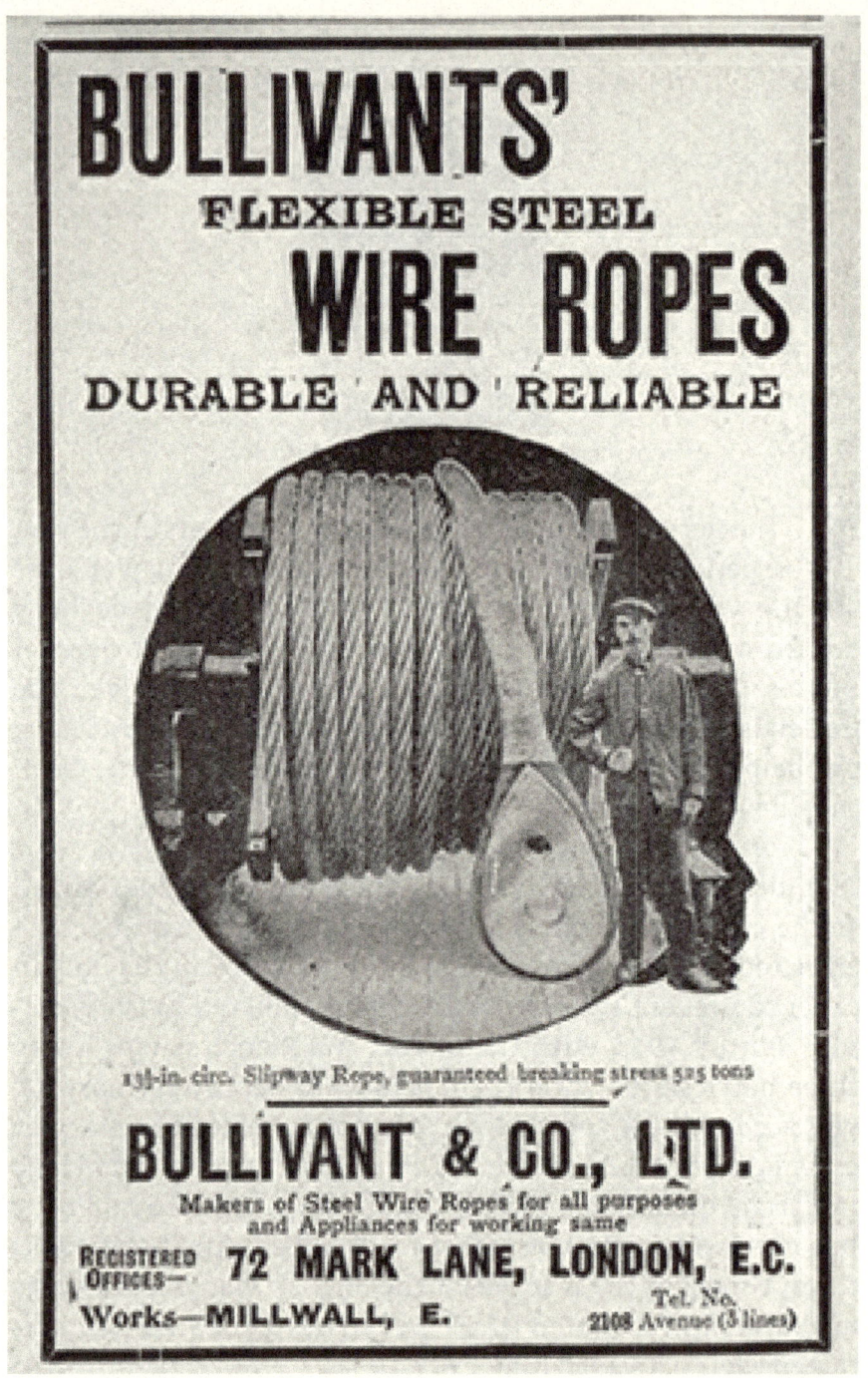

BULLIVANTS'
FLEXIBLE STEEL
WIRE ROPES
DURABLE AND RELIABLE

13½-in. circ. Slipway Rope, guaranteed breaking stress 525 tons

BULLIVANT & CO., LTD.
Makers of Steel Wire Ropes for all purposes
and Appliances for working same

REGISTERED OFFICES— 72 MARK LANE, LONDON, E.C.

Works—MILLWALL, E.

Tel. No. 2108 Avenue (3 lines)

The Bullivant type (named after the London company which

manufactured them) was constructed of steel wire rings and these were joined by a series of smaller steel rings, forming a continuous crinoline and weighed over 1 lb (453.59 g) per square foot. When required they were slung out on 40 feet (12.19 mtr) long wooden booms and were shorter for obvious reasons than the traditional boat poles. The booms were connected to the ships side by a simple hinged fitting and were held in place high above the water level by stays from the derricks or mast heads. Extensive trials by the manufacturer in the late 1890's proved that they were capable of stopping, without damage, a slow moving 14-inch (360 mm) torpedo, which it had been feared might explode and destroy the net. A 16-inch (410 mm) torpedo with a 91-pound (41 kg) warhead proved capable of causing limited damage to the net.

PREVIOUS PAGE.THE TORPEDO NETS DEPLOYED FOR ONE OF THE DREADNOUGHTS. NOTE THE SHIPS BOAT AND THE IMPOSSIBILTY TO LAUNCH HER BY DIVAT WHEN THE NETS ARE DEPLOYED. SOURCE: NAVAL HISTORY & HERITAGE COMMAND.

The booms on the three Tegetthoff's were carried along the sides and stowed under the casements, except possibly for a pair secured at the bow and the stern. The cumbersome netting took a long time to deploy and longer still to stow away. They could only ever be used with the ship was at anchor and were prone (while stowed) to damage in bad weather, sometimes being completely washed away.

[1] Was there somewhere within the Grand Fleet at Scapa Flow a capital ship deploying the nets that had been destined for Pola?

THE PRICE TAG

BATTLESHIP LIEUTENANT

The 1913 edition of The Naval Annual records a cost of £2,500,000 for the Austrian ships. The same volume notes the following process for the empires rivals Dreadnoughts:

Collingwood (Great Britain) £1,193,121,
Nassau (Germany) £1,825,000,
North Dakota (USA) £970,630.

CREW

CORVETTE LIEUTENANT (SUB-LIEUTENANT)

The ship's crew was comprised of 31 officers, 16 petty-officers and 993 men. The Szent István had 38 officers. With an Admiral and his staff on board an additional 37 officers and 16 non-commissioned officers were carried.

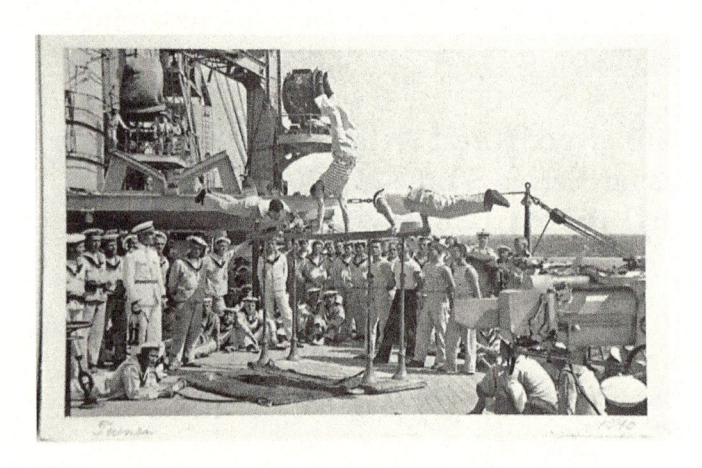

PREVIOUS PAGE.'SPORTS DAY' ON BOARD THE TEGETTHOFF.

THE TEGETTHOFF CLASS.

PREVIOUS PAGE. GIVEN THE SHUTTER SPEEDS OF CAMERAS IN THIS PERIOD, THE ATHLETIC BUT UPENDED CREW MAN MUST BE HOLDING HIS POSE, OTHERWISE HE WOULD BE BLURRED!

ANDY SOUTH

A PORTION OF THE OFFICERS AND CREW FROM POSSIBLY THE VIRIBUS UNITIS.

THE OFFICERS OF THE VIRIBUS UNITS.

THE CREW OF THE VIRIBUS UNITS WITH THE SHIPS CAT. THE FADED TEXT WITHIN THE LIFE BOUY REFERS TO EASTER 1917.

THE TEGETTHOFF CLASS.

A PORTION OF THE VIRIBUS UNITIS CREW (STOKERS?) THE NCAPTION READS "THIS WARTIME, LAST CHRISTMAS" I'M ADVISED BY A HUNGARIAN FRIEND.

CREW MEMBERS OF THE VIRIBUS UNITIS POSE BENEATH THE 30.CM GUNS.

ANDY SOUTH

THREE OFFICERS STAND BEFORE THE MAIN GUNS OF THE TEGETTHOFF. THE BLACK ARMS WOULD IMPLY THE PHOTO DATES FROM JUNE 1914, WHEN THE SHIP ESCORTED THE ARCHDUKES COFFINS HOME.

THE TEGETTHOFF CLASS.

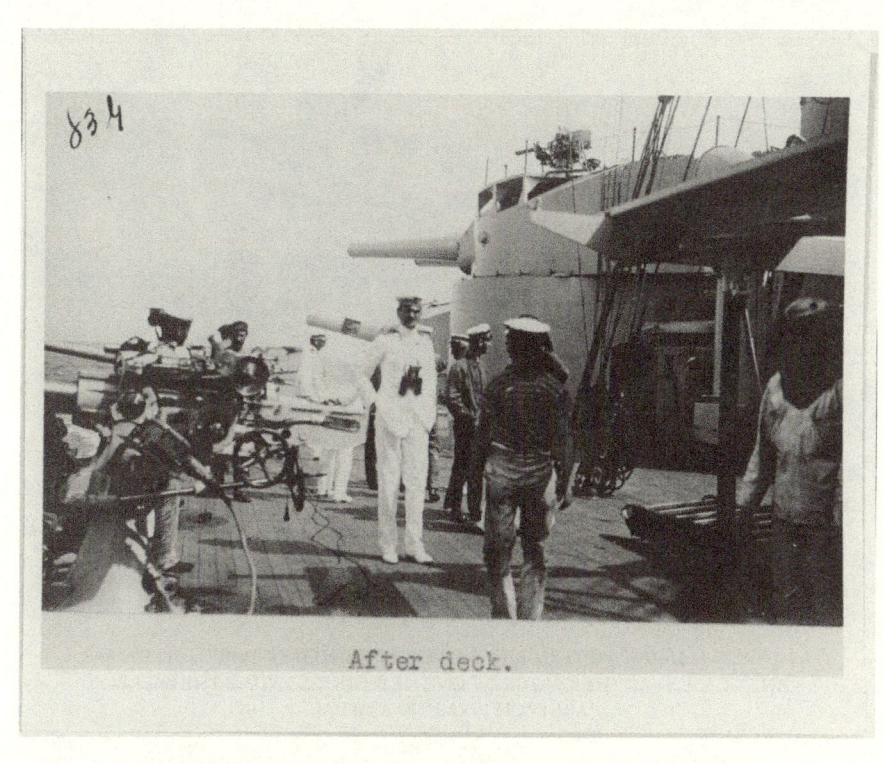

THE AFTER DECK OF THE VIRIBUS UNITIS. SOURCE: NAVAL HISTORY AND HERITAGE COMMAND.

A MUSICAL ELEMENT TO THE CREW'S LIFE. THE PHOTO MUST BE TO CELEBRATE
AN OCCASION AS THE TWO CREW ON THE BUSINESS END OF THE BARREL
ARE EACH WEARING A MEDAL.

THE TEGETTHOFF CLASS.

MANNING BATTLESTATIONS ON THE PORT 7CM BATTERY. SOURCE:NAVAL HISTORY AND HERITAGE

CHRISTMAS DAY FOR SOME OF THE PRINZ EUGENS CREW ON THE 7TH JANUARY 1917. THE 7TH WAS THE DATE THE ORTHODOX CHURCH MARKED THE FESTIVAL SOURCE:CONFLICTS.COM

ANDY SOUTH

A CREW MAN OF THE SZENT ISTVAN IN A FORMAL PORTRAIT, MAYBE TAKEN FOR A SWEETHEART AT HOME?

THE TEGETTHOFF CLASS.

THE VIRIBUS UNITIS CREW AND A 30.5 CM SHELL.

A CREWMAN WRITING HOME

ANDY SOUTH

AUSTRO-HUNGARIAN ANTI-FLASH

CHAPTER 8 : THE SHIPS BOATS.

THE NATIONAL EMBLEM CARRIED ON THE BOWS OF THE SMALLER CRAFT.

The four Tegetthoff's each carried a compliment of over 19 small boats, 8 of which were hung from davits on the ships side. The remainder were lifted from their deck stowage and into the sea by one of the two cranes the ships carried.

SMALL BOAT COMPLIMENT

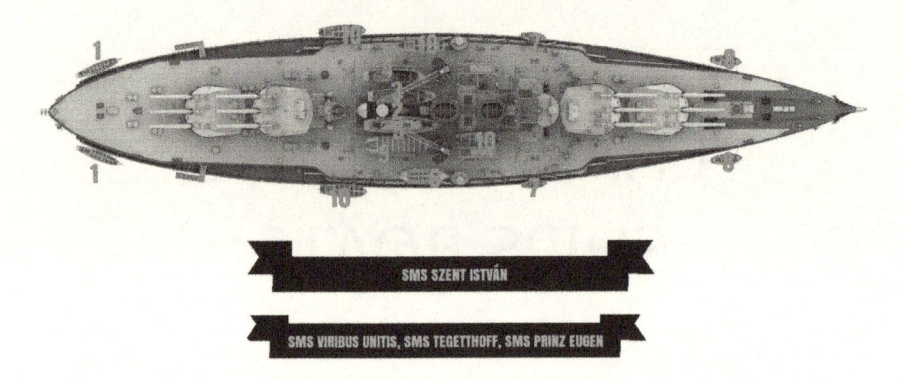

Key: 1=Gigg 1st class, 2=Dinghy 4.28 mtrs, 3=8.5 tonne motorboat. 4=5 tonne motorboat. 5=10-13 tonne motorboat. 6=Rescue cutter. 7=Dinghy 6 mtrs. 8= cleaning dinghy. 9= Motor sailing barge. 10= sailing cutter 1st class.

The 'official' small boat compliment was:

- 10-13 tonne Motorboat x1 (5)
- 8.51 tonne Motorboat x1 (3)
- 5 tonne Motorboat x1 (4)
- Sailing barge class 1 x1 (9)
- Rescue sailer class 1 x1 (6)
- Sailing dolly class 1 x4 (7)
- Gigs class 1 x2 (1)
- Dinghy boat x1 (2)
- Dinghy X2 (10)
- Cleaning dinghy x2 (8)

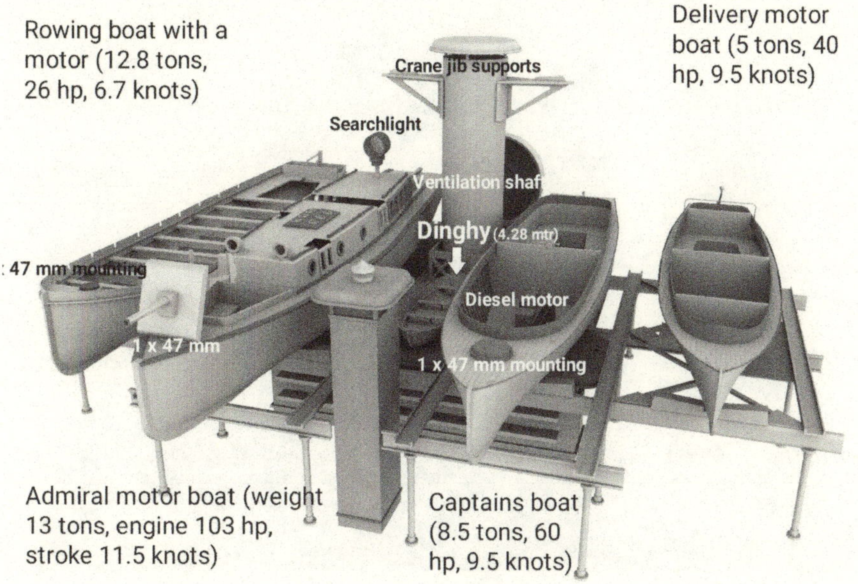
Rowing boat with a motor (12.8 tons, 26 hp, 6.7 knots)
Crane jib supports
Delivery motor boat (5 tons, 40 hp, 9.5 knots)
Searchlight
Ventilation shaf
Dinghy (4.28 mtr)
47 mm mounting
Diesel motor
1 x 47 mm
1 x 47 mm mounting
Admiral motor boat (weight 13 tons, engine 103 hp, stroke 11.5 knots)
Captains boat (8.5 tons, 60 hp, 9.5 knots)

THE BOATS SUPERSTRUCTURE LOCATED AFT OF REAR FUNNEL.

Sighted between the aft funnel and rear conning tower was the 'Boat Superstructure' on which rested combination of the ships largest and smallest boats. Running from the port beam across the ship's width lay the 5-tonne Motorboat, 8.5-tonne Motorboat, the diminutive 4.28-meter dinghy, the 10 to 13-tonne Motorboat and nearest the starboard beam was the Motor Sailing Barge. The dinghy excepted, these the four biggest 'small' boats onboard, where hoisted into the water from their cradles by one of the two 30 tonne cranes that towered over the structure.

The boats stored on the side davits (and possibly the boats inboard) would be jettisoned before an engagement to remove them from the gun crews' line of fire. the emergency cutter would however be retained to rescue men from the sea.

ANDY SOUTH

A BLURRED IMAGE RECORDED THROUGH A GLASS LAYER, BUT IT SHOWS THE SMALL BOATS ALONGSIDE AWAITING WORK.

THE TEGETTHOFF CLASS.

10-13 TONNE MOTORBOAT

THE 10-13 TONNE MOTORBOAT IS THE REAR MOST IN THE IMAGE.

The heavier of these five centrally stored boats was the 10-13 tonne Motorboat, referred to in some sources as the 'Admiral's barge'. The craft had a length of 17.61 meters (17 ft 9 5/6 inches) and a beam of 2.90 meters (9 feet .6 3/16 inches. When unladen, it weighed 10.870 tonnes (10.69 tons), but that increased to 11.548 tonnes (11.365 tons) once her crew of four had loaded her to the maximum capacity. It could carry 30 passengers and had a diesel 60 PS engine giving a speed of 11.5 knots. This the largest of the small boats had the capacity to carry one of the ships two 47 mm (1 27/32 inch) saluting guns on the bow. In addition, a searchlight could be

ANDY SOUTH

mounted on the stern portion of the craft.

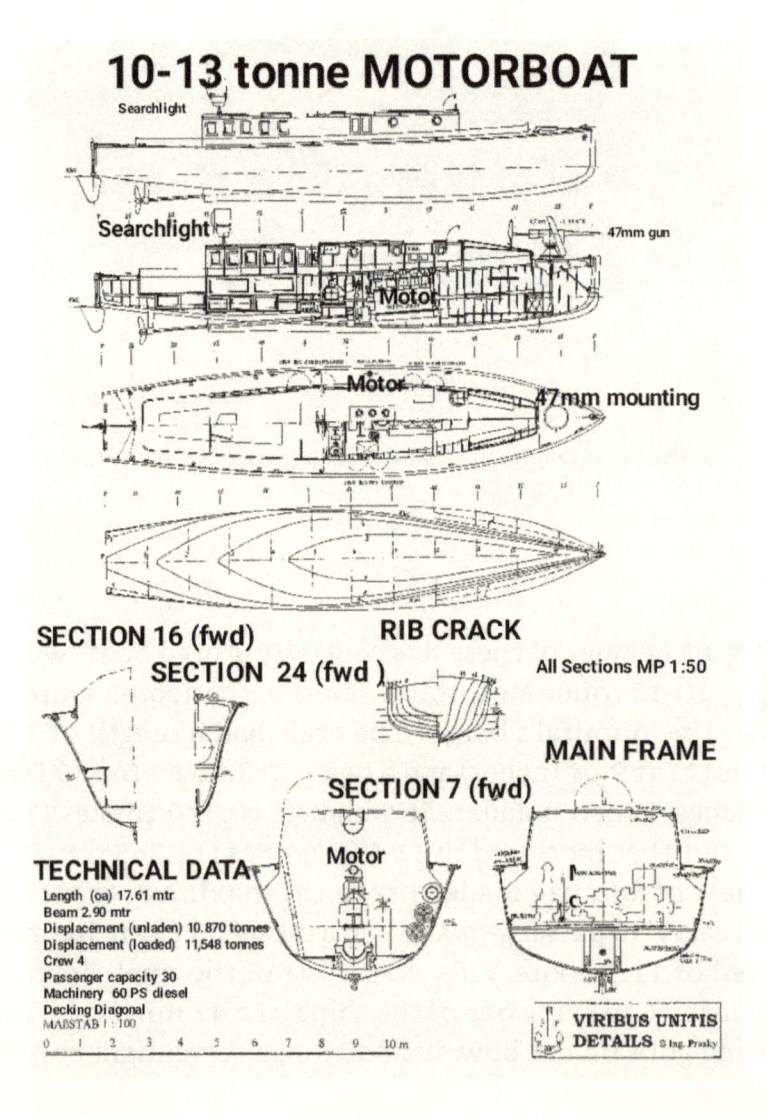

10-13 tonne MOTORBOAT

SECTION 16 (fwd)
SECTION 24 (fwd)
RIB CRACK
All Sections MP 1:50
MAIN FRAME
SECTION 7 (fwd)

TECHNICAL DATA
Length (oa) 17.61 mtr
Beam 2.90 mtr
Displacement (unladen) 10.870 tonnes
Displacement (loaded) 11,548 tonnes
Crew 4
Passenger capacity 30
Machinery 60 PS diesel
Decking Diagonal
MASSTAB 1:100

VIRIBUS UNITIS DETAILS © Ing. Prasky

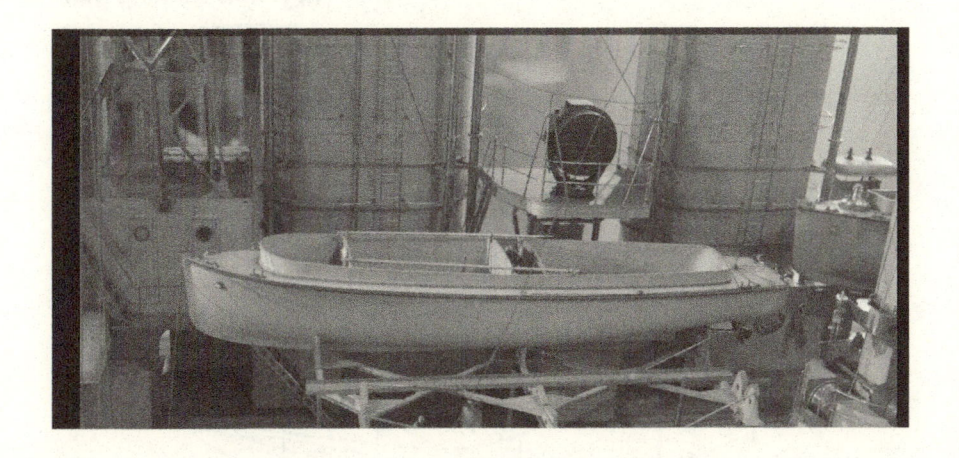

8.5 TONNE MOTORBOAT

Next in a decreasing size order was the 8.5-tonne Motorboat, which had a length of 12.82 meter (42 feet 0 23/32 inches), a beam of 3.02 meters (9 feet 10 29/32 inches) and unladen its displacement was 7.750 tonnes, (7.62 tons) rising to 8.482 tonnes (8.34 tons) fully loaded. The crew numbered two, and it could carry 28 passengers. The power source was a 60 hp diesel giving it a speed of 9.5 knots. It too had the capability to mount one of the 47 mm guns onto her bow.

ANDY SOUTH

1x47mm saluting gun.

Motor

47mm mounting

Rib crack

Section 11 1/2

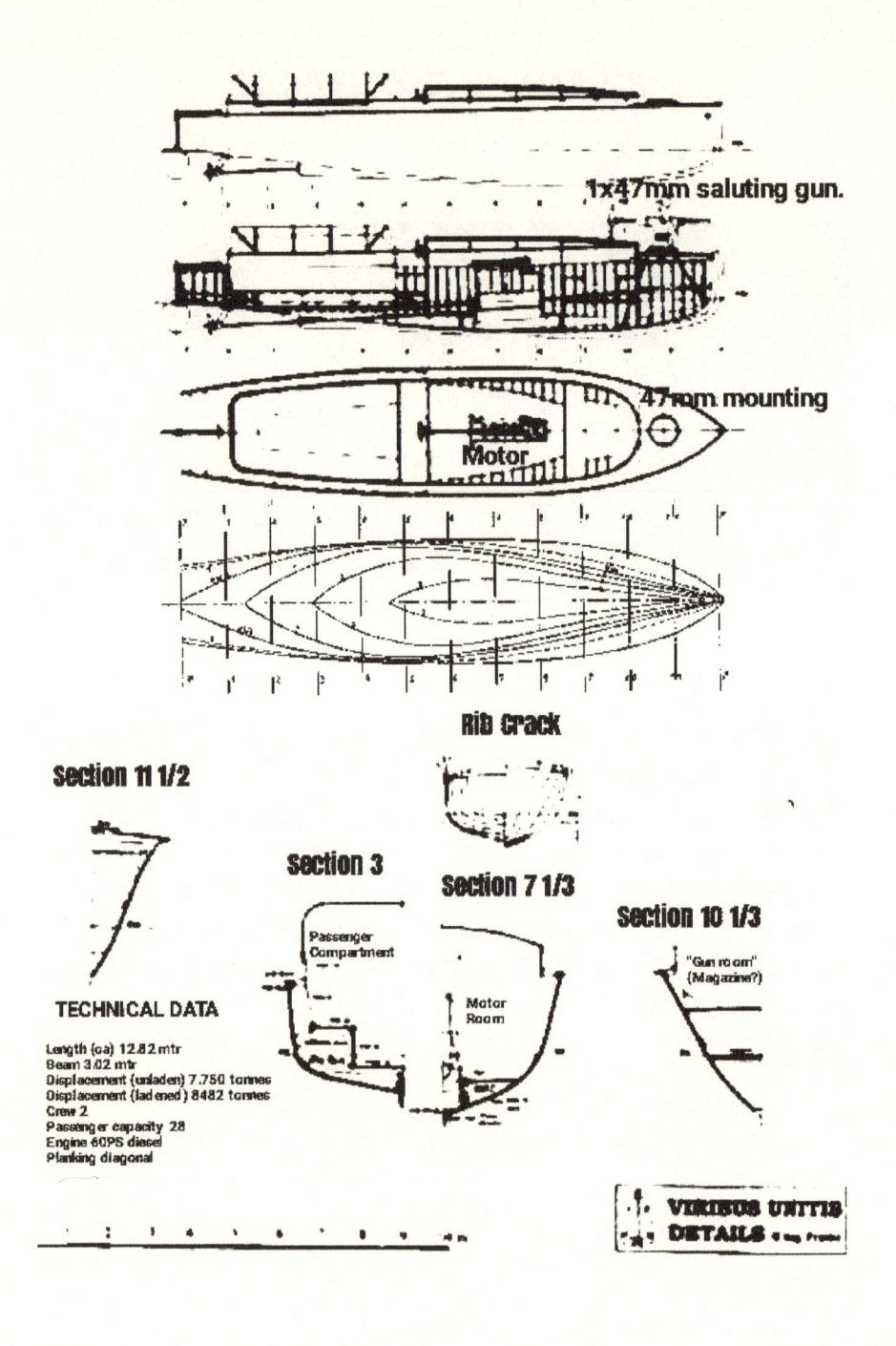

Section 3

Passenger Compartment

Section 7 1/3

Motor Room

Section 10 1/3

"Gun room" (Magazine?)

TECHNICAL DATA

Length (oa) 12.82 mtr
Beam 3.02 mtr
Displacement (unladen) 7.750 tonnes
Displacement (ladened) 8482 tonnes
Crew 2
Passenger capacity 28
Engine 60PS diesel
Planking diagonal

VIRIBUS UNITIS DETAILS

5 TONNE MOTORBOAT

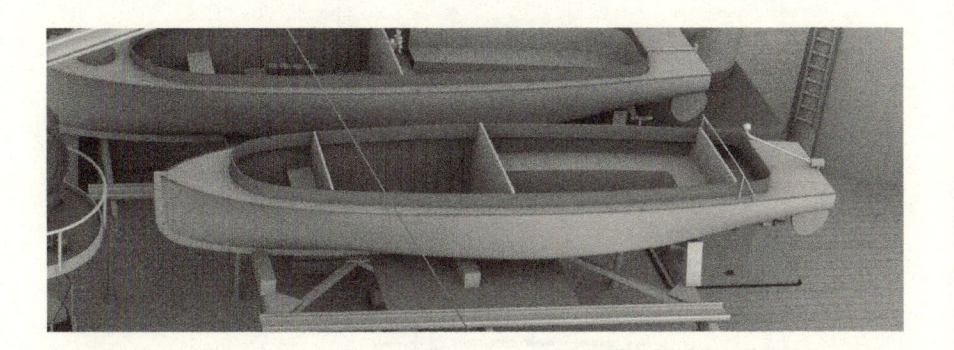

The 5.00 tonne Motorboat was the third in order size. The faded plans I have as my primary source seems to imply it had a length of 11.38 meters (37 feet 4 1/32 inches) and a beam of 2.45 meters (8 feet 0 15/32 inches). Unladen it weighed 3.843 tonnes (3.78 tons), increasing to 4.290 tonnes (4.22 tons) loaded. The crew numbered 2 with a capacity for 16 passengers. The engine was a 40 PS Diesel and unlike her larger companions, there was no armament capacity.

Motor

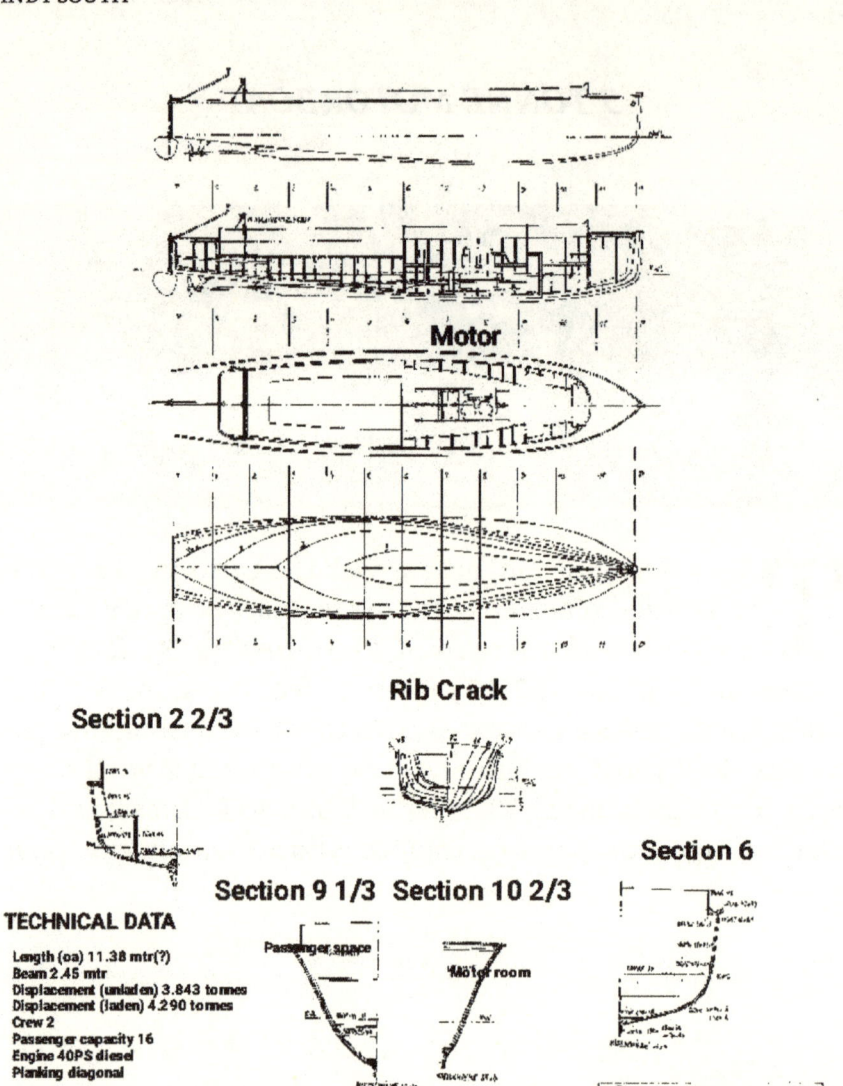

Rib Crack

Section 2 2/3

Section 9 1/3   **Section 10 2/3**

Passenger space   Motor room

Section 6

TECHNICAL DATA

Length (oa) 11.38 mtr(?)
Beam 2.45 mtr
Displacement (unladen) 3.843 tonnes
Displacement (laden) 4.290 tonnes
Crew 2
Passenger capacity 16
Engine 40PS diesel
Planking diagonal

MASSTAB 1 : 100
0 1 2 3 4 5 6 7 8 9 10 m

VIRIBUS UNITIS DETAILS © Ing. Prasky

MOTOR SAILING BARGE

THE MOTOR SAILING BARGE WITH THE 10-13 TONNE MOTORBOAT IN THE BACKGROUND.

The Motor Sailing Barge was the fourth in size order, with its 12.80 meters (41 feet, 11 15/16 inches) length and 3.45 meters (11 feet 3 13/16 inches) beam. Unladen it weighed 4.5 tonnes (4.42 tons) rising to 5.18 tonnes (5.09 tons) loaded. It had both sailing and powered capacity, her sails having a square meterage of 58 m2 (524.30 sq. feet). The power source was a 26 PS petrol engine, or 18 oars and her sail capacity. Without the sail the payload capacity was 110 passengers, but under sail that increased to 146. In addition, the crew numbered two. It is more than likely given its passenger capacity that this craft would have been the liberty boat, ferrying the crew to their shore leaves

ANDY SOUTH

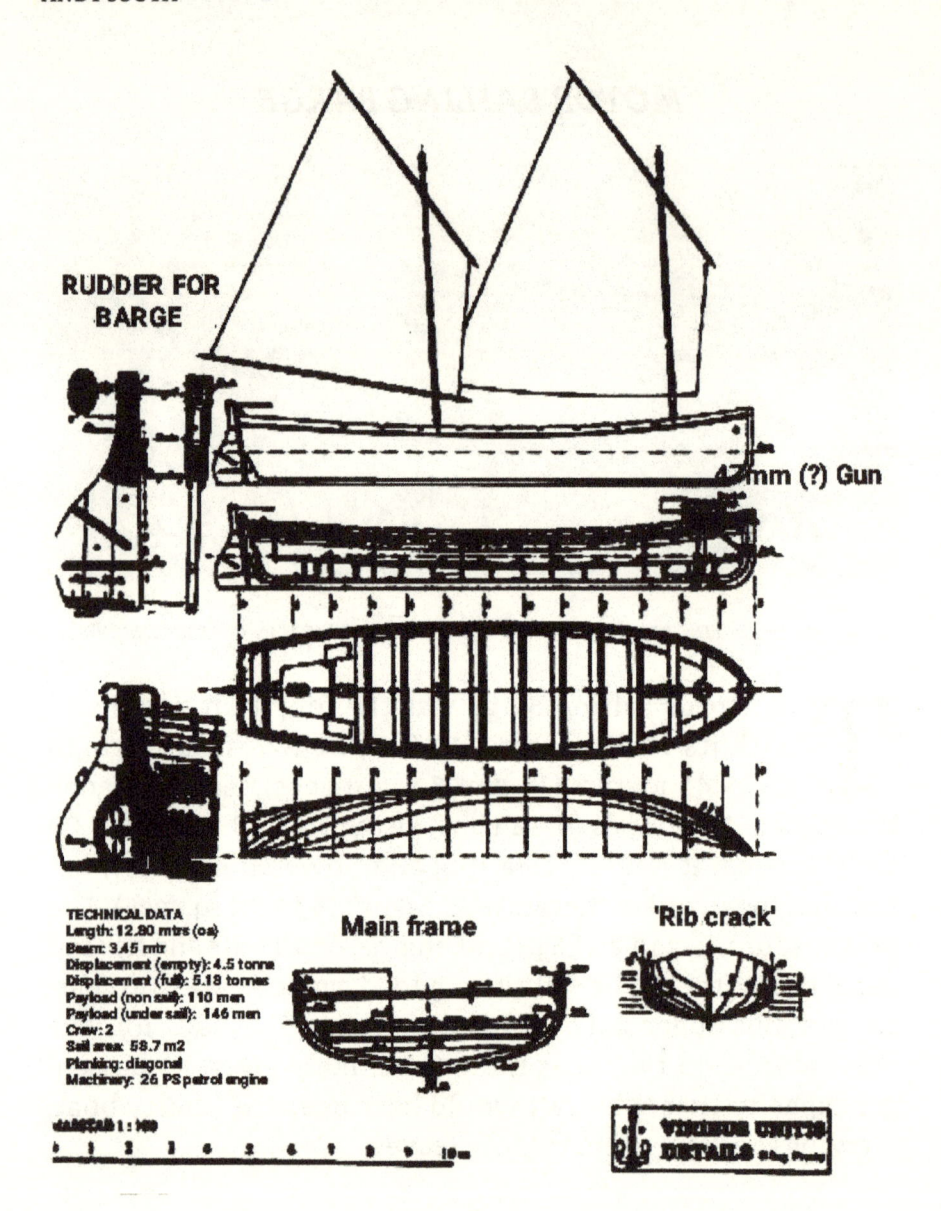

RUDDER FOR BARGE

mm (?) Gun

Main frame

'Rib crack'

TECHNICAL DATA
Length: 12.80 mtrs (oa)
Beam: 3.45 mtr
Displacement (empty): 4.5 tonne
Displacement (full): 5.18 tonnes
Payload (non sail): 110 men
Payload (under sail): 146 men
Crew: 2
Sail area: 58.7 m2
Planking: diagonal
Machinery: 26 PS petrol engine

4.28 METER DINGHY

The tiny 4.28-meter-long (13 feet 9 11/52 inches) and 1.31-meter-wide (4 feet 3 9/16 inches) dinghy lay in the centre of this amidships group, all but lost in the shadows of the looming Admirals and Captains barge. The boat unloaded weighed 210 kg (462 lb.) and her two crew and six passengers this increased to 221 kg (487.22 lb.). The craft was solely propelled by her six oars.

Either side of the bow were two davits mounted boats, which translate from Hungarian as 'Cleaning dinghies'. These two craft appear to be identical to the small dinghy resting amid the ships boat Superstructure.

MAIN FRAME M 1:20

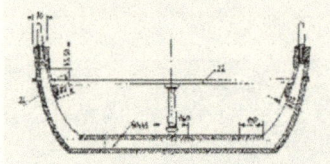

TECHNICAL DATA

Length (oa) 4.28 mtrs
Beam 1.31 mtrs
Displacement (unladen) 210 kg
Displacement (loaded) 221 kg
Crew 2
Passenger capacity 6

RIB CRACK

MABSTAB 1 : 100
0 1 2 3 4 5 6 7 8 9 10 m

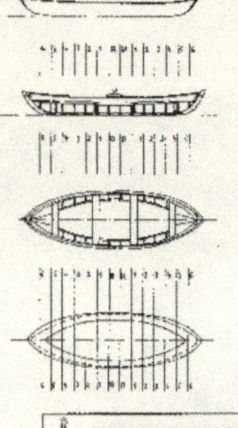

VIRIBUS UNITIS
DETAILS © Ing. Prasky

DINGHY

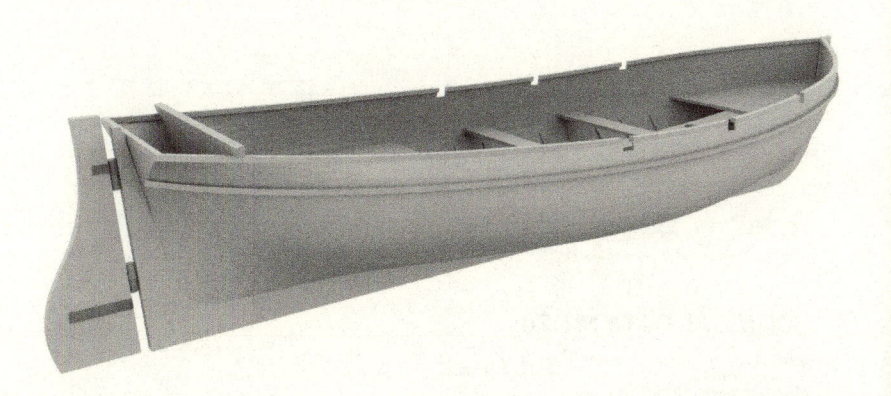

The third and final pair of dinghies were also davit mounted on either beam of the main conning tower. These two boats were 6.00 meters (19 feet 8 7/32 inches) in length with a beam of 1.82 meters (5 feet 11 21/32 inches). Unladen they had a displacement of 715 kg (1,576 lb) and loaded that increased to 785 kg (1,730 lb). The craft had a crew of 2 and under her six oar power a capacity of 16 passengers. But with the sails hoisted this increased to 18 passengers.

ANDY SOUTH

Main frame

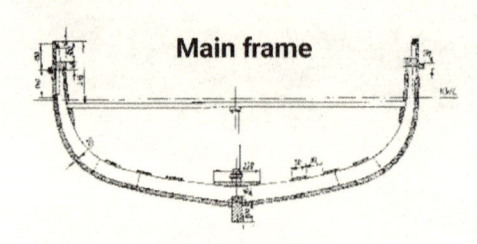

TECHNICAL DATA M1:20

Length (oa) 6.00 mtrs, Beam 1.82 mtr,
Displacement 715 kg
Displacement loaded 785 kg
Crew 6, Payload 16 men,
Payload under sail 18 men

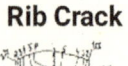

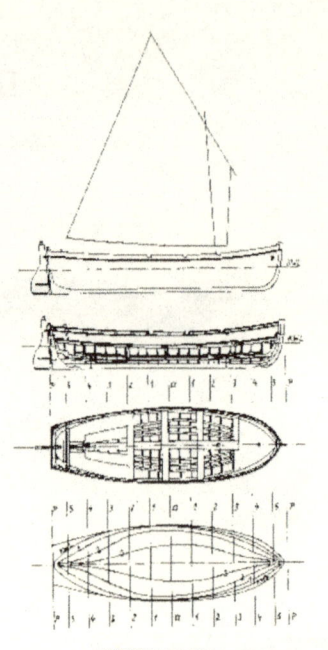

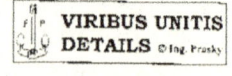

Rib Crack

VIRIBUS UNITIS DETAILS © Ing. Prasky

1ST CLASS SAILING CUTTER

To the starboard of the fore funnel was what appears to be a series of four boat cradles. In the photographs only one is occupied and that is with a 1st Class sailing 'dolly', or cutter. There was an additional pair of these boats' davit slung a few meters further aft. These four boats were 3.17 meters (10 feet 4 13/16 inches) in length and 2.70 meters (8 feet 10 5/16 inches) in their width. Unladen they had a displacement of 1.14 tonnes (1.12 tons), increasing to 1.78 tonnes (1,96 tons) loaded. When powered by the 12 oars it had a passenger capacity of 58, rising to 68 when the sails were used. The planking was diagonal.

ANDY SOUTH

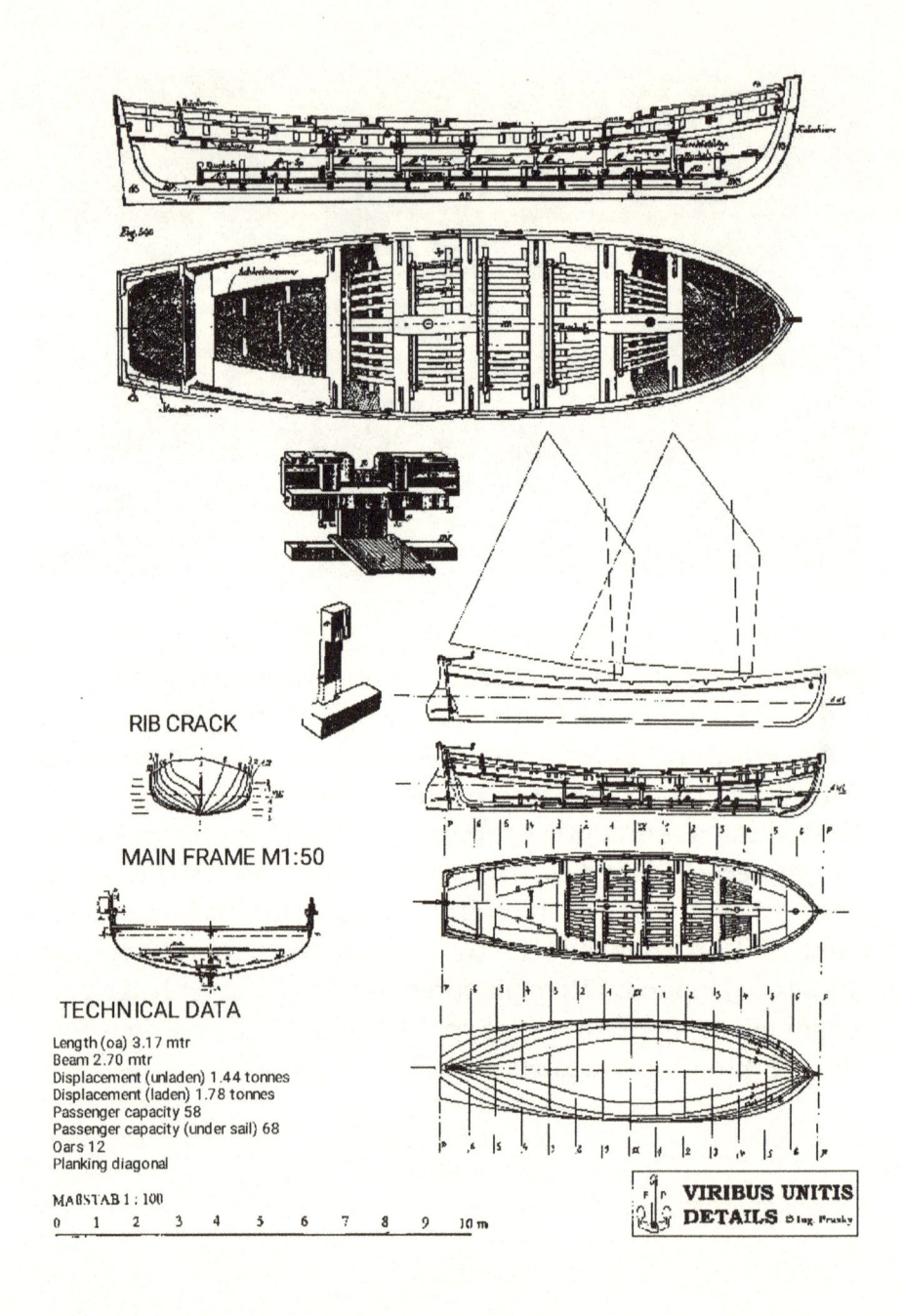

RIB CRACK

MAIN FRAME M1:50

TECHNICAL DATA

Length (oa) 3.17 mtr
Beam 2.70 mtr
Displacement (unladen) 1.44 tonnes
Displacement (laden) 1.78 tonnes
Passenger capacity 58
Passenger capacity (under sail) 68
Oars 12
Planking diagonal

MAßSTAB 1 : 100
0 1 2 3 4 5 6 7 8 9 10 m

VIRIBUS UNITIS
DETAILS

RESCUE CUTTER

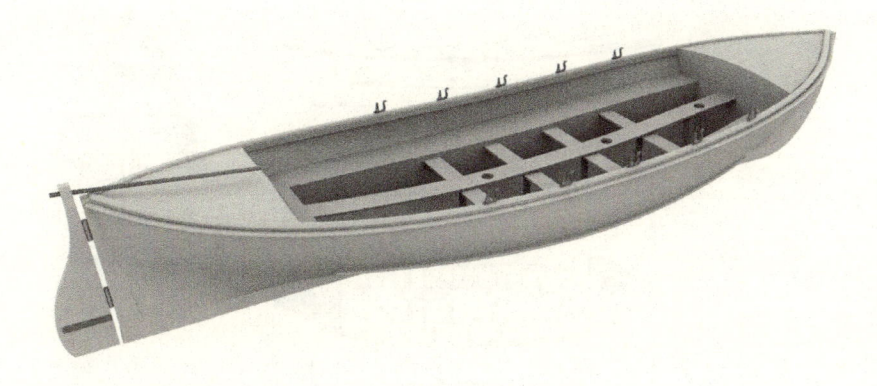

To starboard of the boat crane was the one Rescue Cutter swung from a davit but facing inboard. The boats role was to recover any crew that went overboard, not as a lifeboat.

It had an overall length of 9.18 meters (30 feet 1 13/32 inches) and a beam of 2.50 meters (8 feet 2 7/16 inches). Unloaded it had a displacement of 1.69 tonne (1.66 tons), but that increased to a maximum capacity of 2 tonne (1.96 tonnes). The crew numbered 10 and under ten oars it could carry 38 men, increasing to 45 under the 27.87 square meterage (299.99 sq. feet) of sails it had available.

ANDY SOUTH

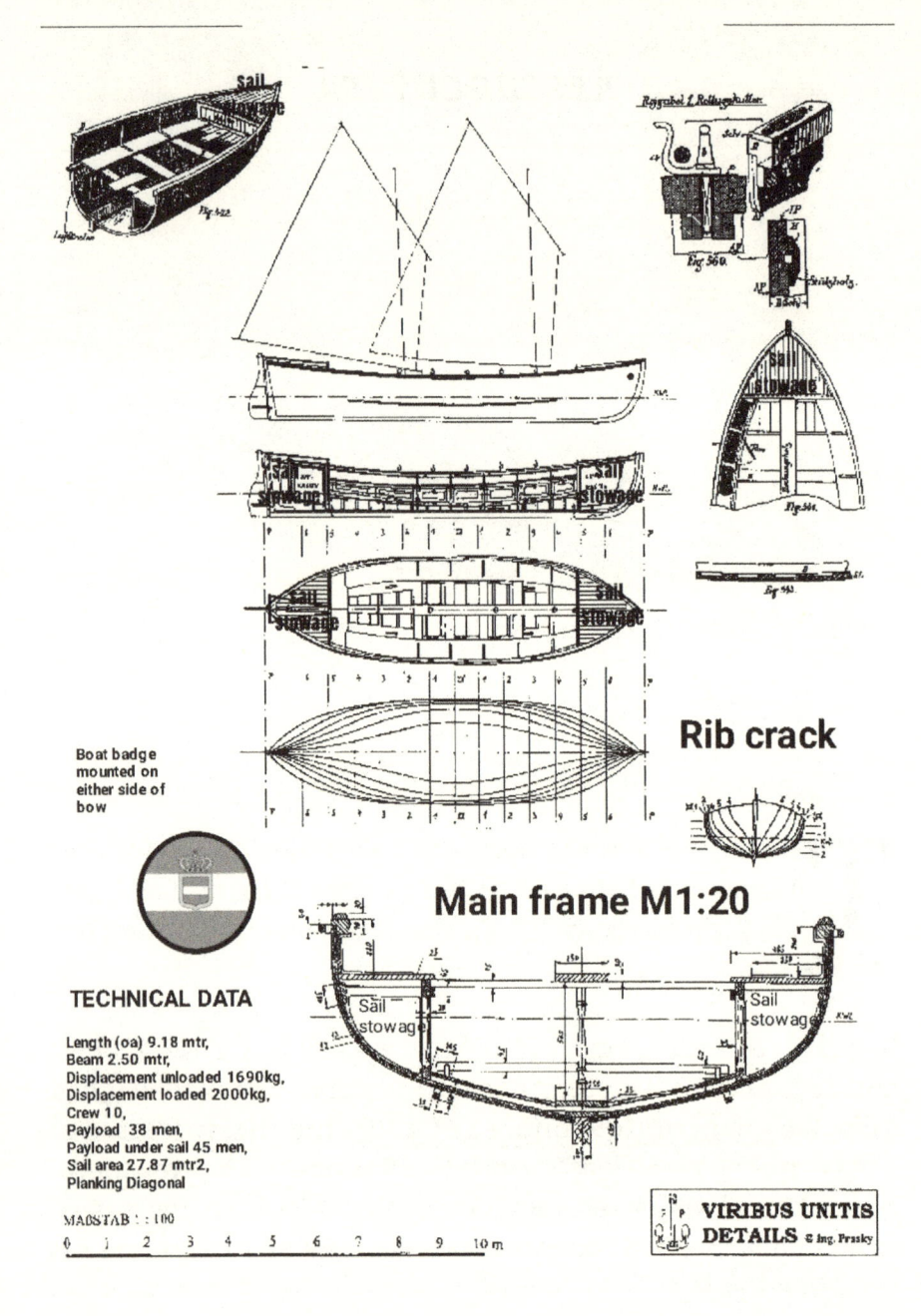

Rib crack

Main frame M1:20

Boat badge mounted on either side of bow

TECHNICAL DATA

Length (oa) 9.18 mtr,
Beam 2.50 mtr,
Displacement unloaded 1690kg,
Displacement loaded 2000kg,
Crew 10,
Payload 38 men,
Payload under sail 45 men,
Sail area 27.87 mtr2,
Planking Diagonal

MAßSTAB 1 : 100

VIRIBUS UNITIS DETAILS © Ing. Prasky

1ST CLASS GIGS

The final two boats were the two 1st class gigs (or Captains gigs) which were davit mounted on either side of the stern. The gig is traditionally a harbour craft and is not an easy vessel to use on open waters, so these would have been used when the ship was at anchor. The boats were 9.17 meters (30 feet 1 1/32 inches) in their length and 1.75 meters (5 feet 8 2 9/32 inches) on the beam. their displacement was 730 kg, (1,609 lb) but that increased to 873 kg (1,924 lb) loaded. They had a crew of 20 under oars and 24 under the 12.88 square meterage (138.63 sq. feet) of sails.

Rudder for easy
& heavy giggs
(for dinghy & 1st class)

BACKREST FOR BOAT

FILLER HANDLE FOR GIGGS

Handbook for Boatswains
Pola 1894

MAIN PART M 1:20

TECHNICAL DATA
Length(oa) 9.17 mtr
Beam 1.75 mtr
Displacement (unladen) 730 kg
Displacement (laden) 873 kg
Crew 6
Payload 20 men
Payload (under sail) 24 men
Sail area 12.88 mtr2
Planking clinker

RIB CRACK

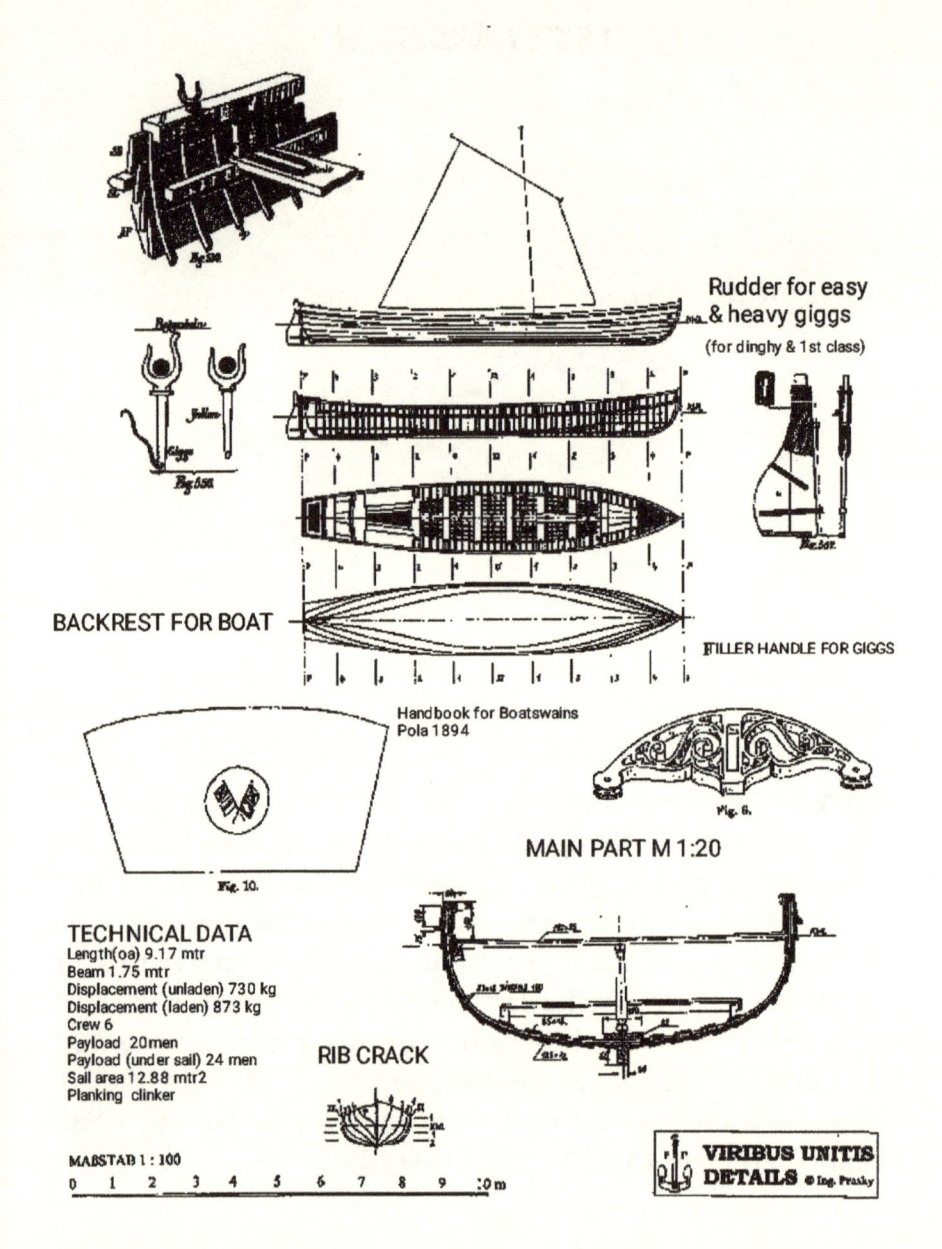

MAßSTAB 1 : 100

VIRIBUS UNITIS
DETAILS © Ing. Prasky

The total weight of all this flotilla was 41.77 tonnes (41.12 tons).

AUXILARY EQUIPMENT

The operation of the small boat flotilla would have necessitated an amount of auxiliary (or support equipment) be made available on board. This would have included a dedicated superstructure, the two 30 tonne cranes, davits and a boom with Jacob ladders, ropes, spare oars...

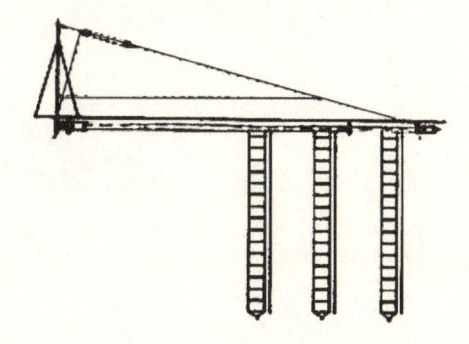

ACCESS WAS BY THE OVERHEAD BOOM. THE CREW WOULD WALK ALONG THE BOOM, USING THE PARALLEL ROPES TO REACH THE LADDER AND THEN DESCEND. ACCESS TO THE BOATS THAT WERE MOORED TO THE ROPES HANGING FROM THE RIGHT OF THE JACOBS LADDERS

The small boat boom was located just below the upper decks and in front of the foremost casement battery. When not in use it was folded flat against the ships hull, but once in port it was swung out by 90 degrees and the three Jacobs rope ladders dropped down from it. Access to either deploy the boom, or to reach the boats at the bottom of the ladders was by two metal ladders secured to the hull. These descended from the main deck level onto the angled deck that ran from before the casements. One ladder was immediately before the foremost 15 cm gun barrel and the other at the far end of the folded boom. Once deployed the boom would have been of sufficient length to reach out beyond the torpedo nets, Like the nets it was solely used whilst the ship was to be at anchor for a significant amount of time.

THE STORED BOOMS FOR BOTH SMALL BOATS AND TORPEDO NETS. THE SMALL BOAT BOOM AND ITS LADDERS ARE FOLDED FLAT TO THE HULL.

The davits would not have reached beyond the nets, so assumedly the boats were put into the water and then both the boom and the nets deployed. The small craft were secured to the boom by ropes and access was gained by walking out along the boom and descending the Jacob ladders. A manoeuvre reminiscent of walking out along the Main Yard of 18th century ship of the line.

THE TEGETTHOFF CLASS.

THE PRINZ EUGEN WITH HER SMALL BOA\T BOOM EXTENDED.

There were two gangways with stairs descending from the quarter deck. These would be for naval personnel carrying both rank and epaulettes on their shoulders, as well as for civilian and VIP guests.

THE GANG WAY STAIRS.

THE TWO 30 TONNE BOAT CRANES.

The ships each carried two large cranes, both of which also housed one searchlight on a circular platform and when not hoisting boats in and out of the water, the cranes would have been employed in lifting the heavier stores and equipment onboard. These cranes would have swung the Archduke Ferdinand and his wife's coffins on-board in June 1914.

THE TEGETTHOFF CLASS.

[Technical diagram with labels:]

- "Rain cape"
- 2 Ropes
- spar
- Fixed point
- 1 Ropes
- Rope clamp for emergency
- Frame for emergency operations (swival)
- Bulk head Swivel control
- Foot control
- Swing motor
- Searchlight platform
- Searchlight platform
- Rope drums
- Device for pinch drive (hub)
- Swival gear Cover for rope drums
- Protective wall
- Searchlight platform
- Cover for maintenance
- Ladder Swing motor
- Band brakes
- Head swivel
- Consol (2x)
- ACCESSORIES CRANE ARM
- Band brake
- Pedestal
- Lateral discs
- Rope pulleys
- Searchlight platform
- Crane arm bearing
- Pedestal
- Gear box
- Stroke control
- Lift operations
- Head of swivel Control
- Ladder
- MASSTAB 1 : 14H
- 0 1 2 3 4 5 6 7 8 9 10 cm

VIRIBUS UNITIS DETAILS

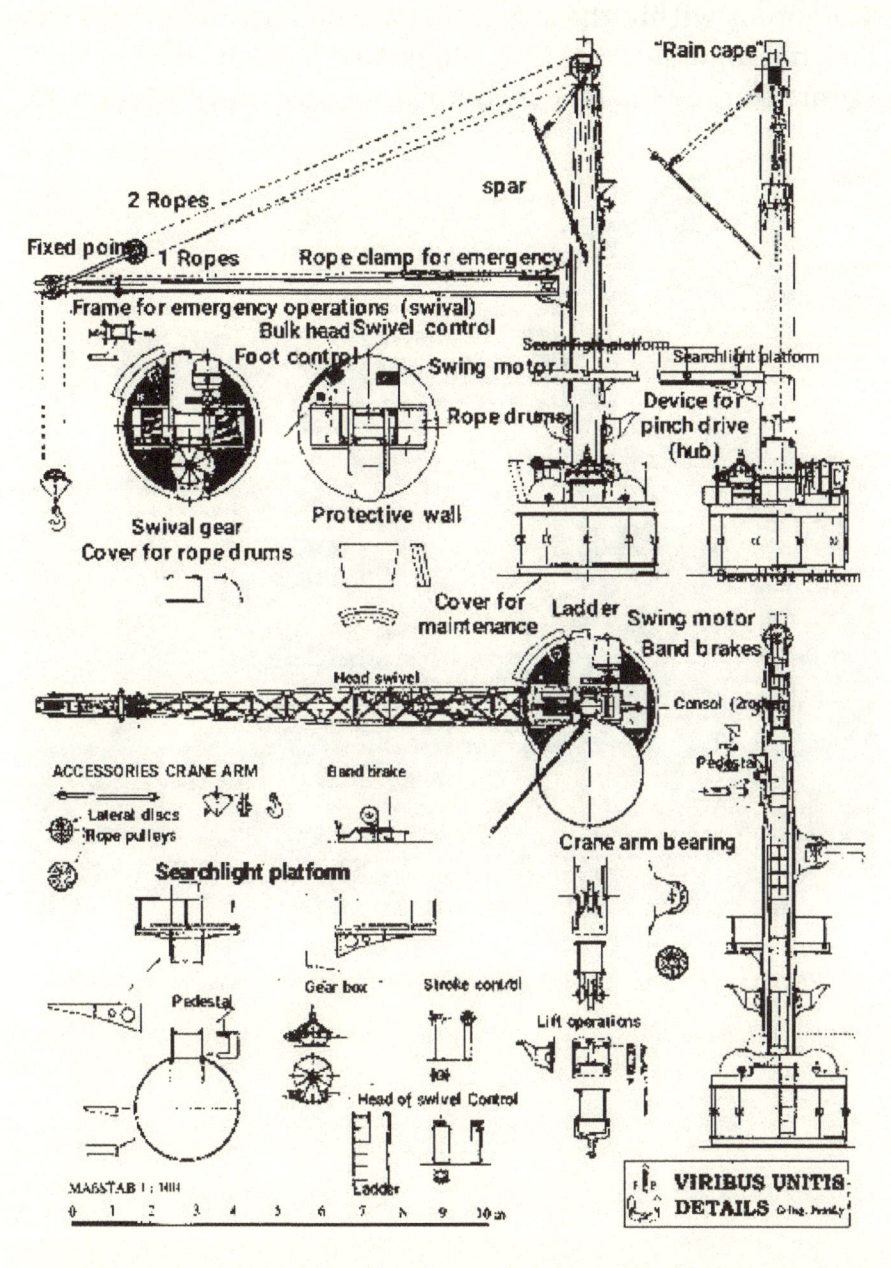

In the centre of the ships main deck, (just aft of the rearmost funnel) was a superstructure which held a series of cradles on its roof for the ship's heavier boats. Deep in the shadows of the motorboats was one of the smallest ship's boats, the dinghy.

The rooms within the structure have no listed use that I can find, but logic suggests it would be the most convenient storage area for the small boat equipment, oars, ropes, life jackets, etc...

THE EXTREMITY OF THE CRANE'S JIBS RESTING ON THE STORAGE SUPPORT BRACKETS.

THE TEGETTHOFF CLASS.

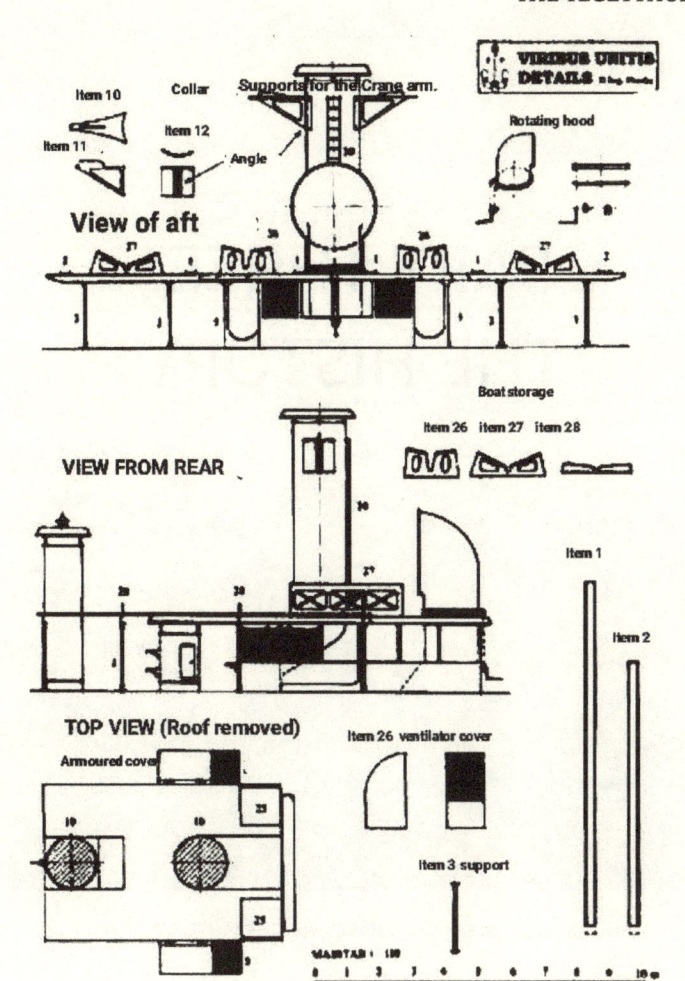

THE SMALL BOAT SUPERSTRUCTURE.

215

PART THREE: THE HISTORY

HABSBURG POWER, THE AUSTRO-HUNGARIAN FLEET AT SEA.

CHAPTER 1: STEEL & RIVETS.

Almost a year after the Italian Dreadnought keel had been laid down, the Austrians laid the first of their four planned keels, when on the 24th July 1910 the *Viribus Unitis*' construction was commenced at the STT yard in Trieste. She was initially to have been named the *Tegetthoff*, but on the orders of the Emperor Franz Josef she was to be renamed and the second ship in the class would carry that name instead. Eleven months after her keel laying, the yet unnamed ship was ready to be launched. With the symbolism and importance surrounding the Empires first Dreadnought launch, the Grand Duke Franz Ferdinand was to attend the occasion. He had been due that day, to be on board an older battleship, the *Erzherzog Franz Ferdinand,* at Spithead, England, attending the fleet review organized to mark the crowning of King George V. But the 'less important' Grand Duke Karl Franz Joseph attended the review in his place on board the *Radetzky*. Also present that day was the wife of the Grand Duke, the Duchess von Hohenberg, who became the Godmother of the battleship, as well as the highest ranks of the army and navy, parliamentary leaders, ministers, and diplomats.

THE VIRIBUS UNITIS STANDS READY FOR HER LAUNCH. THE SIX SPACES IN THE UPPER DECK CLEARLY INDICATE WHERE THE 15 CM GUNS WILL BE EMPLACED IN TIME.

The yet unnamed Dreadnought's launch day arrived and on the 24th June 1911 the ship was sent down the slip way, bearing her new name, the *Viribus Unitis*. The ship's entry into the water was accompanied by the roar of artillery salutes from the battleships *Archduke Franz Ferdinand, Archduke Karl, Archduke Frederick*, and the roar of steam sirens of merchant ships. On her completion the *Viribus Unitis* underwent her trials and Brassey 1913 Naval Annual states the trials were a "success" but that on their completion she was still regarded as "experimental". The volume also states she exceeded her design speed of 21 knots by 4/5ths of a knot. On the 5th December 1912 Viribus Unitis, was to enter service becoming the fleet flagship the following month, having taken 876 days from keel to commissioning, the fastest time for her class. She was also the world's first triple gun turreted ship to enter service.

THE TEGETTHOFF CLASS.

PREVIOUS PAGE. SPECULATION IN BRITISH NEWSPAPERS OF WHAT THE AUSTRIA-HUNGARIANS WERE BUILDING BEHIND ALL THE SECRECY IN THEIR SHIPYARDS,

"TO BE LAUNCHED AT TRIESTE ON 24TH JUNE: AUSTRO-HUNGARIAN FIRST DREADNOUGHT, THE "VIRIBUS UNITIS." THE FIRST AUSTRO-HUNGARIAN DREADNOUGHT WHICH IS TO BE LAUNCHED AT TRIESTE CURIOUSLY ENOUGH ON THE DAY OF OUR OWN CONATION NAVAL PREVIEW AT SPITHEAD, IS THE FIRST OF A SQUADRON CONSISTING OF FOUR SHIPS OF THE SAME CLASS NOW BEING BUILT. THE OTHERS WILL BE READY IN 1913. THE LENGTH OF THE "VIRIBUS UNITIS" IS 151 METRES (ABOUT 400 FEET) HER WIDTH, 28 METRES (91 FEET) DEPTH 8 METRES (24 FEET) DISPLACEMENT 21,000 TONS AND SPEED 21 KNOTS SHE'S COMPLETELY ARMOURED IS DRIVEN BY TURBINES AND CARRIES TWELVE GUNS OF 30.5 CM IN THE FOUR TRIPLE TURRETS AND TWELVE GUNS OF 15 CENTIMETRES SIX ON EACH SIDE."

Two months after that first keel laying, on the 24th September the second vessel, also to be built by STT was laid down. Eight months after work on the keel commenced, (in May 1911), the construction crews went on strike, but they soon returned to work. As the work on the ship slowly progressed, she was referred to as the *"Battleship V"*, while a debate raged over what to name her. The Naval Section of the War Ministry had proposed the name *Don Juan a*nd the Austrian press reported, incorrectly, during her construction that one of the ships was to be named *Kaiser Franz Joseph I*. But that name was already being borne by a cruiser. "Battleship V", on the Emperor Franz Josephs decision, was to be named *Tegetthoff*. The Emperor was to decide on the names of all four Dreadnought, selecting to name the first ship of the class, after his own personal motto, *Viribus Unitis* (Latin: "With United Forces"). On her completion, the *Tegetthoff* underwent her trials and during one of her gunnery assessments, the ship's main guns concussion managed to damage the staterooms of the ship's officers. But despite this, her trials were completed, and she was commissioned on the 14th July 1913.

INSTALLATION OF THE VIRIBUS UNITIS 30.5 CM GUNS. PHOTO COPYWRITE OF NAVAL HISTORY & HERITAGE COMMAND.

With the experience gained from the dreadnoughts launched before the *Tegetthoff,* the CTT engineers were to carry out a much larger amount of work while the ship was still on the slipway. So, a heavy conning tower weighing almost 300 tons was already mounted on the battleship, and the plates of the armour belt in the stern were bolted to the sides (they were absent during the launch of the Viribus). On the 16th January 1912, the future *Prinz Eugen* was the third Dreadnought keel to be laid down at the STT yard. Despite two strikes by the machinists in August 1912 and March 1913, which delayed the construction of the ship's engines, the *Prinz Eugen* was built quickly and was launched later in the year, on the 30th November. On completion she conducted her sea trials throughout March and April with the results declared as "satisfactory". The Austro-Hungarian Navy issued a statement that the ship's trials had concluded her gunnery tests successfully, but no other information could be published. But she was not to experience peace time service, commissioning on the 8th July 1914, just ten days after the assassination of Archduke Franz Ferdinand. The *Prinz Eugen* was completed in 416 days, which amounted to 110 days faster than the Italian ship. The fourth ship, the only one to bear a Hungarian name and last ship of the class, originally referred to as *"Battleship VII"* was laid down in the Ganz-Danubius yard in Fiume on the 29th January 1912. Originally named after Hunyadi János, the Duke Ferdinand recommended the name *Laudon* after Ernst Gideon von Laudon. In addition, the names *Don Juan* and *Corvin Mátyás* were also proposed. But in June 1913, József Ferenc decided on the name of *Szent István* (Saint Stephen), having been proposed by the Navy. [1]

THE SZENT ISTVANS MASTS ARE HOISTED INTO PLACE.

The Ganz-Danubius yard in Fiume had prior to *Szent István's* construction only built torpedo boats and destroyers, alongside smaller commercial vessels such as for the Austrian Lloyd line. Fiume had the sole large Hungarian shipyard within Croatia and the yard had only been awarded the contract in return for the Hungarian Government agreeing to the 1910 and 1911 naval budgets, which had funded the *Tegetthoff* class. But the contract involved large expenses for the Government. The Dreadnought agreement meant the shipyard had to be refitted and enlarged for the building of such a ship, which was five times larger than anything the yard had built prior, delaying the keel laying. The hardness and rocky content of the ground selected for the construction site, proved to be harder than expected and this served to add to the delay.

THE TEGETTHOFF CLASS.

INSTALTION OF THE VIRIBUS UNITIS 30.5 CM GUNS. PHOTO COPYWRITE OF OF NAVAL HISTORY & HERITAGE COMMAND.

But on the 17th January 1914, having prior to the day been renamed *Szent István* by order of the Emperor Franz Joseph, she was launched. It was traditional for either the Emperor or his heir to be present at the launching of a battleship, but Emperor Franz Joseph was too feeble and his heir, Archduke Franz Ferdinand, refused to be there as a result of his anti-Hungarian prejudices. Franz Joseph sent a telegram of congratulations which went some way towards easing the rebuttal by his heir. Finally, the ruler was represented by the the Archduchess Maria Teresa, the daughter of the King of Portugal Miguel I, the third wife of Franz Ferdinand's father and so the stepmother of the Heir of the Throne. The Austrian fleet, including the *Tegetthoff* and *Viribus Unitis*, (as the flagship of the fleet), was present on the day. A compromise had been reached whereby the red-white-red flags of the Navy were red-white-green. The Hungarian guests were István Burián, the minister of the king, Hungarian Prime Minister István Tisza, Minister of Finance János Teleszky and Minister to the Imperial Court Stephan Burián von Rajecz. The German cruiser *Breslau* had recently undergone a refit at Trieste and her officers were also there to attend the ceremony.

SZENT ITSVAN UNDER CONSTRUCTION. THE FUNNELS IN THE FOREGROUND BELONG TO THE HELIGOLAND. HOTO COPYWRITE OF OF NAVAL HISTORY & HERITAGE COMMAND.

At 11:00 Admiral Anton Haus, the chief commander of the fleet, asked the Archduchess to christen the ship, saying:

> "Imperial and Royal Highness! We are preparing for the fourth unit of our strongest battleship division so far today...... The new vessel will bear the unmistakable name of the Supreme Commander of His Maj-

esty, the most ...[?]... Emperor and King, of the first Christian king of Hungary, the great ruler of the holy man to whom all Christian praise. His imperial and royal brilliance devoted to raising the glory of the feast with the office of Christians and for this reason, the Imperial and Royal Emperors of the Navy are the most obedient thanks to the Navy. And now please your imperial and royal majesty, be kind to christen...".[1] The Archduchess answered: ".........may the protection of the Almighty be with you on all your ways!".

Admiral Anton Haus

Archduchess on pressing the button to signal the launch said, *"slide into your element and the Almighty should protect you in all your ways".* As the ship was launched the starboard anchor had to be dropped to prevent the hull from colliding with a boat carrying spectators. The anchor chain had not been securely shackled to the ship, (having been only riveted) and the rudders had to be worked to guide the hull. When the starboard chain broke free from its weak connection, the anchor struck two shipyard workers. One was so gravely injured (the 43-year-old shipyard boatman Giuseppe Pliscovac) that he during the night of 18/19th died in the Civil Hospital from his injuries. The shipyard worker Ermenengildo Piccot had to have his left lower leg amputated. The accident established the widespread opinion that the *Szent István* was an ill-fated ship and that terrible things were going to inflict her. The anchor chains had in fact been checked twice before the launch and no explanation for the use of rivets was ever found.

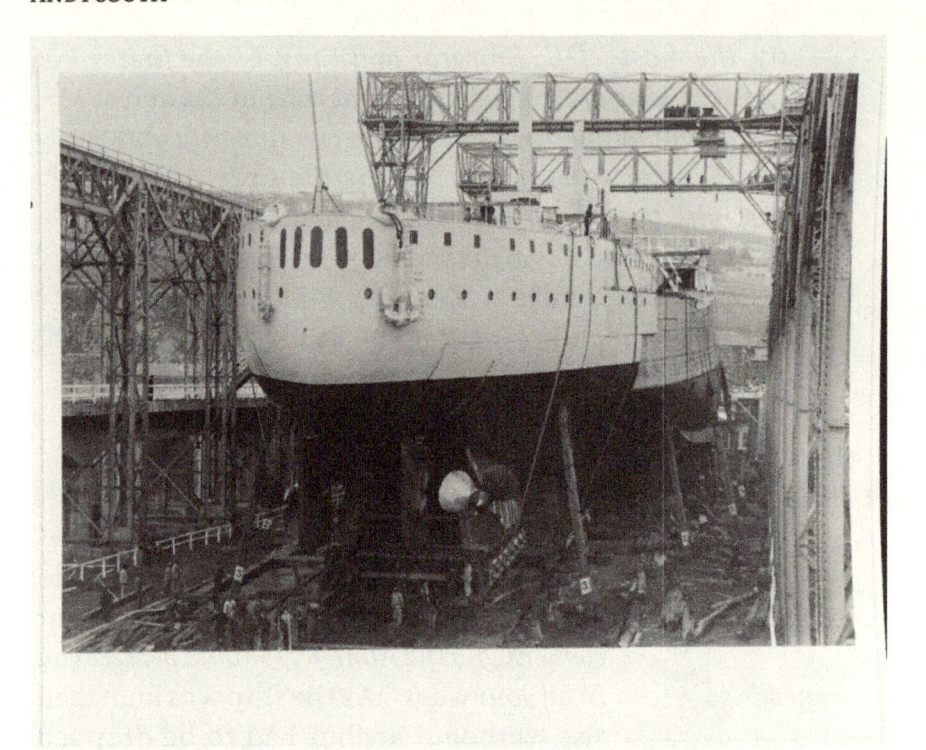

THE SZENT ISTVAN NEAR HER LAUNCH DAY.

Since anchoring was no longer possible, "Hartruder" had to be laid to prevent a collision with the steamer. These manoeuvres brought the newly launched ship dangerously close to her older stepsister, the *Tegetthoff*. The launch was followed by a congratulatory telegram from the Emperor. In it he praised the performance of the Hungarian industry, which after the telegram had been read aloud, the crowd cried *"Long live!"*. The fleet commander, Admiral Anton Haus, noted in his diary:

> *"Sunday 17.1.1914: 7 o'clock, very cloudy. then light rain, in the morning mainly snowfall and cold. 9 1/2 Clock with Toboggan and Reissig in the car to the shipyard, there in the light snow welcomes the arrivals for the court pavilion: Minister Burián,*

THE TEGETTHOFF CLASS.

Krobatin; Georgi, Tisza, Teleszky, Harkányi, Trnka; the ladies of honour Countess Wickenburg, Barry, Guillaume, Pallavicini, Luxardo, Dewseffy. Waited an hour while everyone comes together. Finally, 10.42 o'clock comes the Archduchess Maria Theresia, reception, flowers. Governor introduces the honorary ladies, also three to four main persons, Minister Tisza etc. Then I escort them up the courtyard pavilion, where all others come. Bishop Bjelik inaugurates the ship, when he finally finishes - also all the preparations for the launch - he makes a bow to us, The hydraulic machine starts to work, it takes me four to five minutes, which seem like an eternity to me, finally, the ship sits under the cheers of the audience in motion and slides wrapped in smoke into the water.....in the hotel, moved for the dinner at 2 o'clock. First, receive all the guests in the reception room, at 2 o'clock the Archduchess at the hotel gate, after a short circle I lead the Archduchess into her place and walk around to take her opposite, on the right the Countess Pallavicini, on the left Countess Buquoy. Diner very good, long, rich, cheerful, especially by the conversation with the Countess Buquoy. To the black coffee comes the congratulatory telegram of the emperor, which I ask the Archduchess to read. It contains almost exactly the passage which the heir to the throne deleted from the speech of the Archduchess, namely the recognition of the efficiency of Hungarian industry; it is recorded with "Eljén", Tisza asks me whether it is published in the newspapers. Of course, I am very glad that the Emperor - without knowing it - again repaired a wickedness of the Archduke. Much approval from the Hungarian side. Monday, 18.1.1914:.........All celebrations have been completely successful, not the slightest lapse occurred. Only the absenteeism of the heir to the throne

> has generally been regarded as hostile. This morning I
> received his telegram "Thank you for the message".

While under construction the *Szent István* was filmed to demonstrate to the Hungarian taxpayer how a heavy industry base had been was created with the good use of their taxes (See Appendix E). The film included scenes of her hull on the slipway, her launching, (but with the incident of the anchor chain deleted), her fitting out, the flooding of the dock with the dreadnought standing in it, as well as work at the shell factory.

In February while she was fitting out, a major change was made to her design when the height of the funnels was increased by 1.5 meters (4 feet 11 1/16 inches) and a platform was built around the front funnel, reaching from the command bridge to the rear funnel and the ships search lights were relocated on to it. These changes added 54.4 tonnes of extra weight and increased the centre of gravity of the vessel by 8 mm (5/16 inch), reducing the ships poorer than average stability even further. Her fitting out progressed at a slow pace and the outbreak of the war slowed this even further. With the ship 71.4% complete she was towed to Pola with all her other semi-assembled parts. After long negotiations, it was agreed that the Danubius yard workers could use the local facilities to complete the ship.

THE TEGETTHOFF CLASS.

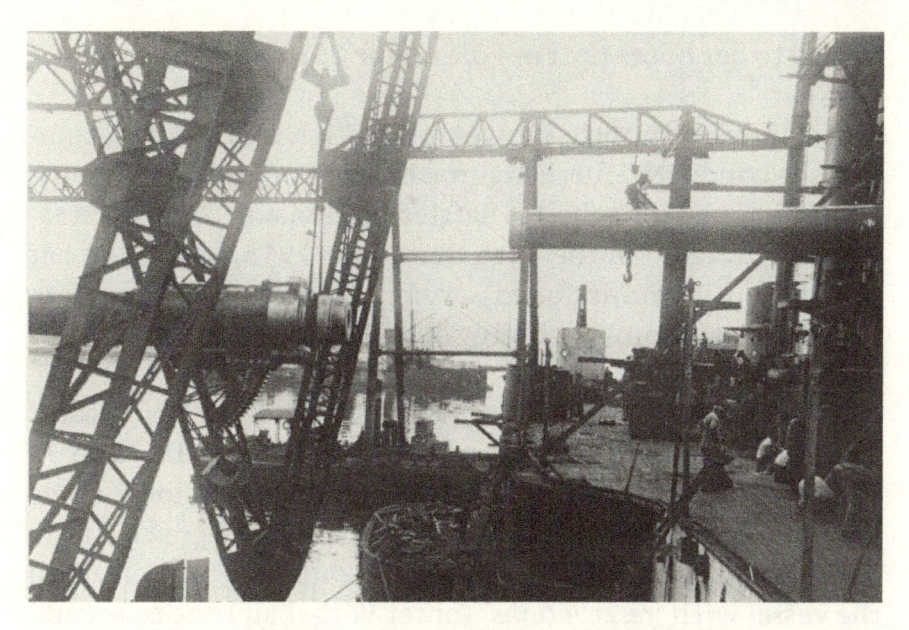

INSTALLATION OF THE 12 INCH GUN BARRELS ON THE SZENT ISTVAN AS SHE IS FITTED OUT IN THE SHIPYARD.

The shipyard workers, wary that once the ship was completed, they could well be called into the army, realized it was not in their interest to quickly complete the ship. As a result, construction progressed even slower. The ship's engine-room tests were finally held on the 14th August 1915 and on the 17th November, she was handed over to the navy.

The next day the *Szent István* commenced her gunnery trials, resuming them the following day. There are reports that during these trials the rivets in the double bottom of the hull were being blown out by the forces from the guns. Not something the crew wanted to see and a portent of 1918. Then on the 20th November, she underwent her machinery trials in the Fasana Channel, during which on the 22nd November, it was reported that she attained an unofficial speed of 21 knots, (the official was 20.4 knots). On the same day, the new Dreadnought conducted torpedo launches from her four torpedo tubes, before anchoring at Fasana for the night. She finally returned to her home port of Pola on the 25th November.

The following month, between the 13th and 23rd December, she conducted further gunnery trials before finally being commissioned into the 1st Battleship Division of the Austro-Hungarian Navy on the 13th December 1915, beginning her 911 days of commissioned service. She was longer in construction than commissioning by 521 days!

After her speed trials it was noted that due to her greater instability, the rudders had to be restricted from 19.75 to 35 degree. It was found that turning sharply at full 'lock' made the foremost turret wet. This resulted in a 15-degree limit on her steering. Edmund Grassberger the ship's captain accepted the vessel with *"reservations"* (unter Vorbehalt) due to several problems experienced. Her guns had been damaged during the two days following the handover and after her trial runs, she was found to have *"great deformations"* beneath the waterline, which could be traced back to the use of sub-standard materials. Over the following two days the guns underwent further trials. Due to the delay in her construction the Navy claimed 312,500 Crowns as compensation from Danubius, which was deferred at the request of the company until after the war and the debt was never settled.

Karl Mohl a non-commissioned officer onboard the new dreadnought, reported during her gunnery trials, rivets from the Szent Istvan's double bottom being blown out, like single shot bullets. Something after her loss in 1918, he would recollect.

The new addition to the fleet was schecduled to be commissioned on the 30th July 1914, but it was not until the 13th December 1915 that she was finally to be accepted ready for service and her ensign hoisted.

[1] "*The navy's name proposals were Hunyadi, Corvin Mátyás (the hero of the Hungarian folk tales as „Mátyás az igazságos" – M. the Rightful - which he wasn't in the real life), Erzsébet Királyné and Szent István. Franz Ferdinand objected the Corvin M. and Erzsébet K. on the ground that they they would fuel Hungarian separatism, He wanted the name Laudon, General Arthur Bolfras the chef of the Emperor's military chancellery shared the views of Admiral Haus that an Austrian name for a Hungarian ship would cause scandal, so he preferred the Szent István. On his advice Franz Joseph (Hung Ferenc József) choose the name Szent István for her*". (XX)

CONSTRUCTION TIMES

VIRIBUS UNITIS

LAID DOWN 24.07.10
LAUNCHED 24.06.11
COMMISSIONED 05.12.12
BUILDING DAYS 867

TEGETTHOFF

LAID DOWN 24.09.10
LAUNCHED 21.03.12
COMMISSIONED 14.07.13
BUILDING DAYS 1026

PRINZ EUGEN

LAID DOWN 16.11.12
LAUNCHED 30.11.12
COMMISSIONED 08.07.14
BUILDING DAYS 905

SZENT ISTVAN

LAID DOWN 12.01.12
LAUNCHED 17.01.14
COMMISSIONED 13.12.15
BUILDING DAYS 1432

THE TEGETTHOFF CLASS.

PREVIOUS PAGE. SZENT ISTVAN STARTS HER JOURNEY DOWN THE SLIP WAY.

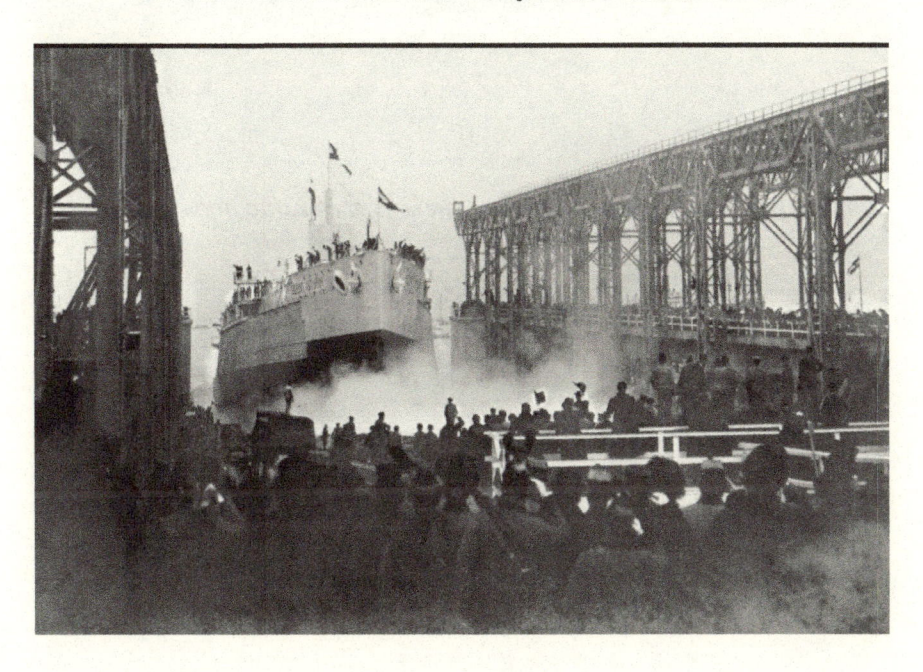

233

SZENT ISTVAN GATHERS SPEED AS THE CROWDS CHEER AND HER STERN ENTERS THE WATER.

PRIESTS BLESSING ANOTHER OF THE CLASS AS SHE SLIDES DOWN INTO THE WAITING WATERS.

THE TEGETTHOFF CLASS.

THE GREAT AND THE GOOD AT ONE OF THE CLASSES LAUNCHES.

SZENT ISTVAN...AND INTO THE WATER FOR THE FIRST TIME.

WITH THE SZENT ISTVAN AFLOAT A TUG PULLS HER TO THE FITTING OUT BASIN FOR HER COMPLETION. THE RECTANGLE PATCH AONG THE FLANK MARKS THE LOCATION OF THE SOON TO BE FITTED ARMOURED BELT.

THE TEGETTHOFF CLASS.

*THE VIPS AT ONE OF THE CLASSES LAUNCHINGS INCLUDING
MARIA THERESIA AND ADMIRAL HAUS*

THE SZENT ISTVAN AND HER TUG WATCHED ON BY THE VIRIBUS UNITIS.

ANDY SOUTH

THE TEGETTHOFF AFTER HER LAUNCH.

THE TEGETTHOFF CLASS.

THE FLEET ATTENDING THE LAUNCH OF THE SZENT ISTVAN. TAKEN FROM RIJEKA.

THE LAUNCH OF THE TEGETTHOFF.. THE FIGURE IS ADMIRAL TEGETTHOFF WHO THE SHIP IS NAMED AFTER.

ANDY SOUTH

THE LAUNCH OF THE VIRIBUS UNITIS

THE TEGETTHOFF CLASS.

THE LAUNCH OF THE PRINZ EUGEN.

LAUNCH OF THE PRINZ EUGEN: SOURCE: NAVAL HISTORY & HERITAGE COMMAND.

ANDY SOUTH

[1] Apologies for the stilted language of the translation, but I was reliant on a translation app to give me the English version.

CHAPTER 2: TIMES OF PEACE (PRE-WAR)

Records on the class's pre-war activities are rare, but two events are noted in the sources. On the 17th March 1913, the British newspaper The Pall Mall Gazette reported how either the *Szent Istvan,* or the *Tegetthoff,* (the article does not name the ship), fired all six guns over the bow simultaneously. The gun crews had vacated the turret and the guns were fired by electrical means. The foremost turret lifted off the roller path placing the ship concerned into dock for some time. Given the timing of the fleets tour of the eastern Mediterranean and its stay in Malta, the report seems questionable? But the British Press were also to report a 'daring' French submarine attack on Pola in 1915, damaging one of the class.

Then in 1918 a second Italian attack was reported, torpedoing the *Prinz Eugen* and sinking her. Midshipman Aomzo was given as the assailant. An event we know to be the by-product of an ill-informed mind, as by the wars end the *Prinz* was still afloat.

THE TEGETTHOFF CLASS.

THE VIRIBUS UNITIS PHOTOGRAPHED IN 1912 FIRING HER MAIN BATTERY.
SOURCE: NAVAL HISTORY AND HERITAGE COMMAND

On Friday 27th March 1914, the German Kaiser Wilhelm arrived in the Empires port of Trieste on-board his royal yacht *S.M.Y Hohenzollern*. As soon as the yacht had anchored the Grand Duke Franz Ferdinand arrived on-board wearing the uniform of a German Admiral. After all due formal greetings both Kaiser and Duke went ashore to the sound of gun salutes. There they met with the Duke's consort the Countess Hohenberg and their family. The party then went on board *Viribus Unitis* for a detailed tour. Afterwards the group departed for Vienna.

Under the command of Rear-Admiral Luzian von Ziegler (and according to one source, prior to her commissioning), the

Tegetthoff and the *Zrinyi*, sailed on a training cruise to the Levant [1]. During the deployment, the ships were to make a number of port calls, including Kumbor in the Bay of Kotor, Smyrna, Adalia, Mersin, Iskenderun, Beirut, Alexandria, Vlorë and Durrës. The ships paused briefly at Malta, a port the Austrian Navy would visit in style just before the outbreak of war in May 1914. But over the intervening months Austria-Hungary proudly showed off her new Dreadnought status to the Mediterranean world.

PREVIOUS PAGE, THE TEGETTHOFF LEADS THE AUSTRO-HUNGARIAN FLEET TO SEA PRIOR TO FEBRUARY 1913 (SOURCE AN OLD POST CARD POST MARKED 16TH FEB 1913)

In the spring of 1914, the *Viribus Unitis* and *Tegetthoff*, (Rear-Admiral Franz Löfler), in company with *Zrínyi* and the coastal defence ship *Monarch* sailed down the Adriatic and then eastward out into the Mediterranean, to the Sea of Sicily and the Levant, visiting the ports of Smyrna, Beirut and Alexandria. While the Squadron was in the port of Alexandria, two of *Monarch's* crew contracted smallpox and cerebrospinal meningitis which resulted in the ship being put into quarantine for several weeks on its return to Pola. Meanwhile the *Viribus Unitis, Tegetthoff* and pre-Dreadnought *Zrinyi* departed the

THE TEGETTHOFF CLASS.

Egyptian port, and steamed westwards towards the island of Malta.

At 10:00 on Friday the 22nd May 1914, the *Tegetthoff* (captain Franz Holub) led a squadron comprising of the *Viribus Unitis,* (captain Konstant Freiherr von Gerlach) and the pre-Dreadnought *Zrinyi,* (captain Maximilian Daublebsky) ,into Malta's Grand Harbour on an official visit. The British Mediterranean Fleet had only just returned to its Malta base after having been in the Adriatic Sea for several days on a visit to Venice (Italian), Trieste, Fiume, Pola, and other ports of the Habsburg Empire. The Austrian Navy's visit to Malta was in return for the visit of the Mediterranean Fleet to the Austrian ports. With spectators occupying every viewing position overlooking the harbour, the three imposing battleships steamed towards the entrance of The Grand Harbour in a single line and at almost their full speed. The *Zrinyi* was the first to enter the crowded bay, passing three British warships that were lying in Bighi Bay, with British and Austrian sailors standing to attention on their respective ship's decks. *Viribus Unitis* led the Habsburg's capital ships into the harbour, while the *Tegetthoff*,(flying the Rear-Admiral's flag) saluted the British flag with a 21-gun salute, just before she steamed past the breakwater. The Royal Malta Artillery returned the compliment from the saluting battery and as their guests steamed into port, the British Admiral Commander-in-Chief Admiral Sir Berkley Milne ordered that the battlecruiser *Inflexible* return the salute. Then as the Austrian flagship drew slowly towards the *Inflexible*, both crews lined their ships decks, while their respective bands played the British and Austrian anthems. The flagship *Tegetthoff* let go her anchor once she lay opposite the British flagship and both ships were con-

captain Franz Holub

nected by a telephone cable. The other ships of the visiting squadron which had preceded the *Tegetthoff* had already exchanged their courtesies with the British ships lying beyond Fort St Angelo and slowly eased into their allotted moorings. *Viribus Unitis* lying opposite the *Indomitable* and *Zrinyi* opposite the cruiser *Warrior*.

IN THE LINED AHEAD, FOLLOWING HER TWO SISTERS IS THE PRE-DREADNOUGHT ZRINYI. THE SHIPS TO THE LEFT ARE OF THE VIRIBUS UNITIS CLASS A WEIN CLASS PRE-DREADNOUGHT AND A ZENTA CLASS CRUISER. THE PHOTO IS UNDATED. COURTESY OF THE INTERNATIONAL NAVAL RESEARCH ORGANIZATION.

Löfler, accompanied by his staff, boarded the *Inflexible* to pay a visit to Berkeley Milne, who then with his own staff in attendance, returned the visit to the *Tegetthoff*. A round of official and courtesy visits were to follow through the succeeding

THE TEGETTHOFF CLASS.

days. Löfler went ashore to pay a visit to the Austro-Hungarian consulate where he held a meeting with the Consul General Kohen von Hohenland. Accompanied by the Austro-Hungarian Vice-consul, Löfler then paid an official call to Archbishop Pietro Pace, who accompanied by his private secretary, returned the visit on board the *Tegetthoff*. The Rear-Admiral and several other officers of the Austrian squadron then returned to the Marina in three motor cars. During the visit, Löfler stayed at Admiralty House in Valletta as the guest of Berkeley Milne.

THE AUSTRIAN VISITORS AT ANCHOR WITH THE BRITISH FLEET IN MALTAS GRAND HARBOUR. IN THE FOREGROUND IS THE BRITISH BATTLECRUISER, HMS INFLEXIBLE.

A programme of receptions and entertainment was planned for the island's visitors. This was to include a tennis tournament, gymkhana, polo at the Marsa, a concert at the Garrison Gymnasium in Valletta, a swimming session at St Pauls Bay, a visit to the dockyard and the Royal Navy Hospital as well as a luncheon given by the Admiral Superintendent at Admiralty House, Vittoriosa. In addition, a special performance was given to honour the visiting officers when the London West End Company presented the play 'Mrs Gorringes Necklace', written by Hubert Henry Davies, at the Theatre Royal. The highlight of the visit was to be a reception held by the consul, von Hohenland in honour of the Austrian Admiral and Officers. It took place at the Union Club and Circolo Għar id-Dud, Sliema with the grounds decorated in both the Austrian and English national flags. The King's Own Band played a select programme of music, which was to include the Overture Imperator, which band master Aurelio Doncich had especially composed in honour of the Austrian Emperor Franz Joseph. A few days before the reception, a special ceremony was held at which von Hohenland had presented Doncich with a diamond scarf pin inscribed with the monogram and crown of the Emperor who had accepted the tribute of the symphony and had ordered that the work should be placed in the library of the Imperial Family.

THE EXCHANGE OF SALUTES AS THE GUESTS ENTER THE GRAND HARBOUR.

Cultural excursions were also held. A party comprising of officers from each Austrian ship were taken on visits to the Chapel of Bones, to the former hospital of the Knights, the Palace, and the Armoury. Other groups visited the Archaeological Museum, the Hypogeum, the Roman Villa, and other places of historical interest under the guidance of Professor Temi Zammit. Two football matches between Floriana United FC and a team from the Tegetthoff were played at the Mile End Sports Ground. Floriana FC won the first game six goals to three. A much larger number of spectators turned up for the return match when rumours spread among football circles that the Austrian team had decided to wipe out the defeat of the previous day. But the local team won again by six goals to one, although the match was diplomatically reported to have been closer. Throughout the visit, local newspapers reported that there was great animation in Valletta as large groups of sailors landed and went to Picture House's and other places of entertainment. For the duration of the visit, the Governor provided 15 horse-drawn carriages for use by the officers of the visiting squadron, free of charge. They each carried a small Austrian ensign and were stationed outside the Custom House and detailed on duty from 10:00 to midnight.

THE AUSTRO-HUNGARIAN FLEET AT SEA IN 1913.

In addition, six dgħajsas, (or water taxis), were provided for the use of Austrian officers, also free of charge. They too flew a small Austrian ensign and two were at the disposal of each ship from 08:00 to midnight. On the 26th at 08:30, the fleet "Dressed Ship" to mark the birthday of her Majesty Victoria Mary Augusta Louise Olga Pauline Claudine Agnes, the Queen Consort of the United Kingdom, the British Dominions and Empress Consort of India, the wife of King George V at 08:30, followed at noon by a Royal Salute of 21 rounds, fired by ships at buoys and the shore battery.

On 28th May, the Austro-Hungarian squadron departed from Malta in the afternoon on route to Pola. The first to sail from the Grand Harbour was the *Tegetthoff*, followed by the *Viribus Unitis* and then the *Zrinyi*. All the men of the British Fleet were lined once more on the decks of their respective ships. Berkeley Milne stood on the Inflexible's bridge, Rear-Admiral

Carden was on one of the dockyard launches and his launch accompanied the squadron as far as the breakwater. As with the squadron's arrival six days prior, large numbers of spectators watched from the Barrakka Gardens and Bastions. In a letter to Berkeley Milne, Löfler later wrote:

> *"Arrived back in our home again. I now offer Your Excellency my most heartfelt and sincere thanks for your kindness and attention, especially that shown by yourself and the English fleet to me, my captains, officers and men in the beautiful harbour of Malta".*

The visit holds a similar feel to the Royal Navy's visits to both Kiel and Tsingtao in the days and weeks before war. There is a sadness to them, at what was soon to be lost to the smell of cordite and blood. Seventy-five days later, the two empires, (Austro-Hungarian and Britannic) would be at war on the 12th August 1914.

THE SHIPS IN THE BACKGROUND INCLUDE FROM RIGHT TO LEFT, A SHIP OF THE TEGETTHOFF CLASS, TWO UNITS OF THE RADETZKY CLASS AND THREE DESTROYERS OF THE ERZHERZOG CLASS. DATED 1913 AT POLA. SOURCE: NAVAL HISTORY & HERITAGE COMMAND.

[1] The term is also used for modern events, peoples, states or parts of states in the same region, namely Cyprus, Egypt, Iraq, Israel, Jordan, Lebanon, Palestine, Syria and Turkey are sometimes considered Levant countries.

CHAPTER 3: THE PATH TO WAR

A month after her visit to Malta, on the 25th June 1914 the heir presumptive to the thrones of Austria and Hungary, Archduke Franz Ferdinand Carl Ludwig Joseph Maria of Austria boarded the *Viribus Unitis* with all due ceremony in the port of Trieste, while his wife, Sophie Maria Josephine Albina Countess Chotek of Chotkow and Wognin, Duchess of Hohenberg, travelled overland by train to Sarajevo. The Archduke made his journey by sea for the less savoury reason that Franz Ferdinand had a fierce antipathy towards Hungarians and wanted to avoid traveling through any part of the empire that was under the control of Budapest.

Once the Archduke and his entourage had disembarked with all due pomp and circumstance from the *Viribus Unitis* as she lay anchored in the mouth of the Neretva River, life onboard the dreadnought returned to normal. Over the next few days, the *Viribus Unitis* was to ride quietly at her anchorage, awaiting the return of her Royal patron. Then on the 28th the news of the double murder in Sarajevo reached the ship. It must have passed through the officers' wardrooms and crews messes bringing both a seismic shock and a wondering of what would result from the murders.

To the north, on receipt of the news the Commander-in-Chief of the Navy Anton Haus sailed south from Pola with an squadron composed of the *Viribus Unities*' sister ship, *Tegetthoff*, the cruiser *Admiral Spaun*, the Admiralty yacht *Lacroma* and several torpedo boat to provide an honour escort for the Viribus Unitis and her two coffins.

Two days after the murder of the Archduke and his wife [1], a 'special' train from Sarajevo bearing the two coffins arrived in the Croatian town of Metkovitich at 06:00. As the train came to a steam shrouded halt, the coffins arrival was met by a military guard of honour lined up on the platform. In addition to the troops, the town's Governor and his Council were present, all dressed in black. School children were also in attendance supervised by their teachers and a crowd filled the station as well as lining the route down to the harbour. A naval detachment was to act as the pallbearers conveying the two coffins from their place on the train to the awaiting horse drawn hearses. Priests blessed the deceased Archduke and his wife, before the horses drew the wreath draped hearses to the waiting yacht. To the tolling of the town's church bells the procession made its way slowly towards the harbour. As it wound its way down to the awaiting river transport, the crowds watched in a stunned shock, with tears and crying marking its passage. The Archduke's coffin was draped with two banners, the military and the Archduke's flag. The Duchess's was draped in only the military banner.

PREVIOUS PAGE. THE COFFINS AWAITING TRANSFER.

Having reached the quayside, the two coffins were laid with great solemnity on board the yacht *Dalmat*, where they were once more surrounded by and bedecked in flowers. With her cargo in place, the yacht slowly made her way down river, a salute by a guard of honour marking her departure. The yacht was proceeded by a lone torpedo boat and in the *Dalmat's* wake came the Governor's yacht with her cargo of the 'important' personages. Every village on the river was draped in black with crowds lining the banks bearing lighted candles. As the villages were slowly passed, the church bells tolled to mark the passage and priests blessed the passing Flotilla.

THE "CHAPELLE ARDENTE" WITH THE TWO COFFINS LAID WITHIN IT.

At the mouth of the river, anchored and waiting with their own flags at half-mast lay the *Viribus Unitis,* now joined by Haus's escorting squadron. As the three-boat cortège eased gently towards the awaiting warship, the *Viribus Unitis* guns fired a salute to mark the occasion. The yacht was secured alongside, and the coffins were transferred with solemnity to the quarter deck, which had been converted to a "Chapelle Ardente", hung with flags and banners. The dreadnought's chaplain and his staff blessed the deceased as the ships officers and governors party watched on. The *Unitis'* crew gathered around and watched as the tragedy was played out on their ship's wooden decks. At 09:00 with the naval flag and the Archduke's flag at half-mast the capital ship and her escort weighed their anchors and slowly moved off. What would on happier days be a short voyage took longer, as the ships moved at a slow pace, they made their way along the coast to the tolling of church bells and crowds watching from on shore.

THE TEGETTHOFF CLASS.

THE VIRIBUS UNITIS ON 1 JULY 1914 WHILE TRANSPORTING THE REMAINS OF THE ASSASSINATED ARCHDUKE FRANZ FERDINAND AND HIS WIFE TO TRIESTE. NOTE AWNINGS AFT OVER THE REMAINS, LARGE FLAG, AND BLACK BUNTING.
SOURCE: NAVAL HISTORY AND HERITAGE COMMAND

THE VIRIBUS UNITIS WHILE TRANSPORTING THE REMAINS OF THE ASSASSINATED ARCHDUKE FRANZ FERDINAND AND HIS WIFE TO TRIESTE. SOURCE: NAVAL HISTORY AND HERITAGE COMMAND.

The procession arrived off Trieste that evening at 19:00, but the Duke and his Duchess's remained on board under a guard of honour. The next morning the harbour was filled with boats, each one crowded with 'spectators'. Amongst the boats an area was kept clear where two barges bearing catafalques [2]. Each barge and its contents were draped in black. At 09:30 one of the *Viribus Unitis* boat cranes, gently lifted each coffin in turn, lowering it into the waiting barge. Then they were towed towards the officials and crowds waiting ashore and as they slowly moved towards the quay the fleet's guns fired salutes to mark the coffins passage. From ashore the church filled the air with the sound of their bells as the tolled. A party of Petty Officers lifted each coffin ashore and lowered them tenderly onto the awaiting hearses. A military guard of honour stood to attention in a salute to the Archduke and his wife. The suites of the two deceased formed around each hearse and the Bishop Karlin, with other priests blessed the coffins. The two hearses, each drawn by six horses slowly moved off, followed by seven carriages, each in turn filled and bedecked with floral tributes. The Archdukes coffin went first, and his wife's carriage followed in the wake of her husband's hearse. All the cities businesses were closed for the occasion and the gas streetlights covered in black crepe. At 09:30 the nine carriages reached the Southern Railway station and the coffins were off loaded and resumed their overland voyage to the Empires capital, Vienna. The crews of the fleet that lay in the harbour that day must have wondered if war was coming to the Empire in the next few days.

THE TEGETTHOFF CLASS.

During the next few weeks, the road to war was to become crowded as Empires rushed to declare war on each other. There was however still 'peace' between the two Empires of Austria-Hungry and Britain on the 7th August 1914, when the Austro-Hungarian fleet was requested by the German Mediterranean Division, (the Battlecruiser *Goeben* and light cruiser *Breslau*), to provide them with assistance. The two German ships were attempting to break out of Messina in Sicily, where they had been coaling before the outbreak of war. But as they communicated via wireless with their allies, British warships had begun to gather off Messina to try and trap the Germans in port. However, despite having started the race to war, the Austro-Hungarian navy had yet to be fully mobilized. But three *Radetzkys* Pre-Dreadnoughts and the three *Tegetthoff's*, with several cruisers and smaller craft, were available to offer aid to the two German ships. The Austrians were wary of causing war between the Habsburg, British and French Empires, until their arthritic mobilization was complete, ordered the fleet to avoid the British ships. They were only to support the Germans openly when they were in Austro-Hungarian waters. On 7th August, when the German ship's broke out of Messina, the Austro-Hungarian fleet, including the *Tegetthoff* class Dreadnoughts, put to sea to offer distant support to their allies. However, at the latitude of Cape Planck, a message was received that the Kaiser's ships had already managed to slip east off Matapan towards Constantinople, so the Austrian battleships set the opposite course. Having achieved extraordinarily little and sailed even less, the ships returned to their harbours.

With the outbreak of the war, *Viribus Unitis* remained the Fleet Flagship of Admiral Anton Haus. Her two sister ships, *Tegetthoff* and *Prinz Eugen* formed an element of the 1st Battle Squadron with Vice-Admiral Njegovan flying his flag from the *Tegetthoff*. Haus was a strong supporter of retaining the Empire's battleships, and the *Tegetthoff* class, in reserve, or as a "fleet-in-being". He believed Italy would renege on her Treaty alliance with the Central powers and eventually side with the Entente. Haus believed that by retaining Austria-Hungary's battle fleet in port and safe, they would be available for an early deployment against Italy.

Through the four years of war that were to follow, the Austro-Hungarian battle fleet was to see little action and was to spend much of its time riding at anchor in its main base of Pola (today's Pula in Croatia). The navy's lack of activity or offensive action was caused, (partly) by a lack of coal, which was to become more of a problem as the war progressed. Before the war, Austria-Hungary's main supplier for coal had been Great Britain, (the perceived enemy of her alliance). In the pre-war years, an increasing amount of coal had come from the mines of Germany, USA, and other domestic sources, but by the outbreak of war, 75% of her navy's demand for coal was still purchased from Britain. The war now removed the British source, although large quantities of coal had been stockpiled before the outbreak of hostilities, ensuring the navy could sail out of port if needed. With the importance of guaranteeing that the navy's new Dreadnoughts had the coal they needed in the event of either a French or Italian attack, or even a major offensive operation, meant the Dreadnoughts remained in port, unless circumstances, demanded their deployment at sea.

In addition, the fear of mines within the Adriatic became a growing concern and a haunting spectre for the navy. The same fear of mines was however also to keep the Italian fleet in its bases for most of the war. *Szent István* was to remain based, as were her sisters, in the port of Pola throughout her period of Imperial service. None of the new Dreadnoughts were to leave the sanctuary of their anchorage except for gunnery practice in the nearby Croatian strait of Fažana, less than 5 miles. Through *Szent István's* long boredom she spent 937 days at anchor or practice, of which just 54 days were at sea, and she was to make only one or two-day trips to Pag Island, 118 miles direct. In total 5.7% of her life was spent at sea and the remaining 94.3% saw her swinging on her anchor back in Pola Harbour. She was never even to go into dry dock to get her bottom scraped clean!

[1] *The story of the murder is well known, but what is less known is the love story that led up to it. How they met is not known. Where or exactly when Sophie first met her future husband and Archduke, but it could plausibly have been at a ball in Prague in 1894. Franz Ferdinand, who was then stationed at the military garrison in Prague, had started to pay frequent visits to Halbturn Castle, the home of Archduke Friedrich. It was not unreasonably assumed that he had fallen in love with Friedrich's eldest daughter, Archduchess Marie Christine. But it was a lady-in-waiting to the Archduchess Isabella, the wife of Archduke Friedrich, Sophie, who was the real reason for his visits. The romance was all too soon unmasked by the Archduchess Isabella, who herself had only been born into a mediatised family (the House of Croÿ). She discovered Franz Ferdinand's locket lying where it had fallen, on the tennis court and on opening it, expected to see a photo of her daughter. Instead, the locket contained a photo of Sophie. Scandal followed.*

Franz Ferdinand had on the suicide of his cousin Crown Prince Rudolf in 1889 and the death of his father Karl Ludwig from typhoid in 1896, become the heir presumptive to the throne. With the reason for his visits now revealed his uncle and Emperor Franz Joseph, informed him that it would not be possible for him to marry a lady-in-waiting, who could never become an Empress Consort. To be a consort for any member of the Imperial House of Habsburg-Lorraine, the bride would need to belong to one of the reigning or formerly reigning dynasties of Europe. Although the Choteks had been noble since at least the 14th century and had been made Counts of the Holy Roman Empire in 1745, they were not of dynastic rank, even though Sophie was a descendant of Habsburgs, from Elisabeth, sister of King Rudolph I of Germany, Franz Ferdinand's ancestor. But having found love, Franz Ferdinand refused to marry 'suitably' and beget an heir to the throne. This only added to the scandal surrounding the death and illicit affair of the Emperor's previous heir. In 1899, under pressure from his family (especially the Archduchess Maria Theresa, the Emperor's somewhat formidable sister-in-law and Franz Ferdinand's stepmother) the couple were finally granted permission to marry. Franz Ferdinand was to be allowed to retain his place in the order of succession and a suitable title was promised for his bride. But to prevent Franz Ferdinand from proclaiming his wife Empress-Queen or declaring their future children eligible to inherit the crown (especially that of Hungary, where morganatic marriages were forbidden by law) once he ascended to the throne, he was ordered appear at the Hofburg Imperial Palace.

He was to attend the Empire's Archdukes, Ministers, and the dignitaries of the court, the Cardinal-Archbishop of Vienna, and the Primate of Hungary on the 28th June 1900, to sign an official document. The wording on the pages of that document stated that Sophie would be his morganatic wife and she would never be raised to the rank of Empress, Queen or Archduchess. He was also forced to acknowledge that their descendants would neither inherit nor be granted dynastic rights or privileges within the Empires boarders. Sophie and Franz Ferdinand were to be married on the 1st July 1900 at Reichstadt (now Zákupy) in Bohemia. The Emperor did not *attend the wedding, nor did any of the Archdukes, including Franz Ferdinand's brothers. The only members of the Imperial family who were present were Franz Ferdinand's stepmother, Archduchess Maria Theresa, and her two daughters. Sophie was given the title Fürstin von Hohenberg ("Princess of Hohenberg") with the style of Durchlaucht ("Serene Highness"). In 1909, she was elevated to Herzogin (Duchess) and accorded the higher style of Hoheit ("Highness"). But all the Archduchesses, mediatized Princesses and Countesses of Austria and Hungary took precedence over her. For the fourteen years of their marriage.*

Sophie was never to share her husband's rank or title. Her position at the Imperial court was humiliating, only made more difficult by the Imperial Obersthofmeister, Alfred, the second Prince of Montenuovo, whose insecurity about his own morganatic background (it's said) prompted him to rigorously enforce court protocol at poor Sophie's expense. Problems of protocol were to prevent many royal courts from hosting the couple despite Franz Ferdinand's position as heir to the throne. Nonetheless, some did, including King George V and Queen Mary of the United Kingdom, who warmly welcomed the couple to Windsor Castle from 17th to 21st November 1913.

The couple were to have four children:

1. Princess Sophie of Hohenberg (1901–1990), married Count Friedrich von Nostitz-Rieneck (1891–1973)

2. Maximilian, Duke of Hohenberg (1902–1962), married Countess Elisabeth von Waldburg zu Wolfegg und Waldsee (1904–1993). Ironically, his descendants married descendants of the Royal Houses of France, Portugal, and Austria (Archduke Joseph Arpad).

3. Prince Ernst of Hohenberg (1904–1954), married Marie-Therese Wood (1910–1985)

4. A stillborn son (1908).

On the death of their parents the now orphaned children were 13, 12 and ten years old.

You gotta admit the guy had quite a backbone and a love for his wife.

I find it a cool slant on what a seen as a stuffy and arthritic imperial court....

Andrew South

[2] Catafalques: a decorated wooden framework supporting the coffin during a funeral or while lying in state

CHAPTER 4: COMBAT (1915)

On the 23rd May 1915, the Italian declaration of war against Austria-Hungary finally came, but the Austrian fleet was ready to respond, launching several attacks on the Marche region of Italy. On the day of the declaration, the destroyer *Dinara* and torpedo boat *TB53* bombarded the port of Ancona. While the destroyer *Lika*, on a reconnaissance mission between Palagruža and Cape Gargano, shelled the semaphore and radio station at Vieste. Defending those waters at the time was the Italian destroyer *Turbine* and an exchange of fire commenced with the light cruiser *Helgoland,* aided by four destroyers. The destroyer *Lika* was to sink the *Turbine* in a pitched battle south of Pelagosa. (The Lika was herself in turn to be sunk by a mine near Durazzo on the 29th December 1915). The same day also saw the destroyer *Tátra* shell the railway embankment near Manfredonia, while the destroyer *Csepel* shelled the Manfredonia railway station.

NEWS OF HOSTILITIES BETWEEN THE HABSBURG AND BRITISH EMPIRES REPORTED THE BRITISH NEWSPAPER, THE SPHERE (22ND AUGUST 1914).
"AUSTRIA'S FIRST DREADNOUGHT, THE VIRIBUS UNITIS FIRING HER NO 2 TURRET"

On the 23rd May 1915, just four hours after the news of the Italian declaration of war had reached the fleet at Pola, the Dreadnoughts in company with other elements of the fleet, left their anchorages to bombard the Italian port of Ancona. The fleet included the *Viribus Unitis, Tegetthoff, Prinz Eugen,* (the *Szent István* was still undergoing her final stages of fitting out) and eight Pre-Dreadnoughts. Whilst some ships bombarded their secondary targets, and others were deployed to the south to screen for any Italian ships making their way north from the Italian base at Taranto, the core of the Austro-Hungarian Navy, led by the ships of the *Tegetthoff* class slipped from their anchorages and set a course for Ancona.

THE TEGETTHOFF CLASS.

AUSTRIA'S FIRST DREADNOUGHT, THE ▓▓▓ ▓▓▓ AS SHE WILL APPEAR WHEN COMPLETED

THE ILLUSTRATED NEWS (AUGUST 1914) "AUSTRIA'S NEW DREADNOUGHT
THE VIRIBUS UNITS AS SHE WILL APPEAR WHEN COMPLETE

THE VIRIBUS UNITS THE FIRST ALL BIG GUN WAS LAUNCHED AT TRIESTE ON THE 24TH JUNE 24. ON A DISPLACEMENT OF 24,000 TONS SHE CARRIES AN ARMAMENT OF TWELVE 12 INCH AND EIGHTEEN 2.7-INCH GUNS. THE BIG GUNS ARE ALL ARRANGED IN THE MIDDLE LINE IN ALL TRIPLE TURRETS, THE SECOND AND THIRD BEING RAISED TO GIVE HER AN AXEL FIRE OF SIX AND A BROADSIDE OF TWELVE. DRIVEN BY TURBINES OF 25,000 HP THE SHIP WILL BE DRIVEN AT 20-21 KNOTS".

WHILE IMPRESSIVE THE ARTISTS IMPRESSION GIVES HER ADDITIONAL MAST STATIONS, A SECOND TIER OF CASEMENT GUNS ETC.

The bombardments across the province of Ancona were to be one, if not the only major 'success' for the Austro-Hungarian capital ship's during the war. In the port of Ancona, an Italian steamer was destroyed by the shelling, another was wrecked on the slipway and three others were damaged. The town of Ancona and the surrounding area was severely damaged by the bombardment. The train yard and port facilities in the city were damaged or destroyed, while the local shore batteries that had opened fire on the attackers, were wiped out. The city's electricity, gas and telephone lines were all disrupted, several shipping piers, warehouses, oil tanks, radio stations and both the coal and oil stores were set on fire by the bombardment. In Ancona, the police headquarters, army barracks, military hospital, sugar refinery and the Bank of Italy's offices all received some damage. During the bombardment, an effort was made to avoid collateral damage, but some of the shells still struck Ancona's cathedral which had become masked by the fires and smoke they generated. A 12-inch shell was to penetrate the walls of the cathedral and there was practically no resistance from the Italian military, the local press referred to the attack as *"barbaric"*. In addition, 30 Italian soldiers and 38 civilians were killed, while 150 were wounded in the course during the attack.

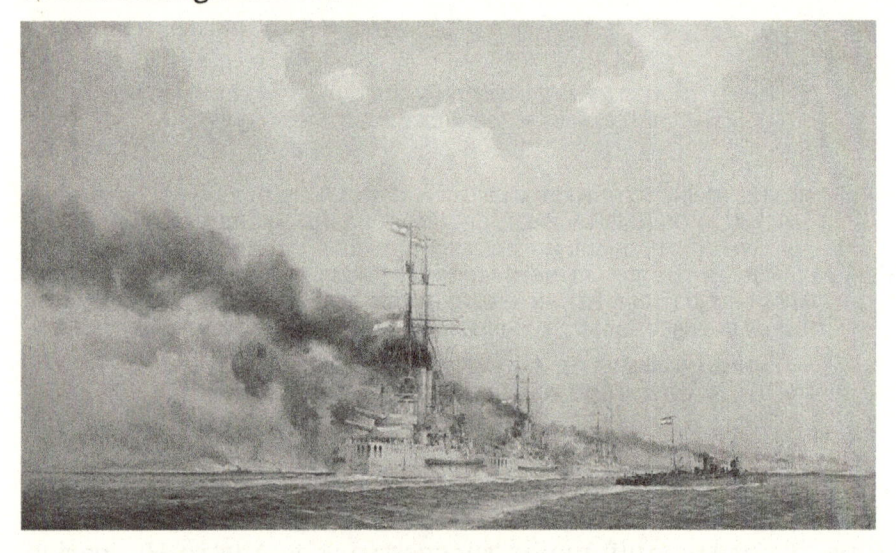

BOMBARDING OF ANCONA,
ARTIST: AUGUST VON RAMBERG (1866-1947)

The Austrian destroyer *Velebit* was to be attacked with bombs by the Italian airship *Città di Ferrara* off Ancona, while the pre-Dreadnought Radetzky and two torpedo boats bombarded Potenza Picena, then returned to Pola. The torpedo boat

THE TEGETTHOFF CLASS.

TB3 was also to be unsuccessfully bombed by an Italian airship. The Radetzky class pre-Dreadnought *Zrínyi*, escorted by two torpedo boats, bombarded Senigallia, destroying a train, damaging a railway station and a bridge, before then returning to Pola. The light cruiser *Admiral Spaun* shelled the Italian signal station at Cretaccio Island, while the *Sankt Georg*, with her two torpedo boats escort, shelled Rimini, damaging a freight train. The destroyer *Streiter* shelled the signal station near Torre di Mileto and the light cruiser *Novara*, a destroyer and two torpedo boats entered the Corsini Channel and shelled an Italian torpedo boat station, a semaphore station and coastal artillery batteries. Finally, Austro-Hungarian flying boats dropped bombs on Venice and airship hangars at Chiaravalle. The Austro-Hungarian ships would move on to bombard the coast of Montenegro, without much opposition and by the time the Italian navy arrived on the scene, the Austro-Hungarians were tucked safely up in Pola.

The objective of the operation had been to delay the Italian Army from deploying its forces along the Austria-Hungary boarder, by the destruction of the areas transport systems. The surprise attack on Ancona would succeed in delaying the Italian deployment to the Alps by two weeks, gaining Austria-Hungary valuable time to strengthen its Italian border and redeploy some of its troops from the Eastern and Balkan fronts. In addition, the bombardment delivered a damaging blow to Italian military and public morale.

PREVIOUS PAGE. ARCHDUKE FREDERICK THE SUPREME COMMANDER OF THE AUSTRO-HUNGARIAN ARMY WITH GRAND ADMIRAL ANTON HAUS ON BOARD ONE OF THE DREADNOUGHTS. 23.2.1916

PPREVIOUS AGE . THE PHOTO IS LABELED AS THE ARCHDUKE ONBOARD THE TEGETTHOFF.

THE TEGETTHOFF CLASS.

THE ARCHDUKE ONCE MORE, BUT ON BOARD THE VIRIBUS UNITIS.

CHAPTER 5: BOREDOM & MUTINY.

As the 'Great Powers' fought their war, 1915 gave way to 1916 and in turn 1917 brought more blood and more death to the European theatre. Through each of those long and terrible years, the four *Tegetthoff's* either rode at their anchor or sailed five miles (45 minutes) to practice their gunnery skills over two-day periods. Then with the practice over, the mighty Dreadnoughts turned about and slunk back the 5 miles to their anchorages. As month followed month the boredom set in for the 4,355 sailors manning the Dreadnoughts. The crew's sea experience must have gradually declined, with all the necessary skills required being practiced on a ship practiced lying at anchor in the harbour or on a brief 10-mile voyage.

During the January of 1917, the newly crowned Austrian Emperor Karl had attended a military conference at the Schloss Pless in company with the German Kaiser and members of both the German Army and Navy. Grand Admiral Haus, along with members of Austria-Hungary's naval command at Pola, accompanied the Emperor to this conference to discuss the future of planned naval operations in the Adriatic and Mediterranean for the coming year. Days after returning from the conference, 66-year-old Haus was to fall ill and, on the 8th February, he died of pneumonia aboard his flagship, the *Viribus Unitis*.

Vice-Admiral Njegovan

On the 17th February, Vice-Admiral Njegovan was promoted to the role of Fleet C-in-C. He had previously voiced his frustration in watching the Dreadnought he had commanded under his predecessor spend its days riding at anchor, slowly rusting and her crew growing more frustrated with each passing day. The new C-in-C had 400,000 tons of coal at his disposal. But despite the change of command, Haus' strategy of keeping the Austro-Hungarian Navy and particularly its Dreadnoughts in port was to remain unaltered. By retaining the *Tegetthoff's* as a 'fleet-in-being', the Austro-Hungarian Navy would be able to continue to defend its lengthy coastline from naval bombardment or invasion by sea with the ports of Trieste and Fiume would also remain protected. In addition, the Italian ships stationed in Venice were all but trapped by the positioning of the Austro-Hungarian fleet, preventing them from sailing south to join the bulk of the Allied forces at the Otranto Barrage. As 1917 passed, both the fleet and its Dreadnoughts were slowly drained of the more promising and experienced crew members who were transferred to serve both the submarine and the torpedo boat flotillas, or assigned ashore to land-based units. Their places were taken by a growing number of reservists who came with less experience.

PREVIOUS PAGE.PRINZ EUGEN SHOWING THE FORWARD PART OF SHIP VIEWED FROM MAIN TOP. NOTE MAIN BATTERY TURRETS, 11 POUND GUNS ON DECK, AND SEARCHLIGHTS ON BRIDGE WINGS.

SOURCE: INTERNATIONAL NAVAL RESEARCH ORGANIZATION

THE TEGETTHOFF CLASS.

The boredom that filled the moored ships was to be briefly broken on three occasions as the ships prepared for parties of Royal visitors. The crews were set to cleaning and polishing their ships making everything ready. First came the new Emperor, Karl I on 15th December 1916. Then in Febuary 1917 to mark the Slavic church festival of Zacchaeus Sunday. Then once more in June of 1917 but this time for the first formal imperial review of the Austro-Hungarian Navy since 1902. This visit was by its very nature far grander than his previous tour of the naval base, with officers and sailors lining the decks of their ships at port and the naval ensign of Austria-Hungary flying proudly from every vessel. The Emperor received the salutes and cheers from the men at Pola, who had spent the past two years doing little more than trying to shoot down Italian air-planes.

IN FEBUARY 1917 THE NEW EMPEROR, KARL I VISTED HIS FLEET IN POLA FOR BOTH THE FUNERAL OF GRAND ADMIRAL HAUS AND THE CHURCH'S MARK ZACCHAEUS SUNDAY (SLAVIC TRADITION). THE SHIP STERN TOWARDS THE SMALL BOAT APPEARS TO BE ONE OF THE DREADNOUGHTS.

ANDY SOUTH

SOURCE: NAVAL HISTORY AND HERITAGE COMMAND.

THE GRAND ADMIRALS COFFIN ALONGSIDE HIS FLAGSHIP, THE VIRIBUS UNITIS. THE PHOTO AFFORDS US A NICE VIEW OF BOTH A 15CM GUN AND ONE OF THE (EMPTY) SMALL BOAT DAVITS.

SOURCE: NAVAL HISTORY AND HERITAGE COMMAND.

THE TEGETTHOFF CLASS.

THE SHIPS CAPTAIN WELCOMES HIS EMPEROR WITH THE 30.5 CM IN THE BACKGROUND. THE PHOTGRAPHS ARER UNDATED AHD WITGH NO BLACK ARM BANDS THEY ARE MOST LIKELY NOT THE ADMIRALS FUNERAL?

SOURCE: NAVAL HISTORY AND HERITAGE COMMAND.

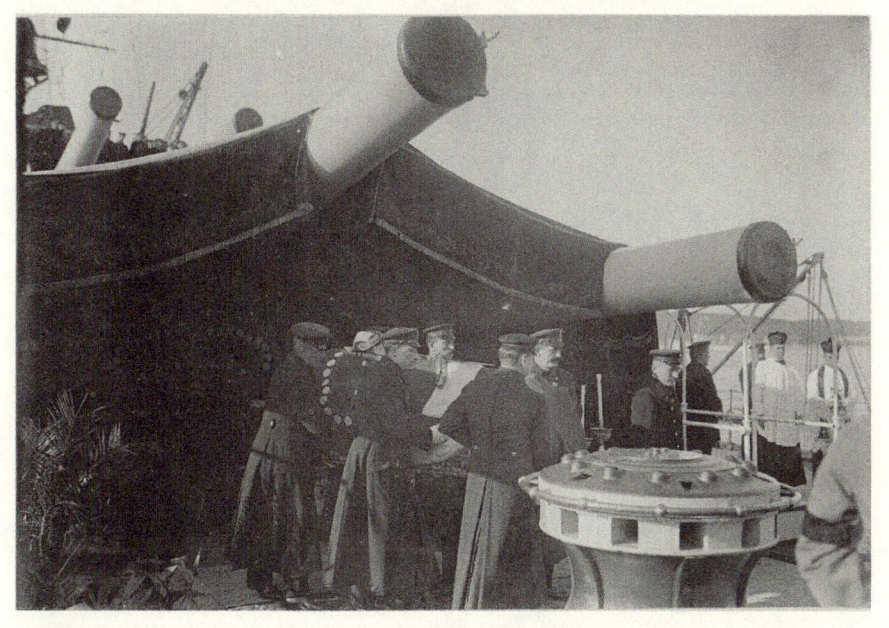

THE COFFIN OF GRAND ADMIRAL HAUS (ESCORTED BY HIS EMPEROR, KARL I) BOARD HIS FLAGSHIP, ON THE DAY OF HIS FUNERAL IN POLA, 10TH FEBRUARY 1917.

SOURCE: NAVAL HISTORY AND HERITAGE COMMAND.

ANDY SOUTH

OFFICERS AND EMPEROR GATHER IN THE SHADOWS OF THE TURRETS
WHERE THE ADMIRALS COFFIN LAYS..

SOURCE: NAVAL HISTORY AND HERITAGE COMMAND.

THE TEGETTHOFF CLASS.

THE CHURCH BLESS THE ADMIRALS COFFIN..
SOURCE: NAVAL HISTORY AND HERITAGE COMMAND.

THE EMPEROR INSPECTS THE SHIPS OFFICERS.
SOURCE: NAVAL HISTORY AND HERITAGE COMMAND.

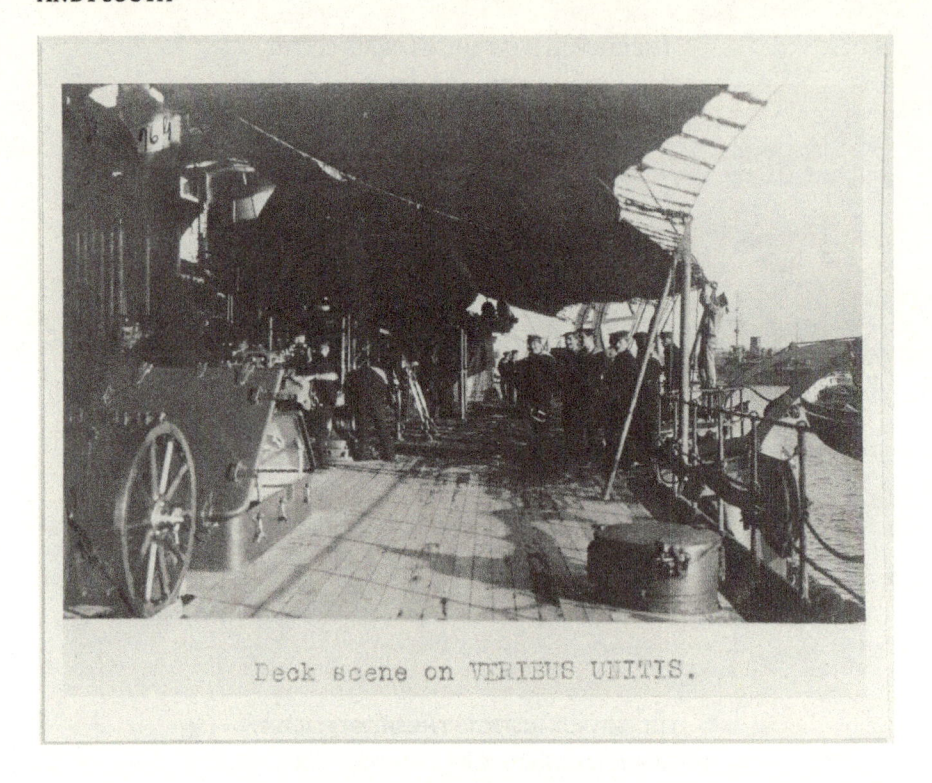

"DECK SCENE ON THE VIRIBUS UNITIS"
SOURCE: NAVAL HISTORY AND HERITAGE COMMAND.

In December 1917 came the German Kaiser Wilhelm II, as he briefly interrupted his inspection of the port's German submarine base. Then the fleet went back to riding at anchor and the occasional practice shoots. In 1918, the sources note the *Szent István* and *Viribus Unitis* participating together in a one-day shooting practice off Giovanni in Pelago, an uninhabited rock off Croatia, located along the west coast of Istria, south of Rovinj. Then back to Pola and their awaiting anchorages.

After four years of near inactivity, in February 1918 the effects of the wartime economic decline and boredom, brought the discipline of some Austro-Hungarian armed units down. In the 984 days since the fleet's return from Ancona, hunger, cold and naval inaction had cultivated in a crop of complaints, desertions and strikes. Revolutionary propaganda was spreading through the ships. The news of Revolution in Russia was debated and raised the men's hopes that things might yet change. Finally, on the 1st February 1918, a mutiny started in the Fifth fleet division moored at the Bay of Kotor naval base on the Adriatic Sea. Sailors of 40 ships joined the mutiny demanding better treatment, but this was soon replaced by political demands and calls for peace. The mutiny was to remain local to Kotor and many units, (including the *Tegetthoff's*) stayed loyal. On the 3rd of February, the loyal Third fleet arrived and together with coastal artillery engaged in a short fight against the mutineers. Finally, around 800 sailors were imprisoned, dozens were court-martialled, and four seamen were executed. Once all was calm, the Commander-in-Chief of the fleet, Admiral Maximilian Njegovan was sacked and replaced by Miklós Horthy, commander of the *Prinz Eugen,* who was promoted to Counter-(Rear)-Admiral. It was announced, at Njegovan's own request, that he was retiring. At the appointment of Horthy, his colleague Admiral Sheer, C-in-C of the German fleet, was heard to exclaim, *"Now, finally, there is the man we need."*

Horthy's promotion was met with wide support by among many of his officers, many who believed he would finally make use of Austria-Hungary's navy to engage with the enemy. But Horthy's appointment did raise difficulties, as his relatively young age alienated many of the senior officers. Austria-Hungary's naval traditions had an unspoken rule that no officer could serve at sea under someone of inferior seniority. This resulted in the Admirals of the First and Second Battle Squadrons, as well as the Cruiser Flotilla, all going into early retirement.

But by March 1918, Horthy's position within the navy was secured and he had begun to re-organize it to his own ideas, with strong support from the Emperor. Horthy used these first few months as Commander-in-Chief to finish his re-organization of the navy and one of Njegovan's final actions had been the movement of several smaller and older ships around to different ports under Austro-Hungarian control. The only ships which remained in Pola aside from the three of the *Radetzky* class, were the four ships of the *Tegetthoff* class, which had now fallen under the command of Captain Heinrich Seitz. Horthy issued orders for the return of as many ships as possible to Pola in order to maximize the threat the Austro-Hungarian Navy could present to the Allied navies. Horthy also used his promotion to take the Austro-Hungarian fleet out of port for manoeuvres and gunnery practice on a regular basis. These operations were the largest the navy had seen since the outbreak of the war.

The gunnery and manoeuvre practices were undertaken not only to restore order in the wake of the mutinies, but also to prepare the fleet for a major offensive operation. Horthy's strategic thinking differed from his two predecessors and shortly after taking command, he planned a fleet action to address the low morale and boredom, as well as to make Austro-Hungarian and German U-Boats access out of the Adriatic and into the Mediterranean easier. At the beginning of June 1918, after sev-

THE TEGETTHOFF CLASS.

eral months of practice, Horthy decided the fleet was ready for a major offensive.

Life at their respective anchorages must have become dismal and monotonous, only broken by a brief 45 minute 'voyage' to Fácán Csatorna for some gunnery exercises. While the empires land armies gave battle, her new and mighty Dreadnoughts lay in the enclosed waters of Pola waiting for the big day, which never seem to come.

On the night of 13th May 1918, on another night of ships in harbour with bored crews and inactivity by the fleet, the ports entrance was as usual illuminated by the dazzling sweeping beams of the searchlights, while the patrols on both land and water guarded the entrance to the fleets home port. But on this evening from out of the darkness, (out near the defense booms) a mechanical clanking broke the silence of the night as alarms sounded throughout the fleet and defensive batteries opened fire. The Italians had arrived at the ports entrance....

As The fourth year of the war had arrived, the Austro-Hungarian Dreadnoughts had remained safely secure at their anchorages, tantalizingly close to the Italian fleet's bases, but still beyond reach. The *Prinz Eugen, Tegetthoff* and the *Viribus Unitis* stayed safe and undamaged as the war dragged ever on.

On the night of 9th & 10th December 1917 the Italian *MAS 9*, commanded by had Lieutenant (tenente di vascello) Luigi Rizzo successfully attacked and sank the Austro-Hungarian Pre-dreadnought *Wien* while she lay in the Bay of Muggia, near

Trieste. Then once more the MAS wrote history in June 1918 with the destruction of the *Szent István*. The value and potential for these small craft had been proven twice and now the Italians wanted to enter the port of Pola itself to attack the anchored fleet as it lay cocooned within its lair.

An attempt to access the harbour during the night of the 1st & 2nd November 1916 had shown the Italians that if they were to taste success again, they would need to find a way to bypass the boom defenses. If under the boom was not an option, then may be a 'jump' over the top? From this logic the Grillo was conceived.

The Grillo (or "Cricket"), was one of the least known Italian small craft of the war and still ranks as amongst the least successful. This small craft was of the MAS gene and was built in the SVAN shipyards having been designed by the engineer Attilio Bisio. They were to be a hybrid tank-MAS, or "jumping boat" according to the initial Barchino Saltatore designation.

They had been designed specifically by Engineer Attilio Bisio to overcome the harbour defenses, which were there in turn to prevent the small MAS boats from rushing in and creating havoc within the Austro-Hungarian ports. The boats were conceived to be a fast craft, of wooden construction and a rectangular, narrow flat bottom, framed on both sides by tracks. They bore a similarity to the rhomboid shaped tanks being evolved on the Western Front, but these 'tanks' were ones that floated on water and not floundered in oceans of mud. These tracks were comprised of a series of narrow 'chains', with every other link having a 'gripping' hook welded on. There were drive sprockets at the front, and large idlers were installed at the boat's stern. The links then circulated with the aid of two more bottom wheels at the front per side, and two tender wheels at the back. The tracks were then laid on the 'bridge' but were raised by the open-air wheel pair at the rear which acted as manageable tension wheels. The rear tensioners and front sprockets acted like toothed pulleys. The aft ones, near the obstacle to be surmounted were coupled to the system. The hooked tracks (or chains) were designed to pull the vehicle over the obstruction and the result was officially known as "Tank Marino".

The armament comprised of two aircraft type light 450 mm torpedoes (the same as carried by the more conventional MAS), each held in a cradle on both sides of the hull.

The nature of the crafts foreseen role in the conflict demanded a high level of quietness, and a pair of 5 hp electric motors were installed for that purpose. The two motors were from Rognini and Balbo with one on each axle, supplying 10 hp in total. The craft made for a top speed of 4 knots with a radius of action of 30 nautical miles [1]. This limited range required the boats to be towed or carried near to the scene of the action. These craft were manned by a crew of only four and were all named after jumping insects, Grasshopper, Cricket, Locust etc...

The 1916 raid on the Fazana channel had already shown the need to use the force of weight to push down the metal obstructions at the mouth of the canal and let the MAS into the harbour. Now with the Grillo the Italians were confident they had the answer. As the Italians schemed and manufactured, the Austro-Hungarian fleet remained at anchor, feeling a confidence in the security Pola's defenses afforded to them.

The first attack by these strange tracked vessels was to be attempted on the 13th April 1918. Two of the boats, Cavalletta (Grasshopper) and Pulce (Flea) were towed into position outside of the harbour of Pola, but the electric motors proved to be too slow and the amount of time required by the craft had been misjudged. Neither vessel managed to reach the booms by daybreak, forcing their crews to abandon their mission.

One month later on the night of 13th May 1918 the Grillo's were once more released near the entrance to Pola and they stole quietly in on their electric motors towards the enemies ships, the raiders wreathed in a cloak of near silence.

Having reached the first the booms the 'secret weapon' was started and the quietness of the night was torn to shreds. The chain mechanism produced a horrendous clatter which immediately negated all the advantage the electric propulsion had afforded the Italians. The noise coming from out of the darkness focused the enemy's attention and all to quickly the raiders were spotted and engaged by shellfire. They had passed four booms, but the fifth was to mark their journeys conclusion. Faced with little chance of success or choice, the Cavalletta (Grasshopper) and Pulce (flea) were both scuttled.

The lone Locust now lay abandoned in her home port, the concept having a flaw that was insurmountable and she would eventually be scrapped in 1920. The curious Austro-Hungarians raised the sunken Italian craft and set about copying them. But by the wars end their version although near completion, never reached even the testing stage.

With the 'excitement' over, the fleet returned to its dull and monotonous port bound routine.

[1] Grillo specifications
Dimensions: Length 52 feet 5 29/32 inches (16mtrs), Beam 10 feet 2 1/16 inches (3.1mtrs), Draft 2 feet 9 3/16 inches (0.7mtrs).
Displacement: 7.87 tons (8 Tonnes)
Crew: 4
Propulsion: 2 screws, 2 electric engines, 20 hp combined Speed: 4 knots (7 km/h)
Range: 30 nmi at 4 kn.
Armament: 2 x 450 mm torpedoes
Armour: None.

CHAPTER 6: SZENT IŚTVAN

With the war dragging on into its third year, the Allied navies began creating the Oranto Barrage across the width of the southern end of the Adriatic, in order to prevent the German and Austro-Hungarian U-boats from attacking allied shipping in the Mediterranean. Rear-Admiral Horthy was also becoming concerned at the fragile state of moral amongst his fleets crews, after years of inactivity. He determined to make use of the fleet in an attack on the Otranto Barrage hoping to repeat the success of his raid on the blockade in May 1917. Horthy was to write after the war in his memoirs [1]

> "It was clear to me that the best way to restore discipline in the Navy, is to lead the ships into battle - a point of view that is completely shared — I knew it very firmly — by my colleagues in the German Navy. The sailors, who had not yet heard the angry peals of volleys, had to shake off their stupor. Therefore, I decided to withdraw the fleet to sea and again attempt to break

the blockade at Otranto. The whole fleet was supposed to take part in this operation, since it was completely clear that after May 15, 1917 (on this day, the Austrian light cruisers Sayda, Novara and Helgoland hit the patrol ships of the Otranto barrage) the enemy will throw his armoured cruisers into battle in order to at least intercept our forces on the retreat. I believed that our fleet would be able to surround and destroy them".

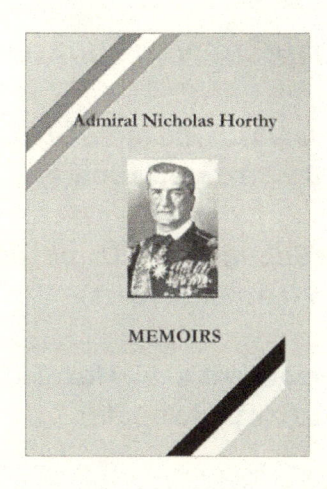

The Admiral planned an attack on the Allied forces on the Barrage making use of his four *Tegetthoff* class ships which would provide the largest component of his force. The three ships of the *Erzherzog Karl*-class Pre-Dreadnought, the three *Novara*-class cruisers, the cruiser *Admiral Spaun,* four *Tátra*-class destroyers and four torpedo boats, would accompany the Dreadnought on their first offensive sortie since Ancona in 1915. In addition, lighter forces comprised of submarines and aircraft would support his force by attacking any enemy ships found approaching the flanks of the fleet. Horthy's plan was to include the following offensive and support squadrons:

THE OFFENSIVE SQUADRONS*

Group 1: *Novara, Heligoland (light cruisers),Tatra, Csepel, Triglav II, Lika II* (destroyers). This group was to attack the Otranto Strait seagoing units.

Group,2: *Admiral Spaun, Saida* (light cruisers), T*B 84, TB 92, TB 99* (torpedo boats) & 8 planes. This group was to attack the Otranto Air Base and naval stations located there.

THE SUPPORT SQUADRONS*

Group 3: *Viribus Unitis, Balaton, Orjen* (destroyer), *TB 86, TB 90, TB 96, TB 97* (torpedo boats).

Group 4: *Prinz Eugen, Dukla, Uszok* (destroyer),*TB 82, TB 89, TB 91, TB 95* (torpedo boats).

Group 5: *Erzherzog Ferdinand Max, Tutul, TB 61, TB 66, TB 52, TB 56, TB 50* (torpedo boats).

Group 6: *Erzherzog Karl, Huszar, Pandur* (destroyers),T*B 75, TB 94, TB 57* (torpedo boats).

Group 7: *Erzherzog Friedrich* (Tugboat), *Csikos, Uskoke (destroyers),TB 53, TB 58* and one *Kaiman* (old torpedo boat).

Group 8: *Tegetthoff, Velebit* (destroyer),*TB 81* and three *Kaiman* (old torpedo boats).

Group 9: *Szent István ,TB 76, TB 77, TB 78, TB 79, TB 80* (torpedo boats).

Groups 8 and 9 would sail as one force.

THE TEGETTHOFF CLASS.

(*The group designations are the author's creation for clarity).

THE FLEET IN POLA, AWAITING THE ORDERED SAILING TIME.(IMAGE CREDIT ANDREW WILKIE WWW.VIRIBUSUNITIS.CA)

In addition, Austro-Hungarian and German submarines would be sent to Valona and Brindisi in order to be in place to ambush the British, French, Italian and U.S warships that responded to the Austro-Hungarian fleet, while the seaplanes from Cattaro would offer air support, as well as screening the ships' advance. The four *Tegathoff's* and the three *Erzherzog* Pre-Dreadnoughts, with their destroyers and torpedo boats were to be stationed in the southern portion of the Adriatic in order to provide cover for the retreat of the cruisers and destroyers, as well as to overcome any Allied Naval units that gave pursuit.

THE SZENT ISTVAN IN THE FEZANA STRAIT ON WHAT WAS MOST LIKELY A GUNNERY EXERCISE.

Horthy's biographer Horthy O. Rutter noted,

"Having received permission from Admiral Kale, [more correctly: Vice-Admiral Keil] *he began to make plans and dedicated only 12 of his closest officers to them. However, even in this case, the possibility of information leakage cannot be ruled out. The Austro-Hungarian fleet did not have a headquarters ship, as was the case with the German ally in Wilhelmshaven, on which all the secret operations of the fleet were developed. Horthy developed his plans within the walls of his own cabin at Viribus Unitis, where there was a single table of suitable sizes to lay out all operational cards on it. During the course of his working day, his constant participation was required in resolving many current issues, so the meetings usually took place at night, and even if no uninitiated could hear what was said there, it was still clear that something is up to. The final plan was a sudden attack on the strait by the forces of cruisers and destroyers, while the battleships providing them had*

to cover the subsequent withdrawal (of light forces) with active operations against any enemy ships that could get out of the way from Valona or Brindisi. All the ships involved in the operation were to take their starting positions for the attack at dawn on June 11."

Between the 4th and 6th June orders were dispatched summoning the ships of the fleet that were operating along the Dalmatian coast to return to port. A redeployment that must have been noted across the Adriatic in Italy? It was also noticeable that the fleet units began to take on combustible materials (or ammunition) and items the ships required, but it was plausible the Italians could see this as a 'ruse' by the Austrians to divert the enemy's attention from the preparations of their armies ground offensive. But despite all this the meeting of the diminutive Italian boats and the towering Austro-Hungarian capital ships was to be ruled by the gods of chance.

Despite the secrecy for the planned operation and the preparations for the fleet's departure, the population of Pola quickly realized that something was being planned. On the 3rd June, a 'leave ban' for staff and crews of the cruiser flotilla and the fleet came into force and all those already on leave were ordered, by telegraph, to return. Then on the 8th of June at 12:00, a full leave and mail ban for the fleet was put into effect.

On 8th June 1918 Horthy finalized his plans to take his flagship, *Viribus Unitis* and the *Prinz Eugen* south with the lead elements of his fleet. The *Szent István* and *Tegetthoff* were to follow along with their escort ships. The battleships and the *Tegetthoff's,* were to use the full power of their main calibre guns fire power to destroy the Barrage and to engage any Allied warships that they found. Horthy hoped that the assault would be critical in securing the decisive victory the fleet and Empire so desperately needed.

The ships crews were excited to finally be departing from the monotony and boredom of riding at the harbour's buoys, where their ships had laid anchored for too many months. They were no doubt uncertain at what lay ahead, and it must have played on their minds, but morale was bound to have improved now they were finally active? It was only once the long-awaited command for lighting all the boilers, did the ship take on a tangible sense of anticipation and the unease settled. On the *Szent Istvan*, all twelve boilers, were in their individual rooms in such a way that every pair stood with their backs to each other. The boiler rooms were the depth of three decks, with access from the armoured deck being through a bulkhead door and a descent of a series of "iron" ladders. The kingdom of the stokers and engine room crew was a self-contained world. The cavernous rooms were fed fresh air through grills by a series of fans and such was the noise that communication was only achievable by shouting.

On Sunday the 9th June at 14:00, Karl Mohl's (First Class Engineer (M.A.Schinenbetriebsleiter Klasse 1)), on the *Szent Istvan* received his orders and with the men under his command they manned their stations within the boiler and engine rooms. Before the ship could even raise its anchor there was hours of work ahead for his crew. With great care every piece of machinery was tested, water pumps, oil pumps, signal cables were checked and both spares and the necessary tools prepared. The ship's two powerful AEG-Curtis steam turbines were preheated slowly over a number of several hours in order to prevent any stress being applied to them and once they were ready, the ships propellers were tested for 20 minutes and all twelve boilers under full steam pressure were by now fully alight. Only then at 22:00 was the message *"Steam Clear"* reported to the Bridge and the Engine Room crew were con-

THE TEGETTHOFF CLASS.

fident that they and their charges were finally ready. Soon afterwards a signal horn for *"Anchor Stations"* was sounded throughout the ship and every crew member rushed to assume his allotted station. Mohl descended into the engine rooms to oversee the orders from the Chief Engineer. The ships Commander, Captain Heinrich Seitz, a well-liked and efficient officer, joined his staff on the bridge and when all was finally ready the anchor chain was looped out of the buoys ring with the command *"Go ahead"*.

THE FLEET DEPARTS POLA FOR ITS VOYAGE SOUTH. (IMAGE CREDIT ANDREW WILKIE WWW.VIRIBUSUNITIS.CA)

On the 8th June as planned, Horthy took both the *Viribus Unitis* and *Prinz Eugen*, with a small escorting flotilla out of port and the following evening (9th June) at 22:25 *Szent István* and *Tegetthoff* and their six-torpedo boat escort followed. On board the flagship was Commander Rear Admiral Horthy with the entire headquarters of the fleet. Several journalists were also invited to join the ship, their role to be providing detailed press coverage of Horthy's upcoming victory, as well as a film crew. The ships steamed southwards as if intending to conduct regular training firing on the Fácán Csatorna. The operation against the Otranto Barrier was set for the dawn of 11th June 1918 and the Austro-Hungarian ships that were moored in the Bocche di Cattaro had orders to depart their anchorages on the actual day of the attack. In turn the capital ships anchored in the fleets main port of Pola had to depart on the 10th and sail south in two groups during the moonless night. The battleship groups orders were that during the day they were to hide in one of the Dalmatian coasts many bays and inlets, in an effort to avoid being sighted by the Allied navies and losing the element of surprise.

THE SZENT ISTVAN LEADS HER GROUP OUT TO SEA. (IMAGE CREDIT ANDREW WILKIE WWW.VIRIBUSUNITIS.CA)

The *Tegetthoff's* group departure from port had been delayed by 45 minutes, as the instructions to open the entrances protective nets were late in being issued. But after the delay had been resolved, the ships finally cleared Pola and steamed

THE TEGETTHOFF CLASS.

out on route to Slano. The nine ships made their way south through the night's darkness, with only dimmed lights, having passed through the harbour nets and the minefields that were laid out in front of Pola. The *Tegetthoff* proudly led the Dreadnoughts and their escorts out on their first operational sortie in three years   But as the ships made their way southward, they were to be troubled by the poor quality of the boilers charcoal. The ships funnels omitted clouds of smoke and sparks and the ships stokers who were partly new to working on board such large vessels, found their inexperienced only served to exasperate the problems.

GROUPS 8 & 9 STEAMING SOUTH FOR THEIR FIRST NIGHTS STOP OVER.
(IMAGE CREDIT ANDREW WILKIE WWW.VIRIBUSUNITIS.CA)

By 22:40 the ships were steaming south at 7.5 knots, then at 16 knots, with orders to increase to 17.5 knots, to close the sea miles between the groups and to be in the required location by sunrise. On the port beam was the *T79*, *T84*, *T78* and on the starboard beam, *T77*, *T76*, and the *T81*. Ahead of the formation went the destroyer *Velebit*. The limited number of escorts available for the two Dreadnoughts caused the crews some concern, given how heavily the Adriatic was patrolled by enemy warships, especially by submarine and motor torpedo boats. A watch was set with "hundreds of eyes", many of them equipped with night-glasses, as they scanned the near and distant waters during the remaining hours of darkness. The *Tegetthoff* flotilla slowly accelerated its speed to the ordered 17.5 knots to reach the Bay of Tajer at dawn (today Tela & čiæa on Dugi Otok), where the ships would await the 10th June's sunset.

PREVIOUS PAGE.
THE MAS 96 -RESERVED TODAY AT THE GARDENS OF THE VITTORIALE
WHILE NOT THE ACTUAL CRAFT IN THE RAID, THE MAS 96 WAS OF THE SAME DESIGN AND TYPE.

Mohl regularly checked the boilers and turbines as the ship pounded its way south through the Adriatic waters. The steam pressure remained constant and initially everything worked well. At midnight, the watch was changed and soon after, (at 00:20) the starboard turbine started to develop problems and the speed was forced to be decreased to 12 knots. When last had the ships systems been worked so hard and for so long? Mohl immediately oversaw the problematic turbine and finally succeeded by both intensive application of lubricants, cooling and loosening the screws to keep the temperature of the bearings within an acceptable limits. As a bucket of lubricating oil was poured onto the hot bearings, the oil pressure was increased, and two thick hoses were used to direct powerful jets of water onto the 40 cm steel shaft. After half an hour the ship speed crawled back to 14 knots. But despite the engine room crews best efforts, the speed of the ship had to be restricted to 14 knots, as to increase beyond that speed merely increased her trail of smoke and spark omissions. The Chief Engineer and the Captain decided to repair the damaged main turbine during the day while the squadron lay at anchor in the Bay of Tajer and then as planned, to continue the next evening on to the Otranto Barrage.

THE MAS 96

At 03:15 on the 10th June the two Italian MAS boats [2] numbers *2* and *15* sighted the plume of smoke and sparks from the

Austrian ships that had worried some of the Dreadnought's officers. The Italians were returning from an uneventful patrol off the Dalmatian coast where they had been measuring the depth of the sea near Premuda and looking for mines, (to enable the operations of their own submarines). The two MAS's were commanded by Capitano di corvetta Luigi Rizzo, the man who had sunk the Austria-Hungarian coastal defence ship *Wien* in Trieste only six months before. The individual boats were commanded by Capo Timoniere Armando Gori *(MAS 2)* and Guardiamarina di complemento Giuseppe Aonzo *(MAS 15)*. They stole slowly towards the source of the smoke, aware that it could only be enemy forces and taking care not to raise a bow wave which could give them away.

AN ITALIAN 'MAS'
(PHOTO CREDIT ANDREW WILKIE COLLECTION www.VIRIBUSUNITIS.CA)

Rizzo decided to draw as close as possible before his two boats launched their respective attacks. He led his boats between the two destroyers that were screening the ships to starboard of the first dreadnought ship. Then to avoid the destroyer to

THE TEGETTHOFF CLASS.

their left, the Italians increased their speed from 9 knots to 12 knots. They managed to slip past the Austrian escorts, passing the two destroyers by 100 meters without being sighted. The two small craft having managed to steal past the escort screen, then parted to widen their potential impact. *MAS 21* launched her torpedoes at the *Tegetthoff,* but one disastrously failed to leave its tube and the other failed to strike home. The MAS 15 in turn fired her two torpedoes from 300 meters at 03:25, towards the *Szent István*. The two torpedoes, both running at the pre-set depth of 1.5 meters (4.92 ft), were sighted by the *Szent's* lookouts from 100 to 200 meters (109-218 yds) off, but their oncoming speed made avoiding them impossible. The ship was struck by the two underwater missiles on the starboard side sending two vast columns of blackish water into the dark morning air. The destroyer *TB76*, to the Italian's left sighted the torpedoes trail and turned towards them, being 100 to 150 meters (109-164 yds) behind the by now retreating Italian boats. The destroyer opened a well-directed fire from a single gun, with the shells striking near the boats. In an effort not to offer a better target, the Italian guns remained silent. But as the destroyer was following directly in the Italian wake a submarine bomb was dropped into her path, but it failed to explode. A second charge followed but this time it erupted before the bow of the Austrian destroyer. The pursuer turned a sharp 90 ° away, as the Italians turned to port and the destroyer was rapidly lost from sight.

PREVIOUS PAGE. THE MAS 96

As the two Italian boats had stolen in to release their torpedoes, a tired and sweat drenched Mohl, with a 12- hour shift of heavy duty behind him wanted nothing more than a change of clothes and the chance to sleep a little. He finally collapsed fully dressed onto his bunk, where tired as he was, sleep was to evade him. His cabin was too hot, and he was unable to switch his mind off.

THE TEGETTHOFF CLASS.

THE MOMENT OF IMPACT BETWEEN THE ITALIAN TORPEDO AND THE AUSTRIO-HUNGARIAN HULL

(IMAGE CREDIT ANDREW WILKIE www.ViribusUnitis.ca)

The two torpedoes struck home on the ships armour belt, when the *Szent István* was 9 nautical miles off Gruizától. The first one struck to the front of the rear boiler room, near the transverse bulkhead that separated the two boiler rooms, damaging it badly. The second was to strike 62 feet (19 mtrs) behind it, hitting the front of the engine "chassis".

As Mohl lay on his bunk trying to sleep, the two explosions rocked the ship and threw him about his bunk. He could hear the joints of the hulls structure tremble and commented later how he had noticed an almost immediate list to starboard. Mohl scrambled from his bunk and rushed to his alarm station in the boiler rooms, sliding and falling down the ladders in his haste. He first went to the aft boiler room and as he opened the thick bulkhead door, hot steam and deafening noises assailed his senses. He found the crew there paralysed with horror. With a growing sense of anger at the damage inflicted to his ship, he screamed orders over the noise at the Petty Officers, who over the years had been tried and tested by the lower ranks, many of whom were reservists. Slowly the crew's senses returned, and the ship's stokers hurried back to their posts, a mixture of fear and discipline gripping them. In the background the phone was ringing uninterrupted and alarms began to add to the cacophony. Mohl and the other officers began to issue a stream of orders and messages were rushed between the control and engine room stations. Although only a few minutes had passed since the explosion, the ship already had a 10-degree list and the Adriatic's water was lapping over the starboard floorboards. Mohl reported the situation to the Engine Room command and Pump Centre and as counter flooding of the magazines and port tanks was ordered by the captain. All the ships pumps were diverted to the boiler room, to try and keep the invading waters at bay. Mohl noted that by this stage the water had already begun to enter from the forward boiler room. The *Tegetthoff's* captain, on news of the sighting of the torpedoes wake assumed them to be of a submarine origin. He urgently ordered his command to steer to port, dropping her out of the formation and zig zagging to throw off any further attacks. He also ordered an increase to her maximum speed. As the huge Dreadnought manoeuvred away, her guns repeatedly fired on suspected submarine periscopes and it would not be until 04:45 that she would return to the aid of her stricken stepsister.

As her sister ship avoided and engaged phantom submarines, the *Szent István's* crew struggled, due to the growing list, to shut those bulkhead doors that von Tirpitz had so advised against. The doors were troublesome and the crew that could have been of service elsewhere in the engine room were kept distracted at a critical time. But the heavy doors were closed

THE TEGETTHOFF CLASS.

finally before the flood waters reached the lower lip of the doorways. Soon afterwards, the water was reported as entering the 'V' and 'IX' compartments, in the boiler rooms and on the engine rooms right gangway. But once more the folly of ignoring the Germanic advice during the design stage, was highlighted as the bulkheads were now leaking water through numerous seams, wires and pipes that pierced the bulkheads. The crew tried desperately with hammocks and other such items to slow or stop the flooding through the bulkhead's gaps.

Szent István's captain ordered that two blue lights be hoisted aloft to signal that his ship was both listing and moving at a much-reduced speed. The searchlight crew tried to signal the zig zagging Tegetthoff but were not to have any success.

SLOWLY TAKING ON WATER, BUT WITH HER TURRETS SWUNG OUT AND HER CREW GATHERING ON THE HIGHER SIDE OF THE DECKS IN A FUTILE EFFORTS TO COUNTER THE GROWING LIST.

immediately after the two explosions, orders had come down from the bridge for the shutting down of the equipment that used the boiler's steam, for the pumps. The captain also ordered the port compartments and the magazine flooded, reducing the list to 7 degrees, with the forward six boilers still being able to keep the pumps working. The ship was able, after a while, to achieve 4.5 knots and a course was made for the shore nearby at Brgulje. It looked at this stage as if the ship might yet be beached and saved.

Below decks, the water continued in its unrelenting invasion of the ship's spaces, something that the ship's 4.5 knots speed aggravated. But before the safety of the shore could be reached, the ship's turbines were ordered stopped to allow for an attempt to lower a collision mat over the ship's wound. But the mats steel hawsers became ensnared on the bilge keel and despite the efforts it failed to take hold. It was only to be learnt years later that the hole they were trying to plug was far larger than the 4 meter (13 feet) square mat, at 5 by 6.7 meters (16 x 22 feet) and the damage area of the hull was around 70 square meters (229 sq. ft) feet).

PREVIOUS PAGE. WITH HER TURRETS SWUNG OUT THE CREW ARE ORDERED TO THE HIGHER SIDE OF THE DECK IN A DESPERATE ATTEMPT TO COUNTER THE GROWING LIST.[3]

Below decks, Mohl noticed that the flooding seemed to have slowed and the list slightly lessened. The captain had ordered the 12-inch turrets swung out to counter the slant, the ready ammunition moved, and the port cells flooded. The crew had to manually rotate the turrets as the ship's ever decreasing source of steam was needed for the struggling pumps. Those that were already on deck were ordered to gathered to one side in a desperate move to counter the growing list. The gun's ready ammunition was moved first to the same side before, it was consigned overboard into the Adriatic's depths.

These desperate efforts succeeded, briefly, to reduce the list by 3 degrees. Down in the boiler rooms Mohl's men struggled, but somehow kept the forward six boilers alight, as the steam was needed for the pumps and the light's dynamos. The order *"Keep boiler operation under all circumstances."* was made a priority, an hour after the torpedoes had struck. At this stage, the eighth boiler room started to take in water and the water pressure on the bulkhead was now so great, the rivets started to fail, popping from their holes, like bullets fired from a gun. The water quickly found the newly vacated rivet holes and poured through them, as the crew attempted to brace the wall with beams. The desperate men tried to slow the leaks with makeshift material *("tarred brans, puke and scraps")*. But slowed as it was, the growing list of the ship reduced the boiler feed, leaving the pumps struggling and to the background of all the frantic activity was the constant ringing of the signal apparatuses from the command bridge.

THE SZENT ISTVAN SLOWLY LISTS AS THE TEGETHOFF FINALLY RETURNS AND LAUNCHES HER SHIPS BOATS. BOTH HER CRANES ARE SWUNG OUT AS HER BOATS ARE HOISTED INTO THE WATER.

Having finally arrived back on the scene, the *Tegetthoff*, (two hours after the attack), tried to take her stricken stepsister in tow. The destroyer escorts only added to the mornings chaos by firing at phantom periscopes. The alarm rang out on *Tegetthoff*, *"Torpedo line from left to right"* and every eye turned in that direction, with the officers and crew taking up the cry from all sides. The order *"Full Force Back"* was given but the ship refused to respond quick enough to the order. Every eye watched the phantom torpedo track, which at about 492 feet (150 mtrs) off, vanished. The *Tegetthoff* returned three minutes later to the stricken *Szent István,* where she saw and felt the 'submarine bombs' the escorts were using to scare off any Allied submarines. Another submarine alert and phantom periscope brought the escorts wrath down on the supposed object, 3,280 feet (1,000 mtrs) off. One source claims that even the *Szent István* herself opened fire with her 7-inch guns.

At around 05:45, Mohl received a message from the Engineering Officer, in whose hands the entire control of the Pump Centre lay. The flood waters were increasing more and more rapidly, and the pumps could no longer handle the sheer volume of water. Despite the deteriorating situation the Engineering Crew remained at their posts and worked harder, as the water continued to penetrate ever deeper into the ship. Mohl's earlier confidence that the ship could be saved was fading, but he and his men worked on, dripping with sweat and fearful of the dangers around them, but with superhuman effort.

Then as if to make their jobs harder, the world around them was plunged into darkness, as the electric lighting failed with the dynamo room finally flooded through the leaky bulkheads. The crew were plunged into a noise filled darkness and their nerves were near to breaking. The men started to scream and curse as panic finally took a hold on them. In their fear and desire to survive they pushed past Mohl, all thought of his rank and any respect due, gone. They made for the ladders and no longer thought of saving the ship or duty, they just wanted to go up to the deck, away from the dark noise and water filling tomb they now inhabited.

Torches and emergency lights were quickly issued but this barely broke through the tomb like darkness. Facing almost certain death, the men were wading up to their knees in cold water, but it flooded in remorselessly and quickly reached up to their hips. The engineering crew struggled and slipped on the sloping iron floor plates, sinking into cold, dirty, black oil contaminated sea water. Mohl yelled orders and screamed till his voice was hoarse, trying to encourage both himself and others. The Petty Officers stood guard at the ladders that led up to the world of light, to rescue and safety. They too shouted as the crewmen scream, pushed, and shoved in their fear and terror.

At 05:30, over two hours since the detonations, only the boilers high on the port side, still stood proud of the water with the growing list and those alone remained operational. But finally, the crew had to blow off the steam from those remaining boilers through the safety valves or risk an explosion. The sound of steam was mixed with the eruption of failing rivets from the bulkheads and as each new rivet popped, the water found fresh access to the compartments that lay beyond. As the boilers were let out, sending the roar of venting steam into the cold night air, the ships fate was finally beyond saving. By this stage of the disaster the ship had developed a 30-degree list and the starboard side was now deep under water, allowing the sea new ways to flood ever further into the hull's interior.

The ships dark engine-rooms that had so recently been filled with the noise of the struggling pumps, the fans and the hiss of escaping steam, now gave way to the sounds of swirling waters and the crewmen's terror. As the surviving senior rank, Mohl tried vainly to communicate with the control centre for further orders, aware of how limited time had become.

But no longer able to reach the Chief Engineer, Mohl finally turned his attention to that of both his men and his own survival. He loosened his shoelaces and prepared his life jacket, as those around him followed his example. Discipline still held at this stage for Mohl as he fought to survive his own growing panic. Loud noises from above could be heard as the men fought to survive in the *"hell"* they now inhabited. Mohl felt the ships bulk shake and he knew that it would only be insanity to remain where they were. But he still could not reach anyone to get orders to leave their posts. As the situation steadily deteriorated, he alone had to finally give the order to abandon the engine rooms. It started a terrible fight for the two narrow ladders, the weaker were ruthlessly pushed back by the stronger, it became about their naked survival, rank and difference forgotten.

He immersed himself into the crowd of 40 men who were around him and reached a small platform where they were struggling to open the bulkhead door. After an effort, the heavy door finally swung open, the tilt of the ship helping it to fully open. The panic-struck crewmen could now race to scramble up the ladders, each giving thanks to his God as they climbed upward. Things were desperate as men struggled to pass each other on the narrow ladders, but after four or five minutes the first crewman stumbled out onto the main deck, which was already under water. The list slowly increased as the decks starboard rail gradually became deeper in its immersion.

A COMPUTER RENDERING OF THE SZENT ISTVAN's FINAL MOMENTS BEFORE SHE ROLLED OVER AND SANK. (IMAGE CREDIT ANDREW WILKIE www.ViribusUnitis.ca)

At this stage in the morning's disaster, Lieutenant Commander Reich was sent by the Captain down to the main deck to line up the crew and prepare the ship's boats to take them off. On the bridge, remaining at their posts was the Ships' Captain, Frigate Lieutenant Niemann and some of the Bridge Crew. The order to gather on deck was not to reach every part of the stricken ship, but *Szent István's* chaplain performed one final blessing for the crew that had made it. The Captain appeared on the quarterdeck, where he stood while the blessing of the crew and his doomed ship occurred. By 05:38 the water had reached the upper deck and the order *"Schiff verlassen! Los vom Schiff! ("Leave the Ship"!)"* was given.

The order to abandon the doomed ship had been issued while Mohl had fought to escape the darkened *"hell"* from below. As he had emerged out onto the sloping deck, most of the crew already there had jumped into the cold waters around the ships capsizing hull. Following his instincts Mohl climbed further up the ships side in his bare feet, as the ship started to roll over. As the speed of the hull's roll increased Mohl ran and slid, cutting himself on the hull's sharp marine growth, as he finally fell into the sea. Within the sinking ships structure half of his men had either lost their way in the ships dark interior, or just could not escape before the ship started to roll over. As Mohl swam he could see the ships Commander, (Heinrich Seitz von Treffen), Lieutenant Rope Maxon and the ships Staff Officers as they were thrown from the "upper levels" into the sea. What had been recently a calm water, was now stormy and violent as the ship finally capsized. [4]

Escaping water from the hulls bottom vents made it difficult for Mohl to swim away and along with other survivors he was thrown about in the stormy waters. But as the ship settled into her new capsized position, the sea briefly calmed and Mohl found he was just ten yards away from a ships boat. Fortunately, the up turned Dreadnought was laying calmly before her plunge into the depths. As she wallowed for five minutes, Mohl made his escape, knowing that when the ship finally sank, she would try to suck the men in the water down with her.

La Marina Italiana nella guerra mondiale 1915-1918

All'alba del 10 giugno 1918 il Comandante Rizzo attaccò con due MAS una forte squadra nemica. La corazzata austriaca "Santo Stefano", colpita da siluro, affondò rovesciandosi sul fianco destro.

TRANSLATION: "THE ITALIAN NAVY IN THE WORLD WAR 1915-1918. AT DAWN ON 10 JUNE 1918, THE COMMANDER RIZZO ATTACKED TWO MAS WITH A STRONG ENEMY TEAM. THE AUSTRIAN BATTLESHIP "SANTO STEFANO", HIT BY TORPEDO. LUNGE SPILLING ON THE RIGHT SIDE."

At this stage in the morning's disaster, Lieutenant Commander Reich was sent by the Captain down to the main deck to line up the crew and prepare the ship's boats to take them off. On the bridge, remaining at their posts was the Ships' Captain, Frigate Lieutenant Niemann and some of the Bridge Crew. The order to gather on deck was not to reach every part of the stricken ship, but Szent István's chaplain performed one final blessing for the crew that had made it. The Captain appeared on the quarterdeck, where he stood while the blessing of the crew and his doomed ship occurred. By 05:38 the water had reached the upper deck and the order *"Schiff verlassen! Los vom Schiff! ("Leave the Ship"!)"* was given. The order to abandon the doomed ship had been issued while Mohl had fought to escape the darkened "hell" from below. As he'd emerged out onto the sloping deck, most of the crew already there had jumped into the cold waters around the ships capsizing hull. Following his instincts Mohl climbed further up the ships side in his bare feet, as the ship started to roll over. As the speed of the hull's roll increased Mohl ran and slid, cutting himself on the hull's sharp marine growth, as he finally fell into the sea. Within the sinking ships structure half of his men had either lost their way in the ships dark interior, or just could not escape before the ship started to roll over. As Mohl swam he could see the ships Commander, (Heinrich Seitz von Treffen), Lieutenant Rope Maxon and the ships Staff Officers as they were thrown from the "upper levels" into the sea. What had been recently a calm water, was now stormy and violent as the ship finally capsized. Escaping water from the hulls bottom vents made it difficult for Mohl to swim away and along with other survivors he was thrown about in the stormy waters. But as the ship settled into her new capsized position, the sea briefly calmed and Mohl found he was just ten yards away from a ships boat. Fortunately, the up turned Dreadnought was laying calmly before her plunge into the depths. As she wallowed for five minutes, Mohl made his escape, knowing that when the ship finally sank, she would try to suck the men in the water down with her.

THE LAST MOMENTS OF THE SZENT ISTVAN. SOURCE: NAVAL HISTORY & HERITAGE COMMAND.

The last half hour of the Dreadnought fate was captured on film footage which survives today on numerous websites, (SEE APPENDIX E). The film was later presented in the United States during the Great Depression but was labelled incorrectly as the *Blücher* sinking. The film remains only one of two, the other being the loss of the British battleship *Barham* in WW2, of a battleship being lost.

Before moving on, it should not be forgotten that Karl Mohl's lecture tour to describe his experiences on the Szent István was 18 years after the event, on 27th November 1936 at the Hotel Brussatti in Baden Vienna as part of a lecture of the "Patriotic Front". Human nature would dictate that he shines both himself and his bravery in a 'heroic' light. So, whilst the core of his recollections should be reasonably solid, he may have 'coloured' his own bravery and duty for the audience before him.

THE SURVIVORS FROM THE SZENT ISTVAN ARE RESCUED BY TEGETTGHOFFS CREW.

The wreck of the *Szent Istvan* was discovered in the mid-1970s off the island of Premuda and today she is now a protected wreck. Only authorised dives on her are permitted. The dreadnought lays in her Adriatic tomb in a depth of 66 meters, with a visibility of around 60 meters. Her bow broke off on her impact on that day in 1918 with the seabed and now it lays immediately alongside the heavily encrusted hull. There are two holes from torpedo strikes, with possibly a third hole emanating from *MAS 21*? Within the debris field lays items scattered from the ship as she fell to the seabed. Amongst this scattering are lone leather shoes which sadly are all that remains of crew members who died with their ship. The human skeleton can in some situations dissolve rapidly through the years and as with the *Titanic,* only the victim's shoes remain today to mark the place of their individual graves. {5}

Divers have gained access to the Admiral's cabin and recovered several bronze lights with intact cut glass infill's, as well as his telephone linking him to the bridge. Close to the cabin was his bathroom, with a bathtub that is still clearly recognizable. The team also were successful in the recovery of some silver cutlery and porcelain from the adjoining cabin.

THE SZENT ISTVAN's ROUTE TO HER FINAL RESTING PLACE.

THE TEGETTHOFF CLASS.

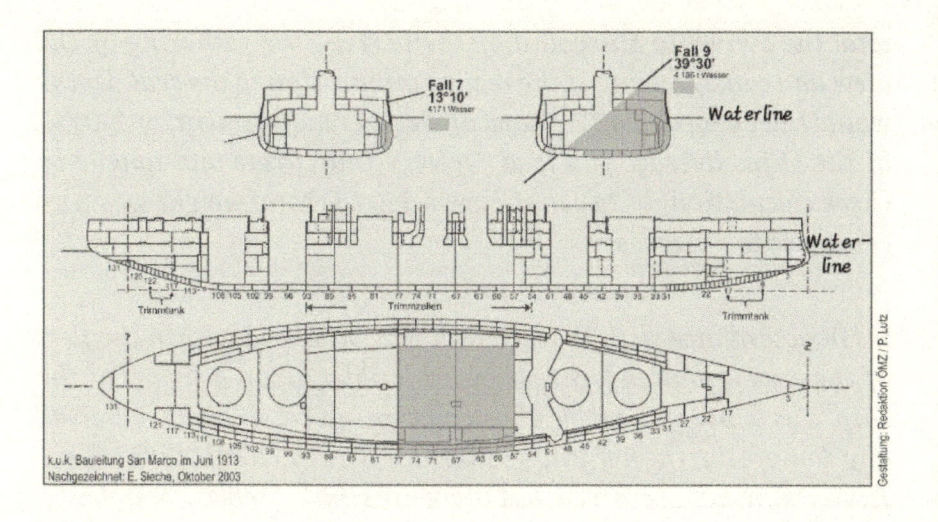

CALCULATION OF WATER LEVEL FRACTURES ON S.M.S. SHIPS TYPE TEGETTHOFF

"AT A HEEL OF 36 DEGREES THE SHIP BEGINS TO ROLL OVER AND AT 53.5 FULL TURN IT CAPSIZES COMPLETELY. THE ILLUSTRATION [ABOVE] SHOWS THAT WHEN THE DOUBLE BIDET AND THE WALKWAY ARE FULL, THE WATER ALREADY PENETRATES AT THE STUCCO DOORS OF THE 15 CM CASEMENTS. IF BOTH BOILERS ARE UNDER WATER THE SHIP CAN NO LONGER BE SAVED"

[1]   https://www.abebooks.co.uk/9780966573435/Admiral-Nicholas-Horthy-Memoirs-Simon-0966573439/plp

[2] *There are a number of definitions of what MAS stood for:*

Motoscafo armato silurante or "torpedo armed motorboat"

Mezzi d'Assalto or assault craft

Motobarca armata SVAN or armed motorboat SVAN.

Motoscafo Anti Sommergibile or Anti Submarine Motorboat.

[3] *As a rough calculation the eight 30.5 cm gun barrels weighed 413 tons. If half her crew gathered on the higher side of the deck their average weigh on mass would have been circa 3.5 tons. The turrets held just over 21 tons of shells as ready ammunition. In*

total the swivel to starboard of the barrels, the gathering of the crew and consignment of the ready ammunition to the seas depths would have e totaled 437.5 tons of weight readjustment, or 2.07% of the ships average full load. A very inaccurate and tongue in cheek calculation, but even if it was 3% the total weight was tiny compared to the mass.

[4] In accordance with the rule that was practised within the fleet of the dual monarchy, the shipyard-builder, upon delivery of the ship, was to present a table of calculations in case the ship received any damage during her years in service. The calculations for Szent István were not preserved, but there are similar tables compiled in June 1913 by the observer for the construction of the remaining three dreadnought. These files illustrate what was planner to happen with 18 different combinations of flooding of one or another compartment of the dreadnoughts. Of particular interest are the three options VII, IX and X. These scenarios suggest the same case that actually happened when the Rizzo torpedoes hit the target:

> **Option VII:** flooding of the compartments between the 77th and 54th frames of 417 tons of water causes a roll of 13 ° 10 '. Alignment by flooding of the compartments of the opposite side leads to its reduction to 0 ° 17 '.
>
> **Option IX:** flooding both boiler rooms and the side corridor, coal pits and side ammunition cellars with 4186 tons of water will create a roll of 39 ° 30 '. By counter-flooding, it decreases to 3 ° 52 '.
>
> **Option X:** flooding the aft boiler room, port turbine compartment, ammunition cellars, side corridors and coal pits 2998 tons of water will lead to a roll of 36 ° 50 '. Counter-flooding reduces it to 6 ° 50 '.

It should be note at this point that the theoretical modelling of such situations does not allow for such factor as the total loss of power by the ship due to the failure of the boilers in the flooded boilers.

It should be added that at a roll of 19 ° the water would reach the lower edges of the ports of the 15 cm guns, and at 30 ° it is narrower than the upper deck. It was at this degree of list that the main deck begins to submerge and that the peak of the dreadnought stability curve was (30.5 °). The repairing moment vanishes at a roll of 58.5 °, after which the ship capsizes.

{4} The latest research raises the possibility that the Szent István was struck by three torpedoes that day. It suggests that she was the victim of two torpedoes from the MAS 15 and one by MAS 21. Due to the visibility at that time of day, (twilight) MAS 21 probably attacked her and not Tegetthoff as tradition reports. The information has not be officially confirmed.

CHAPTER 7: THE ENQUIRY, BLAME & THE WRECK.

Szent István's captain was to write of his crew:

"The Tegetthoff and the torpedo boats took part in the rescue of the crew by dropping their boats. The officer's behaviour deserves all the praise. Only a small fraction of the crew had to be alerted by the officers to their duties. The majority of the crew was very well behaved and in many cases brave and self-sacrificing acts had taken place. Finally, I must add that some construction of the ship proved to be inadequate and in our case, the ever-oppressive disaster was particularly prevalent".

The Austro-Hungarian 'expert' opinion on the loss of the ship was completed on the 1st August 1918, but it failed to establish any personal responsibility for the loss of one quarter of the Empire's Dreadnought fleet. The Captain, Heinrich Seitz was given a written warning that the use of the emergency signalling, (by horn) had not proven effective enough. His Master Chief, Charles Masjon, was held to be responsible for the ships delay in departing Pola, as he had not checked the necessary orders for opening the security nets had been issued. The *Tegetthoff's* Commander von Perglas was not reprimanded for his ship being absent for two hours, following the explosion. It was held that with his ship under attack and the fear that the navy did not want to see two of its Dreadnoughts lost he was correct with his sequence of orders. But it was pointed out, that if he had taken his stricken sister ship in tow soon after the attack she may well have been saved. At the time of her loss, the *Szent István* was 10 kilometres (6.21 miles) off the island of Premuda. If the *Tegetthoff* had started towing her at 04.40, making use of a slow speed and at 6 knots she might have made shallow waters. But it is likely, in fact its more than probable, that the bulkheads under the immerse water pressure from a forward progress would have given way at just 4 knots.

Perglas was to retire after the attack having been promoted to Rear-Admiral. The main cause of the loss was summarized in the following sentence:

> *"The inadequate distance between the longitudinal torpedo armour blocked bulkhead and the wall of the 15-inch fire chamber is a serious mistake, which is likely to have contributed to the enlargement of the torpedo. It is recommended that this be communicated to the ship's designer, Admiral Siegfried Popper, shipbuilding engineer."*

According to the building regulations, the armour belt had to be assembled in a cold state, but the civil engineers noted that in the *Szent István's* case (and in order to save time), it was undertaken while still warm. As the belt cooled it would have contracted, there by coming under tension. In the event of a detonation, the shrunken metal would lack any flexibility to absorb the force and therefore be very susceptible to damage by an explosion. Because of this, the Austrian Government blamed the loss of the ship as one of the consequences of the joint Austria-Hungarian relationship. According to Karl von Puchner, the sister ships seals were subjected to strong pressure after the loss. Unsurprisingly none of them could withstand the pressure of water.

If we look at the loss from purely a design side, it is the designer Siegfrid Popper who should be held responsible for the sinking of the ship. When he was planning the torpedo bulkheads, he simply ignored the German data and advice provided to him by Koudelka. If enough distance had been left between the inner wall and the torpedo partition, the two explosive forces would most likely have failed to penetrate all the way through the defences. But for Poppers arrogance and insistence that he knew better, men would have not died.

In turn, the Danubius shipyard is also partly responsible for the poor performance of the ship's watertight bulkheads. After the sinking, several of the yards staff recounted how they had warned of a series of construction errors, but their observations were simply ignored. It must however be borne in mind that the shipyard only had practical experience at building far smaller and less complex vessels. In addition to the above, it should also be remembered that when designing the ship, Montecuccoli had insisted that the Dreadnought must be armed with a 30.5 cm main calibre, 280 mm of armour and with 25,000 hp engines but that it should not exceed 21,000 tonnes. Since the above could not be challenged, only with the structural elements of the vessels could weight be saved. As a result, both the hull and the watertight bulkheads only met with the minimum.

Erwin F. Sieche has provided us with a glimpse of the wreck, following his dive to the site:

> *"The seabed is about in 65 m, consists of sand and is slightly sloped in direction of Premuda island. The wreck lies in direction 50° pointing to the island. It is capsized, bottom up and presents itself to the visitor as a huge metal dome, all superstructure being smashed under the hull. The very great surprise is that all three triple turrets are still in place, trained to port as we know it from the well-known sinking film. Mr. Prasky pointed out that the turrets could be locked by clamps onto the roller path to fix them against unwanted revolving. This might be one of the reasons why they are still in place. The other reason might be that there has not been enough time for them to fall out due to the narrow distance the sinking dreadnought had to go down before he impacted on the seabed. The wreck lies on the roofs of the two superimposed turrets and has a 12° list to port. This angle results from my own drawing as a hypothesis, the actual situation might differ. The superimposed turrets are buried in the sand as 20.000 tons of steel are lying on them. This means that the whole line of the - former - port deck edge is free while the - former - starboard deck line is partially buried and partially free. Both triple turrets are free, the 12" barrels point out in the water. The forward and aft triple turrets are buried deep in the sand, only the tips of the 12" barrels peer out from the seabed at their slight 12° angle. As said before, all superstructure and the funnels were knocked flat and form a deadly labyrinth of*

smashed steel girders and plates. On tapes showing this area nothing is recognizable even to the trained eye with the exception of a boat crane with the searchlight sponson and some 7 cm QF guns now hanging from the ceiling. The second very big surprise is that the whole forecastle has broken off during the impact on the seabed. At the moment there is no exact determination of the exact position of this break, but we can guess that this happened exactly in front of the forward bulkhead of the most forward triple tower. This might be a logical point for structural weakness. Also, it is not clear if the bow has completely broken off if it is still connected to the hull in some way or if it has turned away. One oral report states that the parts are some 8 meters away from each other. The ammo chambers are at the bottom of the ship, which is now on top, we should find 12" shells there. A photograph gives the proof. Both masts are broken off and lie on the seabed nearby, the distinctive spotting tops clearly visible. Surprisingly, they are 'befreed' of the mast and might be an easy object to be recovered by lifting bags. On one video tape of a scooter equipped diver we find a distinctive hole in the ship's starboard side wall, the undamaged, meaning unerupted, longitudinal torpedo bulkhead just behind is fully intact. During the last seven decades the hull has been covered by some 30 cm of marine growth. The Teakwood deck is still intact. The Czakó expedition of September 1995 managed to clean the stern letters and unscrew the letters Z and E and recover them. Unfortunately for the Hungarians this valuable relic will go to the Rijeka Naval Museum (together with the two plates mentioned earlier). Regarding the few time to be spent on the ground there has been no wider search for other debris lying around the wreck. 89 men have drowned with the *dreadnought, most of them inside, locked in the machinery space, so there has been not proof of human bones. Both screws and the rudders are entangled with broken fisher nets indicating that cursing local fishermen knew very well that this was a dangerous spot for fishing".*

CHAPTER 8: THE LAST YEAR OF WAR

Through the long course of the war, Pola was to be subjected to numerous air raids by the Italian air force. On the 17th July 1918, Pola was struck by the largest air raid to date. Sixty-six Allied planes dropped over 200 bombs, but none of the three remaining *Tegetthoff's* were hit or damaged in the attack.   The surviving logbooks of the fleet's 1st Division give us a glimpse into the intensity of the Italian air raids on Pola. As the Italians passed over the port, the ships anti-aircraft artillery would join the land batteries in the defence of the anchorage. During 1916, the fleet and coastal defences were to be assailed from the air 35 times and in 1917 that number increased to 42. The attacking forces would at times include up to a dozen airships and 150 aircraft, but the damage caused by them was in relation, small. The slow and fragile and aircraft were forced to stay at high altitudes, but even in these conditions, the Austrian anti-aircraft gunners were often successful. From 1917, while engaging the overhead Italians, in addition to their standard steel helmet, the

THE TEGETTHOFF CLASS.

gun crews were ordered to wear gas masks as there was a growing fear of gas bombs being dropped by the enemy aircraft.

THE VIRIBUS UNITIS TAKEN BY AN AIRCRAFT, (ITALIAN?)

The Austrian historian E. Zihe has compared, (using the logbooks of the *Szent István*), the total time spent by the four Dreadnoughts at sea, as against the time at their anchors in Pola. The logbooks revealed that during the ship's entire period in commission, (17th November 1915 to 10th June 1918, a total of only 937 days), she was only absent from her anchorage for 54 days. That equates to only 5.6% of her life at sea, while the remaining 94.4% remained riding at her anchorage. Of these 54 days, the dreadnought only once made one two-day sea voyage to the island of Pago. The rest of her time away from Pola was to conduct firing exercises at the Fácán Csatorna (Pheasant Canal) and back, a 'voyage' of three quarters of an hour.

By the autumn of 1918, the war was all but lost and the

disintegration of the Austro-Hungarian Empire was becoming evident to those in 'power'. On 6th October, the National Council of Slovenes, Croats, and Serbs (SCS) was founded in the city of Zagreb. The Serbs who were in the council represented their countrymen resident in Croatia, but not Serbia. On 29th October, the Council ordered all political and diplomatic ties severed between Croatia and Austria and Hungary, and established the State of Slovenes, Croats, and Serbs, comprising Croatia, Slovenia, and Bosnia (Drzava SHS, in Croatian). Emperor Charles I in order to avoid having to surrender his fleet to the Entente Powers, ordered its transfer wholesale, with the Empires merchant fleet, all its harbours, arsenals and shore fortifications to the newly formed State of Slovenes, Croats and Serbs.

On the 26th October Austria-Hungary had informed Germany that their alliance was over, while in Pola the navy was in the process of tearing itself apart along ethnic and nationalist lines. The C-in-C, Admiral Horthy was informed on the morning of 28th October that an armistice was imminent and to maintain discipline or control he published the news to try and retain some semblance of order. Whilst the crews were not too mutiny at the news, tensions remained high and morale was low. The situation had deteriorated so badly and had become so stressful for the officers that the captain of the *Prinz Eugen,* (Alexander Milosevic), committed suicide in his quarters aboard the Dreadnought. On the morning of the 31st October the transfer of the navy to the newly formed State of Slovenes, Croats and Serbs was begun. Horthy met with the representatives from the South Slav nationalities aboard his flagship, *Viribus Unitis.* After a not unsurprisingly *"short and cool"* series of negotiations, the arrangements were settled, and the handover was scheduled to be completed that afternoon.

At the agreed time, the transfer was commenced and as the red and white Austro-Hungarian flag was being lowered on the masts of the ships in port, the Emperor's hymn 'Gott erhalte unseen Kaiser' was sung for the last time. With the fleets transfer completed the thousands of Croatians in harbour began to sing the Croatian hymn 'Lijepa nasa'. As the hymn was played, the Croatian flag was raised on the masts of the ships. Whilst the Croatians were busy singing, the Hungarians, Slovenians, Austrians, and many others were heading for home, as they felt the war was already over. With the transfer completed and the new flag aloft Horthy no longer had a fleet to command. Gathering the portrait of Emperor Franz Joseph which the late-Emperor had presented to the ship, plus the ceremonial silk ensign of *Viribus Unitis* and Horthy's own personal Admiral's flag, he departed his former flagship.

JANKO VUKOVIĆ DE PODKAPELSKI

That evening the Viribus Unitis was renamed *Yugoslavia*. The remaining two Dreadnoughts however were to retain their Imperial names. At 17.00 on the 31st October 1918 Janko Vukovich de Podkapelski took over command of the fleet. He was both a capable and respected soldier and sailor from Jezerane in Lika.

The National Council of SCS promoted him to the rank of Rear Admiral and dispatched notes to the Governments of France, Italy, United Kingdom, United States of America and Russia, stating that the State of SCS was not in war with any of the allied nations and that the Council had taken over the entire Austria-Hungarian fleet. But there was to be no response and officially the war went on. Austria was to finally be asked for an armistice on 29th October and negotiations for the armistice were to begin on 4th November.

CHAPTER 9: LOSS OF THE YUGOSLAVIA

Early in 1918, the Italian naval Lieutenant, Raffaele Paolucci, a naval surgeon, had realized that it might be possible to launch an attack on the Austro-Hungarian ships as they lay at anchor in Pola, by employing Italian divers swimming through the obstacles and into the harbour while carrying explosives. Paolucci contacted the Italian Army in May about his idea and while the army was unsure if the plan was even feasible, it decided that training should begin.

In July Paolucci was to meet with Major Raffaele Rossetti, who had adapted a German torpedo, allowing it to carry two persons, in addition to explosives. With this modified torpedo, Rossetti and Paolucci believed they could travel under water at a speed of 1.63 knots. The torpedo was propelled by two propellers which were powered by compressed air. Having been equipped and supported by the Italian Army, the two men spent three months in the Gulf of Venice planning their mission and training.

On the evening of 31st October, with the transfer of the Empires fleets to its new owners still widely unknown, the two men of the Regia Marina, Paolucci and Rossetti boarded their torpedo boat, *MAS 95* and headed out into the Adriatic bound for Pola. A few miles short of the harbour entrance they donned their waterproof rubber suits and left the *MAS 95*. Rossetti expected that the operation would last only five hours and he ordered the crew of the MAS to rendezvous with Paolucci and himself in the same location at 03:00. They mounted their modified torpedo, (nicknamed the *Mignatta* or *"Leech"*) and submerged it until only their heads remained above the water's surface. Then at 22:13, the motor was started before they made their way in towards Pola's harbour entrance.

As the two Italians quietly stole into the harbour, a small number of Italian agents based in Pola where ready to help Rossetti and Paolucci to pass through the barricades undetected.

While the Italians made their way towards their intended targets, the Croatian crews were happily celebrating on those brightly lit ships (after all a cease-fire had been signed!), completely unaware of the danger drawing slowly nearer. The celebrations distracted the ships crews and the sentinels who oversaw the boom every night were not to be posted. The patrol boats with their searchlights and machine guns were also absent, their crews ashore partying.

At 22:30 Paolucci and Rosseti reached the first obstacles to the harbour entrance. These comprised of three-metre-long floating metal cylinders, connected by thick steel cables. The entrance was in addition watched by the former Austro-Hungarian, but now Croatian guards, who made use of several searchlights. Unable to submerge and ride beneath the barricade, the Italians decided to push their vessel over the obstacle. But this was to prove to be both dangerous and noisy.

However fortunately for them, the guards missed the noise. As the Italians slipped into the harbour, a former Austria-Hungarian submarine passed them in the opposite direction, with only its conning tower above the water. Paolucci and Rossetti somehow remained undetected and continued their ride towards the fleet's anchorage.

They finally drew close to the seawall that protected Pola's anchorage. Here Paolucci dismounted from the torpedo and swam along the wall searching for a way passed it. He was to finally find a gate, constructed from heavy pieces of wood and with protective metal spikes. But in the time Paolucci had taken to explore the wall, the tide had turned. As he swam back towards Rossetti, he found he was swimming against the tide and in addition it started to rain. Faced with these growing difficulties they had not foreseen, the two Italians considered if they should abort the mission. But they finally decided to continue and again they pushed their craft over the gate. Luck was still with them as the noise was masked by the rain and hail that had now started to fall heavily.

At 01:00 on the 1st November and with the seawall finally behind them, the Italians continued towards the brightly lit and anchored warships that were now visible. But they had additional obstacles to overcome first in the form of the anti-submarine nets with attached mines. It took two hours for them to find a way pass these. By the time they were finally clear, it was 03:00 and they had now fallen behind their schedule, as they had planned to be back on their MAS by this point in time. Instead, they had yet to even reached their target. They continued making their way down the long row of illuminated and anchored warships, passing three *Radetzky* class pre-dreadnoughts (*Radetzky, Erzherzog Franz Ferdinand,* and *Zrínyi.*). Next, they slipped past the huge bulks of the *Prinz*

Eugen and the *Tegetthoff*. Their goal was the fleet flagship, the *Viribus Unitis (Yugoslavia)* and she was the last in the long line and the deepest within the enclosed harbour.

It was not until 04:45 that the brightly lit shape of their goal loomed out of the early morning gloom, the dawn light having started to appear on the horizon. As the Italians drew alongside the massive steel cliff that was the *Yugoslavia*, one of the intake valves on their torpedo opened and their craft started to sink to the harbour's seabed. But fortunately, Rossetti was able to quickly fix the problem. He then took one of the two Mignatta's limpet mines (200 kg / 400 lbs of TNT) that their torpedo was carrying and attached it to the hull of the *Yugoslavia*. With it securely in place, he set the timer to detonate the mine at 06:30.

At 05:00, as they were slowly easing away from the mined warship, the Italians were finally spotted by the guards on board the ship. Knowing they had now been sighted, Rossetti and Paolucci tried to reach the shore, but a boat which had been launched from the Yugoslavia and was rapidly closing in on them. Realizing that they are about to be captured, the Italians scuttled their torpedo and were pulled out of the water by the boats crew.

Their 'rescuers' brought them on board the mined dreadnought, their guards assuming them to be downed Italian airmen, (in rubber wetsuits!) something their prisoners did not dissuade them of. With the Croatians convinced their war was over, they welcomed their captives with open arms. But as the 'expected' time of the mine's detonation drew closer they were brought before Admiral Vukovich. Rossetti who had only wanted to sink the ship and not kill the crew, now advised the Admiral that his ship was mined and that he should take steps to save his men. But he refused to reveal neither the time the mine was set to explode nor its location on the hull. Admiral Vukovich calmly listened to the warning and ordered that the crew abandon ship quickly. In the alarm and confusion, while hundreds of sailors were frantically abandoning their ship, Rossetti and Paolucci asked Vukovich whether they could save themselves. With the war all but over, Vukovich agreed to the request and the Italians clambered onto the ship's railing and dived overboard.

But once back in the water, they were captured by a group of sailors who returned them back on board the ship. There they were surrounded by agitated crew members who demanded to know where the mine was and felt that the Italians should also die on their ship if it was soon to be blown up. Seeing what was happening Admiral Vukovich approached the sailors, where Rossetti and Paolucci were demanding the status of prisoners of war. Admiral Vukovich now ordered the crew not to harm the Italians. It was 06:20.

The next ten minutes passed, and the sailors continued to threaten Rossetti and Paolucci. In turn Admiral Vukovich continued to make efforts to calm the sailors and to restore some form of order. At 06:30 there came a loud explosive sound of......... nothing. There had been no explosion, causing Rossetti and Paolucci to believe that their mine had malfunctioned and that their mission had been for nothing. They also believed that they would now be unable to avoid imprisonment and a trial. Their whole nights effort seemed to have been wasted. By this point in the night's drama, most of the crew of the *Yugoslavia* were in the ship's boats, rowing around the ship, uncertain whether to return to back on board or not. Then as all seemed to reek of failure and disappointment for the two captives, a quiet roar was heard and everybody aboard the ship felt a shudder. A huge column of the harbours water rose into the air on the ship's starboard side of the bow and then, as the column collapsed, water started falling on the fore deck in what resembled a waterfall. The Mignatta had finally exploded, all be it fourteen minutes late, at 06:44.

THE YUGOSLAVIA SLOWLY HEELS OVER TAKEN FROM THE SHIP ASTERN OF HER, THE TEGETTHOFF. SOURCE: NAVAL HISTORY & HERITAGE COMMAND.

THE TEGETTHOFF CLASS.

Those crew members that were still on board, started to leave the ship in panic and haste, mostly jumping into the harbours water. In the confusion, Rossetti and Paolucci asked once more of the Admiral, if they could leave the ship. Vukovich agreed a second time and shaking their hands, shouted to one of the lifeboats near the hull to pick up the Italians after they abandoned the ship. Once on board the small boat, Rossetti and Paolucci watched as the doomed ship sank. They were taken on board the *Tegetthoff* (a second source lists the pre-dreadnought *Habsburg*, as the ship they were taken to. But she appears not to have been in the port that night), as prisoners and from there they were transferred to a hospital ship to recover.

A low standard in underwater protection was one of the poor characteristics of the *Tegetthoff* class Dreadnought, but these ships still had coal bunkers designed in such a way that should have acted as additional underwater protection. Unfortunately, the coal bunkers of the *Yugoslavia* were empty that night, so the force of the explosion was not alleviated. The damage to the starboard part of the bow was too extensive and neither the ship's watertight compartments nor the pumps could cope with the huge intake of water now flooding in. The *Yugoslavia* started slowly listing to her starboard side. The rate of sinking steadily increased and at 07:00, the 21,000 ton Dreadnought, with the Croatian flag flying from her mast, capsized and sank quickly taking around 300 members of her crew and her Admiral with her, as the people of Pola watched helplessly on. Janko Vukovich de Podkapelski, who was the commander of the Croatian fleet for only 12 hours, was last seen at the final moments of the ship's death, standing serenely on the stern, waiting for death to come to claim him.

The nights final drama was from the abandoned Mignatta,

which with its second mine, drifted down the harbour, drawn by the current. It finally bumped against the merchant ship *Vienna* (7376 grt), which was now serving as depot ship for the German U-boats in Pola. The mine exploded and a second ship that night sank to the harbour's seabed.

THE REMAINS OF THE MIGNATTA'S LIMPET MINE RECOVERED FROM THE SEA BED.

Four days after the sinking, Italian troops entered Pola (France and the United Kingdom had 'gifted' large parts of the Croatian coast to Italy, as an incentive for entering the war on their side). On the 9th November 1918 the italian naval ensign was hoisted to the mastheads of the former Hadburg dreadnoughts. The next day they were surrendered to the italianss in Pola. Both the Tegetthoff and the *Prinz Eugen* were to have been transfered to the new states that emerged from the empire, but the Italian occupation of Pola made that not possible.

After the Armistice, Italian divers were to locate the wreck and then tear it apart with explosives, before raising several parts of the ship. The main mast, from which the Croatian flag had briefly flown, was to stand until the 1950's at a depth of some 15 metres, but then it vanished. Parts of the wreck remain today on the harbour bed, but they do not cause any problems or hazards to other vessels using the waters.

The much-debated question about whether the Italians knew of the note sent to them before the attack, has never been satisfactorily answered. But while researching the event I have come to puzzle as to why the two Italians asked to be set free, not the course of action a POW would ask or realistically seek? Why did they fear trial and imprisonment and not a POW camp? Did they know of the note and know the true situation? All conjecture on my part, but...

Rossetti and Paolucci were to be freed by the Italian army on the 5th November 1918 and on their return to Italy were treated as national heroes, receiving golden medals, as well as 1,300,000 lire (£349,173 in 1918).

The remaining two Dreadnoughts were to be captured by the Italians when they had marched into Pola. On the 25th March 1919, the *Tegetthoff,* (in company with the Pre-Dreadnought *Archduke Franz Ferdinand*) made the 83-mile voyage between Pola and Venice, their flags hoisted to half mast, in company with an Italian over-watch. On that same date Italy held a *"Marine Victory Parade"* under the slogan:

"LISSA AVENGED!".

The news agency Reuters reported:

"DREADNOUGHTS AT VENICE

RECEPTION OF SURRENDERED AUSTRIAN WARSHIPS.

Venice Monday (received today).

The large battleships of the surrendered Austrian Fleet entered the port of Venice today, and were greeted by an enormous crowd which had assembled on the quays despite the persistent rain. The town and all the ships in the harbour were gaily be-flagged.

The King, the Minister of Marine, and representatives of the Senate and the Chamber were on board the Italian destroyer Audace with the Director of the Naval Department. The Naval Attaches to the British, French and Japanese Embassies, the Brazilian Naval Mission, and other notabilities were on board other vessels.

As the Austrian Fleet anchored opposite the Church of St. Elizabeth the crowd raised enthusiastic cheers for the King and the Italian Navy while systems hooted and blow in all parts of the city".

THE TEGETTHOFF CLASS.

THE TEGETTHOFF UNDER ITALIAN OWNERSHIP IN VENICE.

The former Austro-Hungarian capital ships were thrown opened to the public as they rode at their new Venetian anchorage, "trophies of war". As the ship was toured by the public, a few publications speculated that plans existed for the introduction of the surrendered dreadnought into the Italian Navy to replace the *Leonardo da Vinci*. The Italian capital ship had capsized in Taranto harbour on the night of the 2nd/3rd August 1916 in 36 feet (11 meters) of water due to a magazine explosion while loading ammunition. But the economic situation in the early 1920s, when even the completion of existing battleship plans remained financially impossible, made her salvage unviable. It was however to be the Washington agreement of 1922 and her wartime allies that finally put an end to this idea. The other Great Powers would not sanction Italy commissioning her enemy's capital ships into her navy.

The *Tegetthoff* was to have her moment as a film star (see

Appendix E) in a re-enactment of the sinking of the *Szent István*. But her fate was set, and she was finally to be sold for scrap in 1924. Between the years 1924 and 1925 *Tegetthoff* was slowly disassembled for any salvage and valuable metals, having been transferred to the port of La Spezia.

TEGETTHOFF IN THE PORT OF VENICE IN 1919.

In turn the *Prinz Eugen* went to France as a war-trophy. Four French tugboats arrived in Pola to take the ship in tow for passage to Toulon, where the convoy arrived on 5th September 1920. The French marine experts were primarily interested in the design of the 30.5-cm triple-gun installations of the former Austrian dreadnought. Between 15th January and the 15th March, the *Prinz Eugen* had all her artillery disassembled and hoisted out onto the dockside by cranes. Her new owners initially intended to use the 30.5-cm turret as part of their coastal defence system, but because of technical difficulties, they idea was soon abandoned. The 30.5-cm guns were initially stored in the arsenal of the French fleet, but as a use could not be found for them, they were subsequently transferred to the army. In 1940 after the occupation of France by German troops, the guns of the *Prinz Eugen* fell into the hands of the victorious Germans. From that stage their subsequent fate is unknown, but there is speculation that they were later used to create fortifications within Hitler's Atlantic Wall. The 150-mm and 66-mm guns of the *Prinz Eugen* were in turn dismantled for sale overseas.

With the guns removed, the turrets armoured roofs were re-installed to enable a series of tests to be conducted examining their stability in experiments with armour-piercing air bombs, as the USA would undertake with the former German dreadnought, *Ostfriesland* in July 1921. But by the spring of that year, in addition to her artillery, any mechanisms the French deemed of interest were removed from the ship. The turbines, dynamos, machinery, optical and electrical systems, as well as most of the pipelines and electrical cables were salvaged from the former warship. Holes were cut into the decks and bulkheads for the extractions, which were then later temporarily sealed again. Two months before the East Coast USA *Ostfriesland* trials, at the end of May the *Prinz Eugen* was sunk at the bottom in Alikaster Bay, having been bombarded by naval aircraft with smoke, gas, and high-explosive bombs. The speculated destructive power of the damage had been over estimated and was initially assumed that after these raids the ship would be so irreparably damaged, all other experiments would have to be carried out on an obsolete French battleship. But the *Prinz Eugen* had stood up to her assaults. Once the ship was re-floated in June the experiments were continued. On the 28th July the airship *AT9* off Toulon, dropped three 410 kg pierced bombs onto her decks which exploded below. Salvage tugs were set to work with pumps, and she was towed to a dry dock for a closer examination of the damage.

On the 27th January 1922, the ship was towed to Sen Bay and a tightly packed warhead of a torpedo was exploded against her hull. As a result, one compartment in the stern was completely flooded and she sunk by 12 meters aft. Leaks in the hull and deck hatches gradually allowed the ship to fill with water and she settled on an even keel on the bottom of the bay with her bow resting at a depth of 10 meters and her stern at 13 meters. Attempts to lift the ship were halted by bad weather but as she was eventually raised, the ship suffered from exceptional instability due to an unsystematic alternation of the already drained and still flooded compartments. In the end to level the water level in the interior, it was to prove necessary to perforate the armour deck with gas cutting torches. Then with the simultaneous action of 10 pumps, the water was sucked from the hull and pumped over the side. The surfaced ship was then towed once again to Toulon. The salvage time for the dreadnought recovery was to be more than a month. Later the French *AT9* airship once more dropped a 400 kg bomb on the dreadnought. Then on 2nd November a fire broke out on the *Prinz Eugen* and she was left a *"gutted skeleton"*.

The *Prinz Eugen's* final fate was on the 28th June 1922, when she was sunk off Cape Serpe, south of Toulon, with heavy artillery fire from the battleships of the French Mediterranean squadron. The dreadnought *Paris* fired 25 shells from her 34-cm guns, twice piercing the main armour belt, destroying one of the main turrets, the command, the range-finder post of the secondary armament and demolishing a funnel. As the dreadnought begun to sink, the *Jean Bart* and the *Paris* opened fire once more, this time with 305-mm. The *France* was the next ship to have her turn and it was during her shots that sent the long-suffering *Prinz Eugen* to the bottom.

THE TEGETTHOFF CLASS.

THE PRINZ EUGEN LAYS NEGLECTED IN THE BACK GROUND, WITH BRITISH
DESTROYERS IN POST WAR POLA. THE QUALITY OF THE IMAGE IS POOR, BUT
ITS THE BEST IN THE ARCHIVES AND WORTH REPRODUCING HERE.

349

CHAPTER 10: TO CONCLUDE.

I think we can say at the start of any conclusion or summary of the *Tegetthoff's,* that they were a flawed creation. In addition, no other nation entered the Great War and emerged with 50% of their Dreadnought force lost through enemy action. (The Kaiser's fleet lost 0% of its Dreadnoughts prior to the Armistice and 16.66 % of its Battle-cruisers, or one from a total of 6, Blucher excluded). As I researched and wrote this 'book' I found it hard to recall another Dreadnought that had such a flawed foundation, both in its design and those who brought them into the world. So, if we start from the point where we acknowledge they were not the finest examples of the Dreadnought genre, how did they compare when placed against the Italian first generation Dreadnought, the *Dante Alighieri?*

The Italians were the first of the two nations to lay a keel down, but they were easily trumped by the Austrians in the number of days from keel to commissioning. Only the *Szent István* took longer to build than the *Dante Alighieri* and she had a war to blame her slow completion time on. The *Tegetthoff's* were 52 feet 5 29/32 inches (16 mtrs) shorter, 2 feet 11 7/16 inches (0.90 mtrs) wider and 1 foot 1 3/78 inches (0.34 cm) shallower than the Dante. The Austrian hull was 134 tons lighter at standard, but 211 heavier when full. So, the Austrian ship was shorter, wider, and marginally shallower, but even though she started lighter, as the hull was loaded, she put on more weight. But the goal had always been for a shorter ship with the triple turrets. Despite the Austrian navy comments (post the *Szent István's* sinking) that Montecuccoli had handicapped the design with his limitations, the Italians squeezed the same gun configuration into a smaller sized hull for less weight. So, do the Austrian comments on the design restrictions apply to the Italian's?

The *Tegetthoff* carried 2,111 tons of fuel giving a range of 4,200 nsm at 10 knots. For 3,610 tons the Dante achieved 600 nsm greater at the same cruising speed. This resulted in the Austrians achieving 0.50 miles per ton of fuel (MPT) and the Italians 0.69 MPT. To give the MPT figures a comparison, the *Dreadnought a*chieved 0.60 MPT and the French *Courbet* left them all in the dust at 0.86 MPT. So, the Italian vessel could go further on one ton of fuel. However, these were two Mediterranean powers, with no worldwide empires to speak off, based in a sea that was from Tangier's to Beirut only 2028 nsm in length. How far did the two Admiralty's want or expect their vessels to go?

Now we come to the reason for their existence, the big guns. Both ships carried twelve 12-inch guns mounted into triple turrets, with the Italian turrets being 645 tons as compared to the Austrian 620 tons, so hardly much in it. But the *Tegetthoff's* turrets were heavier than designed, caused structural problems, and added 1.5-inches (or 34 cm) to the draft. Bizarrely the *Tegetthoff's* were as we mentioned about 0.34 cm shallower than the Italian hull when full.

Full train and elevation rates are not available for the *Dante* so we move on to what came out the barrel and how far it could go. We cannot compare the damage the shell did on impact as we only have the Austrian weapons details. The *Tegetthoff's* could send a 450 kg (992 lb) shell out to 24,000 meters (26,246 yds), while the *Dante* sent a 415 kg (914.91 lb) shell out to 26,240 meters (28,696 yds), so once the Austrian Captain steered his ship 2,240 meters (2,249 yds) within the maximum Italian range, he could deliver a heavier shell on target at the same rate of fire, 2 shells per minute. But the Italian captain had a 2-knot advantage and if he were good at his job, he could keep the range open and pound the *Tegetthoff* with his lighter shells. The Austrians had the heavier broadside, but they had to close that 2000+ meter gap to make use of it.

Now we come to armour and protection. The trouble here is we know already the Austrian design, for whatever reason was deeply flawed below the water line, so they start at a disadvantage. Plus, we know of the turret's ventilation problems. The Austrian belt was 1-inch thicker, but unlike the Italian belt it stopped short of the bow and stern. The Tegetthoff's maximum turret armour was another of those inches thicker, the decks half an inch and the conning tower an inch thinner. I also have no way of judging if the *Dante Alighieri* had 'other' problems with her armour scheme, such as the *Tegetthoff's* had, so it is hard to draw a fair comparison.

Post the *Szent's* loss, additional failings were to be revealed on the *Tegetthoff*. The overlapping gun turrets caused the centre of gravity of the ships to be too high. In addition, the finished turrets were over Škoda's original guaranteed design weight. In the case of *Szent István* the searchlight platform that was to be built around the funnels only aggravated the situation. It increased the centre of gravity for the vessel by 8 mm (0.31-inch), which then added to the boat's list by almost 9 °. On her trials at twenty knots and with a 35 degrees steering wheel, the ship was inclined to 19 ° 45 '. This was due to the searchlight platform. We also know one of the class had limitations placed on its rudder use and generally they coped badly with the sea. But I have no comparative data on the Italian Dreadnought.

Finally, we need to look at their life achievements. Neither class fired a shell in anger, except at land targets and both rode at anchor for a large part of their wartime services. Both were a heavy drain on their nation's expenses and their manpower. Aside from the bombardment of Ancona I could not find one positive employment of the *Tegetthoff's*.

The Mediterranean arms race has few parallels with the one conducted within the North Sea. It was a short lived and unique race. The 'winner' in 1914 is unclear, but if you transferred both classes to the respective battle lines at Jutland on the 31st May 1916, they would have (I believe) been out classed by the North Sea fleets and out of their depth.

But all this is handicapped in the large holes we have in our technical knowledge of the *Dante Alighieri*. There is so much we do not know. They were both very much an even group of Dreadnought, but if I must concede to one or the other, then it is to the Italians I award the prize. But Austria comes away with a sheer entertainment medal and the "You have to smile", bar to that medal.

ANDY SOUTH

APPENDICES

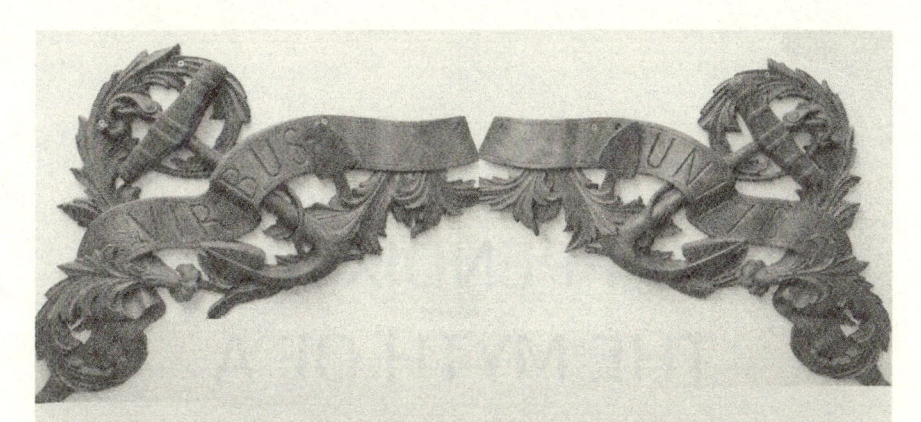

VIRIBUS UNITIS STERN ORNAMENTS

APPENDIX A: THE MYTH OF A UNUSABLE GUN TOWER: LEGEND OR REALITY?

(by Mihály Krámli).

The article is in it's original form written in Hungarian, but it's worth the translation and the full text included with these pages as it lays to rest a often quoted flaw in the class.

The original source is :https://arsmilitaria.blog.hu/2020/04/05/ erdekessegek_a_tegetthoff-oszta lyrol_i

PARTIES ABOUT THE TEGETTHOFF CLASS I.
THE MYTH OF A UNUSABLE GUN TOWER: LEGEND OR REALITY?

The cannon towers of the only dreadnought-class battleship class of the former Austro-Hungarian Navy, the TEGETTHOFF class, were widely believed to be useless on the Internet, various websites *and forums. Namely, they write, because in a combat situation the ventilation system had to be shut down so that it would not suck in the gunpowder, and as a result, the oxygen in the tower ran out in a quarter of an hour. A serious claim, if true, means that the four battleships that cost the Monarchy taxpayers 73 tons of gold didn't cost much more than a pile of junk.*

The weight of the above statement is increased by the fact that it feeds not only from some source obtained from the air, but from a real, official document. This is nothing more than a report written in 1916 by the commander of the battleship VIRIBUS UNITIS at the request of the Navy about his ship. This began to spread in the public consciousness following René Greger's 1980 article (Who Was Responsible for The Faults of the Tegetthoff-class) in Warship. Over the years, this statement of the report has been referred to in several scientific or semi-scientific works. What they have in common is that (at least what I have read so far) they repeat what is described in the report, but they make no attempt to pursue the matter.

This question has been a concern since I first met it. After all, if you think about it, how can a navy afford a technical solution that degrades its latest battleships into expensive steam yachts. On the other hand, from the point of view of common sense, how could such a mistake have occurred when gun towers had been designed and manufactured for more than a decade and a half, operating on more than a dozen ships without such a problem. We would believe that such an organization could not allow such a mistake, or if it did, immediate steps would be taken to remedy it. Of course, there is always fumble for a man named de. I would mention just one example of this: the British Navy had been aware of the lousy quality of its large-caliber grenades since 1911, yet they did nothing. It was only after the battle of Jutland / Skagerrak that they set out to remedy the problem, after their grenades had spectacularly failed in the clash. I therefore believe that this case is worth an investigation, if not Sherlock Holmesi, but at least one of Dr. Watson's investigations.

First of all, let's get to know a little more about the subject of this short post, the turret. The largest type of warship, formed in the last third of the 19th century, carried the main armament of the battleship, heavy guns, in rotatable gun turrets. Until 1906, there were usually two of these on a ship. After 1906 it was called dreadnoughtThey already had four or seven gun turrets, each with cannons of the same caliber. Our main characters, the TEGETTHOFF class ships, each had four turrets, two at the front, two at the stern, behind and above each other, staggered. In such a tower were placed three 30.5 cm caliber cannons. The barrel of the cannon was 13.5 meters long, weighed 54 tons, and could fire its 450-kilogram grenade 19 km away. The gun turret itself weighed nearly 700 tons, with the above-deck rotor containing the cannons protected by 28 cm thick armor. Inside it was the so-called. Cannon Square. Under the cannons, the cylindrical rotor reached five to six floors / deck depth all the way to the stern of the ship. It housed electric motors for various purposes (e.g., tower rotation), ammunition elevators, and other necessary equipment. The rotor was surrounded by an armored cylinder, this was called a barbette. The staff of such a turret consisted of 90 people who performed either hard physical work or tasks that required strong concentration, so they were in great need of a constant supply of fresh air.

And now let's look at the ominous report itself. On April 8, 1916, the Naval Department of the Joint Department of War ordered the masters of the TEGETTHOFF-class battleships to write down their experience of their ship in a report. The reports were completed in the summer and fall of 1916. Reading through the four reports, it can be seen that the most detailed, elaborate material was born from the fleet's flagship, VIRIBUS UNITIS. The artillery section of

THE TEGETTHOFF CLASS.

this report contains this much-cited statement. The other three commanders do not mention a similar problem. The report reads as follows.

"Tower and Gunpipe Ventilation: The air intakes for the tower ventilation are on the main deck. In a combat situation, these must be shut off to prevent smoke and gunpowder from entering the tower interior, with the result that the oil lamps go out after a short time due to a lack of oxygen. Gun fans are too weak and small." So far, the text of the report. Next to it is a manuscript note to which previous references have not paid much, more precisely no attention. It says, "Is there anything that can be fixed now?" Beneath it is a large SOS, next to it a huge, thick check mark with a visibly different ink. From the latter we can deduce that some sort of solution has been found, but it is also possible that they have only looked more closely at the matter.

After that, let's look at what other sources about tower ventilation are showing us. We are not particularly rich in these. The operating documentation for the triple gun tower has not been found by anyone so far, so we can't find a clue here. In chronological order, Stabilimento Tecnico Triestino, the first and perhaps most important of the four Trieste factories to build three ships, has a technical drawing of tower ventilation with a huge red seal marked "Geheim" (secret). Based on the drawing, it can be seen that one air intake per tower was on the main deck, right next to the barbette, and could be closed with a lid. The air duct reached tightly past the barbette all the way to the bottom of the tower, connecting from the bottom center to the turret rotor, which reached almost to the bottom of the ship. The air flow was provided by a fan with a capacity of 3 cubic meters / second. At the same time, under the main deck, on the closed-air battery deck, there was another opening in the air duct that could also be closed with a lid. We know from the report on the test of the tower ventilation of the SZENT ISTVÁN battleship that in case of bad weather or firing with guns, the opening on the main deck was closed with the lid and the opening on the battery deck was opened. The system then sucked air from the battery deck. The ventilator on this deck was away from the gun towers, so it sucked in less smoke. The tower ventilation was operated on SZENT ISTVÁN for two hours without any problems. or in the case of gunfire, the opening in the main deck is closed with the lid and the opening in the battery deck is opened. The system then sucked air from the battery deck. The ventilator on this deck was away from the gun towers, so it sucked in less smoke. The tower ventilation was operated on SZENT ISTVÁN for two hours without any problems. or in the case of gunfire, the opening in the main deck is closed with the lid and the opening in the battery deck is opened. The system then sucked air from the battery deck. The ventilator on this deck was away from the gun towers, so it sucked in less smoke. The tower ventilation was operated on SZENT ISTVÁN for two hours without any problems.

The system itself could have operated, although its exact description is not available, by continuously blowing air into the turret rotor from below, while facilitating the upward flow by constantly running the three flue gas exhaust fans at the top level, in the gunpowder, whose air intakes next to them, they were in line with the barrage.

The reports of the May 24, 1915 shooting of Ancona also provide interesting, albeit indirect, additions. As is well known, Admiral Anton Haus, commander of the Navy, shot down the entire fleet of Ancona and the Italian east coast following the Italian war message. Three ships of the TEGETTHOFF class took part in it, SZENT ISTVÁN was still under construction. The commander of VIRIBUS UNITIS was then Captain Edmund Grassberger, who was transferred to SZENT ISTVÁN in November 1915. Grassberger was otherwise known throughout the fleet for his awareness and ten-

dency to giggle. The three dreadnought shot Ancona from 6,000 meters for twenty minutes sometime between 5:30 and 6:00 in the morning. In doing so, they handled the ammunition very sparingly, firing only 6-8 30.5 cm grenades per ship.

We have pretty much this information about the issue right now. The fact is that the TEGETTHOFF class had a number of design flaws. This was already pointed out by several people during the construction of the ships. It is conceivable that those who officially described them in a formal form were much less restrained in informal conversations, especially if they even consumed alcoholic beverages. Some of these stemmed from unrealistic expectations of the department, as it was a serious trick to crowd twelve 30.5 cm cannons into a 20,000-ton water displacement, but others could have been avoided with more careful planning. Most of these errors were irreparable in retrospect.

Tower ventilation was not one of those irreparable mistakes, in fact, I don't think it was a mistake in the sense of the others. Here, one statement contrasts with several, to the contrary. The strongest of the latter is the technical documentation, which shows that the system did not work quite as described in the report of the commander of VIRIBUS UNITIS. Moreover, by this time an expert report had already arrived from Germany, which showed that in the battle of the Skagerrak, the crew in a gas mask was able to perform their service indoors even in the event of a smoke burglary. Unfortunately, apart from the marginal note already quoted above, we are not aware of any further reaction by the Navy to the assertion of the report. What is certain, however, is that the marginalist has questioned several other statements here.

The fact that the system continued to operate after the main deck opening was closed was justified by the criticism in other reports *that the ventilation of the turrets, and even the ventilation in general, was poor. They were no better off anywhere else, after the battle of Skagerrak, the Germans complained about it. It is a telling fact that while the TEGETTHOFF class triple gun tower had a ventilation capacity of 180 cubic meters per minute, the World War II American 40.6 cm triple gun tower, which had a maximum cubic capacity of twice the Austro-Hungarian tower, was 877 cubic meters per minute.*

Based on the above, I believe that the gun turret, which becomes unusable due to lack of oxygen, belongs to the realm of legends rather than to reality. And this is a quarter of an hour of functionality in particular, as neither the original report nor the more serious literature mentions time, so something folk tales could have been added to the story. Ergo, a theorist, never happened, in the case of the clash with the Austro-Hungarian dreadnought, the opponent could not trust that it would be an easy thing to do, as their gun turrets would silence on their own in a quarter of an hour. Here we come to the end of Watson's reasoning, but we know from many stories that after the good doctor presented his theories, Sherlock Holmes smiled a little and said, "Dear Watson," and then took them to taste in minutes.

Mihály Krámli

APPENDIX B: THE 'COMPETITION' ENTRIES.

Between the years 1909 and 1910 the 'competition' that was run to find a Dreadnought design deemed to be worthy of the Austro-Hungarian Empire (and its navy) brought a series of 'entries'. Fifteen designs were to be produced in the evolution process, covering every conventional layout of main calibre turrets. The process would evolve from an almost pre-dreadnought design to the triple turrets 'winning' format. It was this final shape that would lead to the *Tegetthoff* class.

DESIGN 'I'

The first design, number 'I' (March 1909) had a waterline length of 151.5 meters (497 feet 9/16 inches), a beam of 26 meters (85 feet 3 5/8 inches) and a draught of 86 meters (282 feet 1 3/16 inches). She had a 20,000-tonne displacement (1,968.41 tons) and her four steam turbines produced 25,000 shp culminating in a 20.5 rate of knots.

The armour was 230 mm (9 1/16) along the waterline belt and 48 mm (1 7/8 inch) decking. She had four twin 30.5 cm cal (12 inch) mounted turrets, two forward and two aft. The latter of each pair was super firing, and this gave her a broadside of eight guns and with four also firing both forward and aft. Based on a 450 kg shell her broadside would equate to 3600 kg (7837lb).

Her secondary armament comprised of ten single 19 cm 50 cal (7 feet 15/32 inch) mounted into amidships casements, one battery on each beam. She in addition had twenty singly mounted 7 cm guns 45 cal (2 3/4 inch) guns, two of which were mounted onto the roofs of turrets two and three. Her torpedo armament was of four 53 cm (20 7/8 inch) single tubes.

THE TEGETTHOFF CLASS.

Battleship Pre-project I (March 1909)

Item	Description
Dimensions:	151,5 (wl) x 26 x 8,6m
Displacement:	20.000tons (standard)
Engines:	25.000shp Steam Turbines, 4 shafts
Speed:	38km/h (20,5knots)
Armour:	48mm Deck, 230mm Belt
Armament:	4x2 30,5cm/50 Cannons 10x1 19cm/50 Casemated Guns 20x1 10cm/50 Guns 2x1 7cm/45 Guns 4x1 53cm Torpedoes

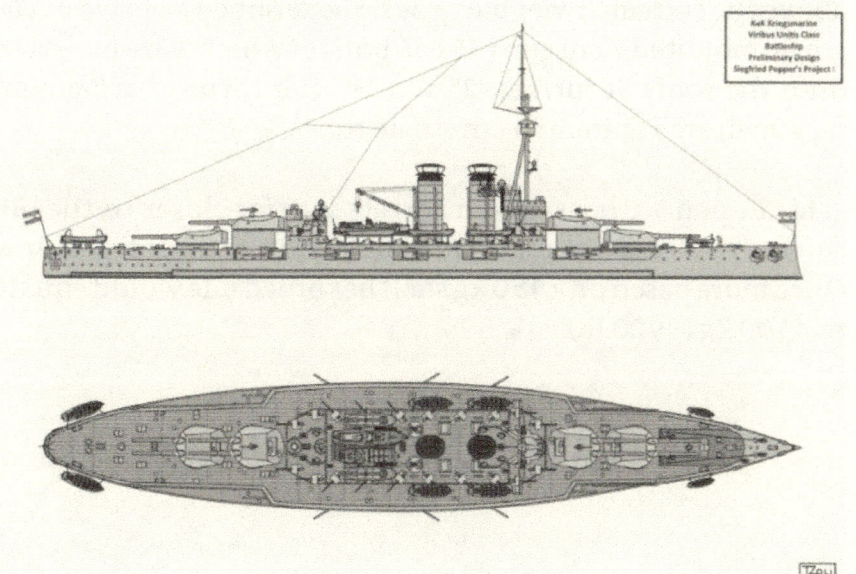

DESIGN 'II'

The second design 'II' (March 1909) was identical to its predecessor in every area, (as would be all the succeeding designs (I-VIII) due to the 'competition rules'), except in the armament configuration they carried.

The four 30.5 cm turrets became five in number and retained the super firing profile, but the fifth turret was set amidships with the capability to fire on either beam. Her broadside brought an increase of two guns, rising from eight to ten.

The major difference was the addition of four twin 19 cm (7 15/32 inch) turrets, two mounted either side of the conning tower and the remaining two on each beam, just aft of the second funnel. Her casemates now held twenty single 10 cm 50 cal (3 15/16 inches) weapons, with sixteen retained in the same format as design "I", bringing eight to each beam. But the two remaining pairs were mounted in a second tier of casements, above the sixteen lower batteries. She retained just two of the single mounted 7 cm guns 45 cal, both of which were mounted onto the roofs of turrets "2" and "3". Her torpedo armament was unaltered at four 53 cm single tubes.

This design with its 19 cm turrets was far closer to the obsolete Pre-Dreadnought in both its layout and configuration. Once more based on a 450 kg shell her broadside would equate to 4500 kg (9920 lb).

THE TEGETTHOFF CLASS.

Battleship Pre-project II (March 1909)

Item	Description
Dimensions:	151,5 (wl) x 26 x 8,6m
Displacement:	20.000tons (standard)
Engines:	25.000shp Steam Turbines, 4 shafts
Speed:	38km/h (20,5knots)
Armour:	48mm Deck, 230mm Belt
Armament:	4x2 30,5cm/50 Cannons
4x2 19cm/50 Guns
20x1 10cm/50 Casemated Guns
2x1 7cm/45 Guns
4x1 53cm Torpedoes

KuK Kriegsmarine
Viribus Unitis Class
Battleship
Preliminary Design
Siegfried Popper's Project II

DESIGN 'III'

Design 'III' (March 1909) was once more, (armament aside), identical to the preceding designs 'I' and 'II'. She retained the five 30.5 cm turret configuration, but the 19 cm were no longer included. She too had two batteries of casemate guns, but these were reverted once more to a port and starboard battery on a singular level amidships and fourteen single 10 cm 50 cal guns sighted in groups on the amidships main deck. Three single 7 cm 45 cal guns were mounted on the roofs of turrets '2', '3' and '4'. Once more based on a 450 kg shell her broadside would equate to 4500 kg (9920 lb).

THE TEGETTHOFF CLASS.

Battleship Pre-project III (March 1909)

Item	Description
Dimensions:	151,5 (wl) x 26 x 8,6m
Displacement:	20.000tons (standard)
Engines:	25.000shp Steam Turbines, 4 shafts
Speed:	38km/h (20,5knots)
Armour:	48mm Deck, 230mm Belt
Armament:	5x2 30,5cm/50 Cannons 10x1 15cm/50 Casemated Guns 14x1 10cm/50 Guns 3x1 7cm/45 Guns 4x1 53cm Torpedoes

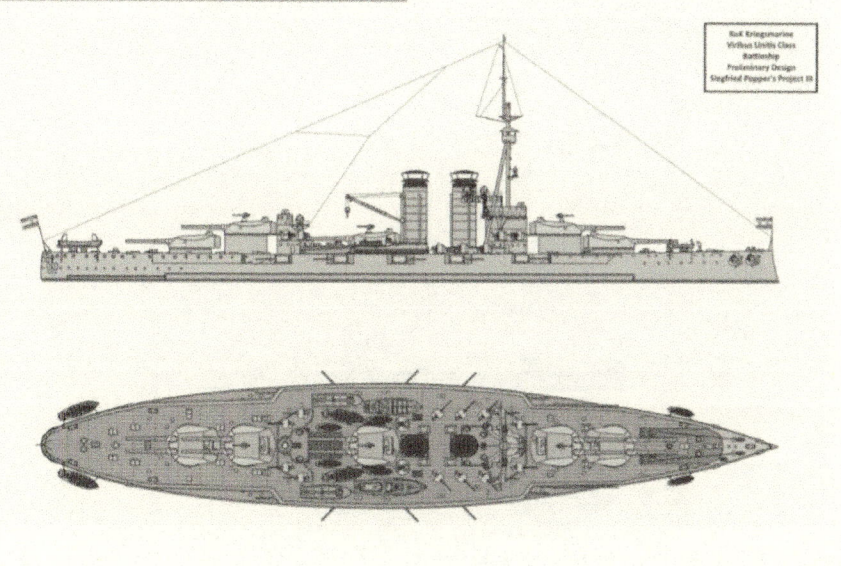

369

DESIGN 'IV'

The next Design 'IV' (March 1909) in turn retained the five twin 30.5 cm turret configuration and the three 7 cm's located on the turret roofs. But her casemated battery was increased in their size to 12 cm, (4 23/32 inches) with 7 on each beam. The torpedo configuration remained unchanged. Again, based on a 450 kg shell her broadside would equate to 4500 kg (9920 lb).

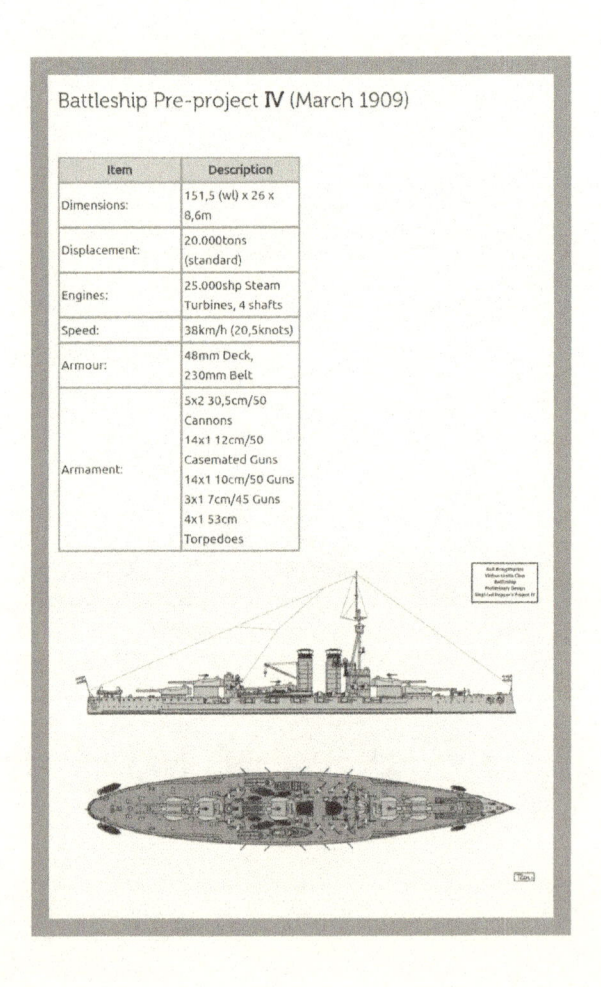

Battleship Pre-project **IV** (March 1909)

Item	Description
Dimensions:	151,5 (wl) x 26 x 8,6m
Displacement:	20.000tons (standard)
Engines:	25.000shp Steam Turbines, 4 shafts
Speed:	38km/h (20,5knots)
Armour:	48mm Deck, 230mm Belt
Armament:	5x2 30,5cm/50 Cannons 14x1 12cm/50 Casemated Guns 14x1 10cm/50 Guns 3x1 7cm/45 Guns 4x1 53cm Torpedoes

DESIGN 'V'

The fifth design, 'V' (March 1909) brought some changes from her four predecessors. An additional twin 30.5 cm (50 cal) turret had been added, increasing the number to twelve guns in six turrets. Turrets '1', '2', '5' and '6' remained as super firing, with one pair forward and the second on the aft.

The two new turrets were sighted just aft of amidships, with the pair sat side by side on opposite beams. The hulls beam was not increased in its width and within the retained dimensions it was planned to place two main calibre turrets with their barbettes side by side. The strain on the ship's hull would be of some concern? The broadside would be on this design (and the 'V.a' & 'V.b') ten on each beam, four forward and four aft. The wing turrets would lack the clear decks to fire directly forwards, but they would have had a wide arc of fire on the beams. Despite the additional turret, the new configuration retained a broadside 4500 kg (9920 lb).

She had her 10 cm weaponry raised in number to twenty-four, of which seven sat on each beam within casements. The reminder was located on the fore and aft superstructure's, each gun within a shield. The turrets '2', '3', '4' and '5' each had a 7 cm mounted on their individual roofs.

Battleship Pre-project **V** (March 1909)

Item	Description
Dimensions:	151,5 (wl) x 26 x 8,6m
Displacement:	20.000tons (standard)
Engines:	25.000shp Steam Turbines, 4 shafts
Speed:	38km/h (20,5knots)
Armour:	48mm Deck, 230mm Belt
Armament:	6x2 30,5cm/50 Cannons 24x1 10cm/50 Casemated and Shielded Guns 4x1 7cm/45 Guns 4x1 53cm Torpedoes

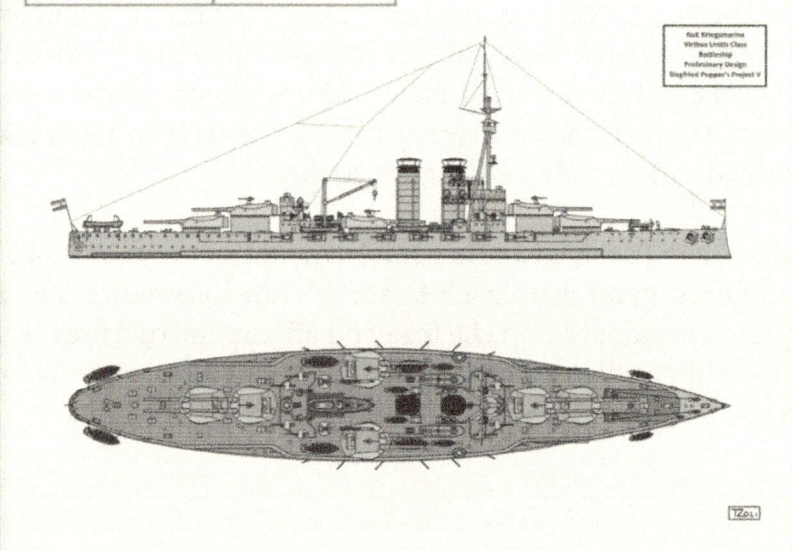

DESIGN 'V.a'

THE TEGETTHOFF CLASS.

Design 'V.a' was dated July 1905 and brought an amendment in the secondary armaments. The 10 cm guns were removed and eight 15 cm 45 cal were placed into the casements in their stead. The four 7 cm became 16 in number. Turrets '2','3', '4' & '5' now mounted two of the weapons on their roofs, where before there had been just one. But the format of the main calibre remained unchanged from design.

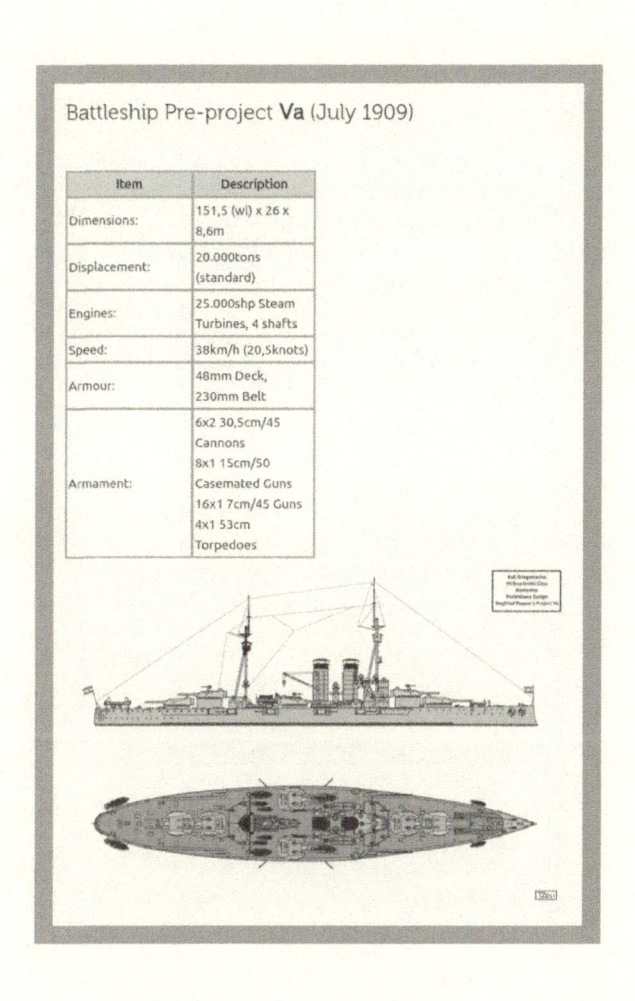

Battleship Pre-project **Va** (July 1909)

Item	Description
Dimensions:	151,5 (wl) x 26 x 8,6m
Displacement:	20.000tons (standard)
Engines:	25.000shp Steam Turbines, 4 shafts
Speed:	38km/h (20,5knots)
Armour:	48mm Deck, 230mm Belt
Armament:	6x2 30,5cm/45 Cannons 8x1 15cm/50 Casemated Guns 16x1 7cm/45 Guns 4x1 53cm Torpedoes

DESIGN 'V.b'

Design "V.b" dating from July 1909 was identical to "V.a", in layout of her weaponry, but the 15 cm (45 cal) now numbered eighteen, all mounted into two casemented batteries.

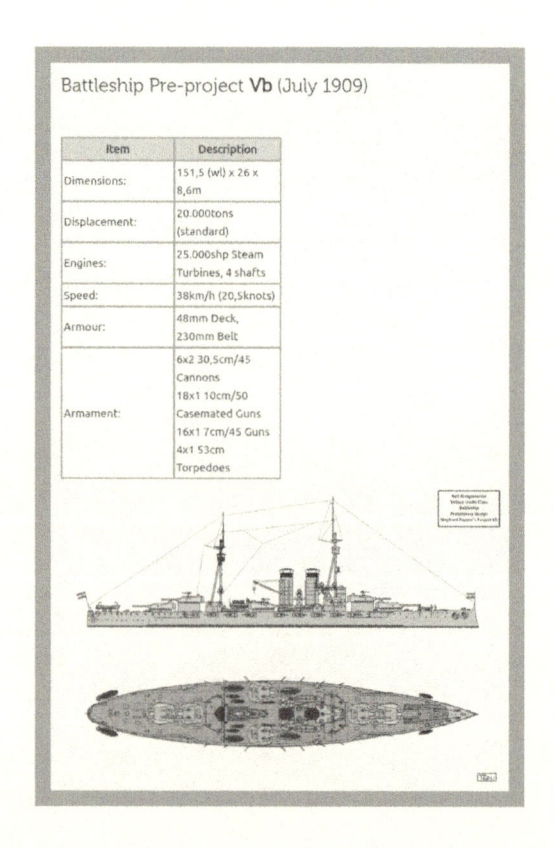

Battleship Pre-project **Vb** (July 1909)

Item	Description
Dimensions:	151,5 (wl) x 26 x 8,6m
Displacement:	20.000tons (standard)
Engines:	25.000shp Steam Turbines, 4 shafts
Speed:	38km/h (20,5knots)
Armour:	48mm Deck, 230mm Belt
Armament:	6x2 30,5cm/45 Cannons 18x1 10cm/50 Casemated Guns 16x1 7cm/45 Guns 4x1 53cm Torpedoes

DESIGN 'VI'

Design 'VI', (dated rather bizarrely March 1909) brought the return of all the turrets (numbering five in total) to the ships centre line. Turrets '1' & '2' were forward mounted, '3' was amidships with the capacity to fire on either beam or turrets '4' & '5' were mounted on the aft portion of the hull. The ships broadside would have been ten on either beam and four over the bow or the stern. The design had fourteen singly mounted 17 cm 50 cal guns in casements, seven on each beam. Eleven 7 cm 45 cal single mounted, three guns carried on turrets '2', '3' & '4.' The remaining eight were split between the forward and aft superstructure. The number of torpedoes was decreased by one to three 51 cm torpedo tubes located beneath the waterline. Her broadside would equate to 4500 kg (9920 lb).

Battleship Pre-project VI (March 1909)

Item	Description
Dimensions:	151,5 (wl) x 26 x 8,6m
Displacement:	20.000tons (standard)
Engines:	25.000shp Steam Turbines, 4 shafts
Speed:	38km/h (20,5knots)
Armour:	48mm Deck, 230mm Belt
Armament:	5x2 30,5cm/50 Cannons 14x1 15cm/50 Casemated Guns 11x1 7cm/45 Guns 3x1 53cm Torpedoes

'DESIGN 'VI.a' & 'VI.b'

Design 'VI.a', dated April 1909, retained the central aligned turrets, but her casement guns were reduced to 15 cm 50 cal, the 7 cm increased to fourteen in number and the torpedo tubes remained at three. April also brought the 'VI.b', retaining as with the two preceding designs, her turrets on the centre line. Her casements guns numbered fourteen 15 cm 50 cal, supported by eleven 7 cm guns. The torpedoes remained at three in number.

THE TEGETTHOFF CLASS.

Battleship Pre-project **VIa** (April 1909)

Item	Description
Dimensions:	151,5 (wl) x 26 x 8,6m
Displacement:	20.000tons (standard)
Engines:	25.000shp Steam Turbines, 4 shafts
Speed:	38km/h (20,5knots)
Armour:	48mm Deck, 230mm Belt
Armament:	5x2 30,5cm/45 Cannons 14x1 15cm/50 Casemated Guns 14x1 7cm/45 Guns 3x1 53cm Torpedoes

Battleship Pre-project **VIb** (April 1909)

Item	Description
Dimensions:	151,5 (wl) x 26 x 8,6m
Displacement:	20.000tons (standard)
Engines:	25.000shp Steam Turbines, 4 shafts
Speed:	38km/h (20,5knots)
Armour:	48mm Deck, 230mm Belt
Armament:	5x2 30,5cm/45 Cannons 14x1 15cm/50 Casemated Guns 11x1 7cm/45 Guns 3x1 53cm Torpedoes

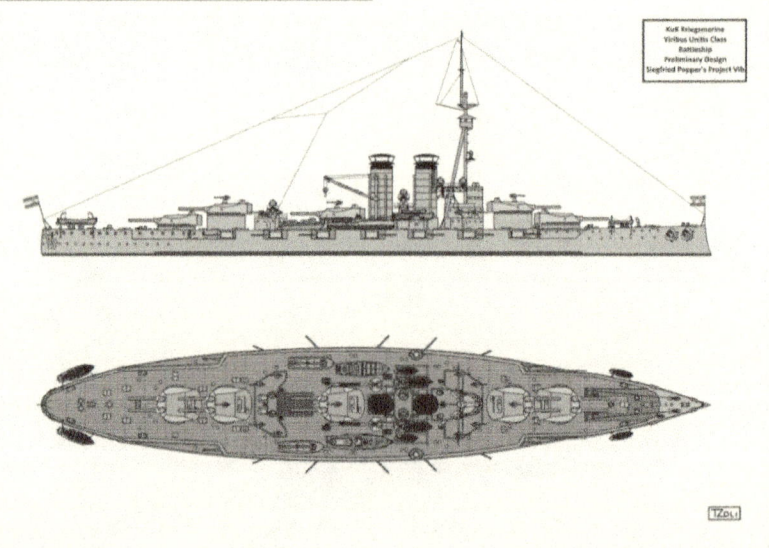

DESIGN 'VII'

Design 'VII' was dated in this distorted calendar, March 1909. She too retained the five centre line turrets, but her casement batteries were 12 cm 50 cal, numbering nine on each beam. The 7 cm and torpedo armament remained unaltered form 'VI.b'.

Battleship Pre-project VII (March 1909)

Item	Description
Dimensions:	151,5 (wl) x 26 x 8,6m
Displacement:	20.000tons (standard)
Engines:	25.000shp Steam Turbines, 4 shafts
Speed:	38km/h (20,5knots)
Armour:	48mm Deck, 230mm Belt
Armament:	5x2 30,5cm/50 Cannons 18x1 12cm/50 Casemated Guns 11x1 7cm/45 Guns 3x1 53cm Torpedoes

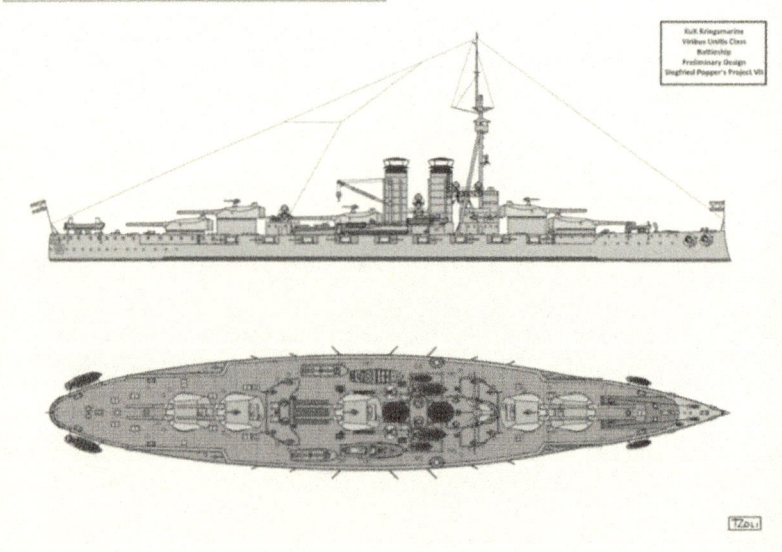

DESIGNS 'VIII a' & 'VIII b'.

THE TEGETTHOFF CLASS.

The March 1909 'VII.a' was identical to 'VII.b' except the 7cm batteries were now increased in number to fourteen.

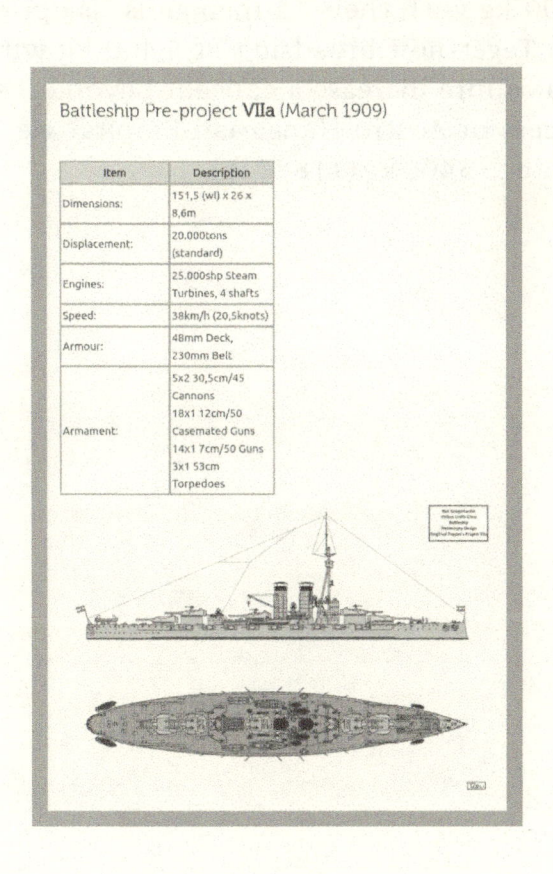

Battleship Pre-project VIIa (March 1909)

Item	Description
Dimensions:	151,5 (wl) x 26 x 8,6m
Displacement:	20.000tons (standard)
Engines:	25.000shp Steam Turbines, 4 shafts
Speed:	38km/h (20,5knots)
Armour:	48mm Deck, 230mm Belt
Armament:	5x2 30,5cm/45 Cannons 18x1 12cm/50 Casemated Guns 14x1 7cm/50 Guns 3x1 53cm Torpedoes

DESIGN 'VIII'

It was design 'VIII' (April 1909) that finally introduced the triple turret configuration. She had four centre line 30 cm 45 cal turrets, giving her a broadside of twelve and four over either the bow or stern. Her casemate guns were 15 cm 50 cal with 5 on each beam. Turrets '2' & '3' mounted pairs of 7 cm 50 cal on their roofs. The remaining ten 7 cm were in a number of sites on the main deck. The torpedo tubes were increased to four in number.

The goal of the triple turrets was always more weight of broadside on a standard hull size, which the triple configuration did within the Austro-Hungarian navy. But in Germany the new eight broadside firing Baden class were achieving around 6000 kg with their 15 inch guns, as opposed to the twelve-gun Tegetthoff broadside of 5,400 kg with their 12 inch. Was a calibre increase a concept beyond the manufacturing process of Austro-Hungarian Empire? Her broadside would equate to 5400 kg (11880 lb).

THE TEGETTHOFF CLASS.

Battleship Pre-project VIII (April 1909)

Item	Description
Dimensions:	151,5 (wl) x 26 x 8,6m
Displacement:	20.000tons (standard)
Engines:	25.000shp Steam Turbines, 4 shafts
Speed:	38km/h (20,5knots)
Armour:	48mm Deck, 230mm Belt
Armament:	4x3 30,5cm/45 Cannons 10x1 15cm/50 Casemated Guns 14x1 7cm/50 Guns 4x1 53cm Torpedoes

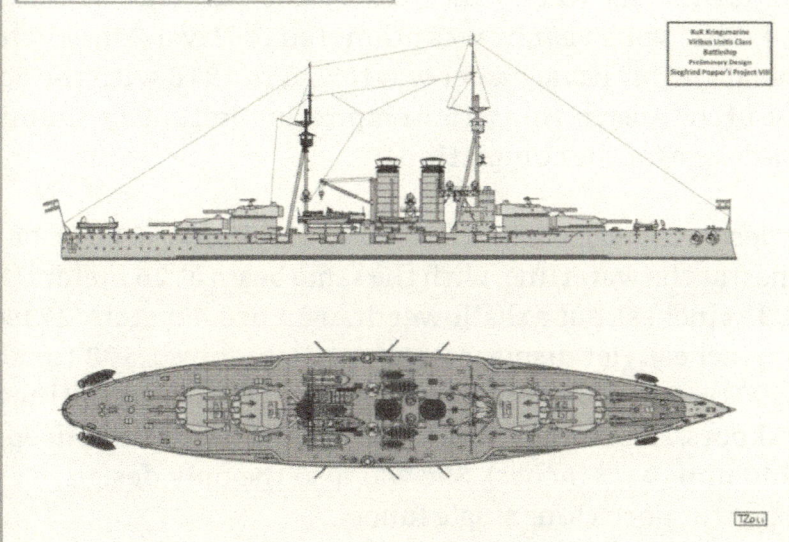

FRANZ PITZINGE

Two additional designs were submitted in time for the competitions closing date. One was by Franz Pitzingers in 1909 and the other by Thedor Novotny in 1910.

Pitzingers (22nd May 1858 – 10th October 1933) was during the late nineteen and early twentieth century a naval architect in Austria-Hungary. He had joined the Austro-Hungarian Navy in 1886 and was to spend a considerable percentage of his career at the naval arsenal in Pola. He had a significant amount of input into the design for the *Erzherzog Karl* class, as well as the ships that preceded the *Tegetthoff's*, the *Radetzky*-class battleships. After the completion he went onto oversea the design of the *Ersatz Monarch*-class Dreadnoughts which were ultimately to be cancelled by the outbreak of war in 1914. That same year he was promoted to Naval Constructor General and his naval career was to end in 1918 with the collapse of the Austro-Hungarian empire. But in 1909 he submitted a design for the completion.

His design envisaged a hull that was 153 meters (501 feet 11 5/8 inches) at the waterline, with the same beam at 26 meters (85 feet 3 5/8 inches), but a shallower draught of 8.4 meters (27 feet 6 23/33 inches). Her displacement was lighter by 1,500 tons at 18,500 tons and her 4 shafts produced 25,000 shp equating to 20.5 knots. Her armoured belt was 10 mm (13/32 inch) deeper at 240 mm (9 7/16 inches). She was also the only design in the process to sport a lone single funnel.

The main armament was comprised of the 30.5 cm 50 cal within five twin turrets. These were mounted along the hulls centre line and gave a broadside of ten guns. Her secondary armament was the single 15 cm 50 cal mounted most likely into casements. The roofs of turrets '1' '2' and '3' each sported single 17 cm 45 cal guns. She most likely had three 53 mm underwater torpedo tubes. Her broadside would equate to 4500 kg (9920 lb).

Franz Pitzinger's Proposal (1909)

Item	Description
Dimensions:	153 (wl) x 26 x 8,4m
Displacement:	18.500tons (standard)
Engines:	25.000shp Steam Turbines, 4 shafts
Speed:	38km/h (20,5knots)
Armour:	48mm Deck, 240mm Belt
Armament:	5x2 30,5cm/50 Cannons 14x1 15cm/50 Casemated Guns (Probably) 3x1 7cm/45 Guns (Probably) 4x1 53cm Underwater Torpedo tubes (Probably)

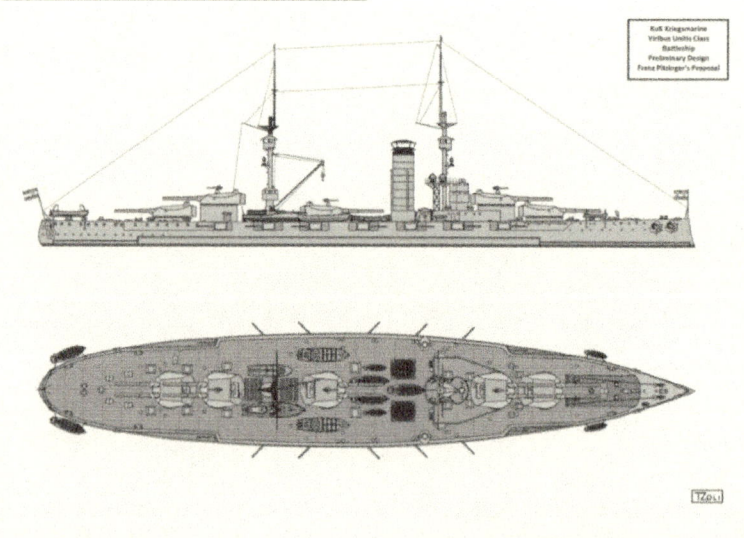

THEDOR NOVOTNY

Thedor Novotny was between 1890 and 1891 a shipbuilder overseeing the construction management of the cruiser Kaiserin Elisabeth and between 1891 and 1893 the cruiser Admiral Spaun. He was between 1910 and 1912 to serve as the construction manager at the Stabilimento Tecnico Triestino and oversaw the construction of the Viribus Unitis class built in the yard. During the war he oversaw the design of several ship's and like Pitzingers his career ended with the events of 1918.

Novotny's design had a length of 153 meters (501 feet 11 5/8 inches) a beam if 26 (85 feet 3 5/8 inches) meters and a draught drawing 8.4 meters (27 feet 6 23/32 inches) of water. These figures produced a hull 3.5 meters (11 feet 5 25/32 inches), a meter longer and the same draught. Her displacement was the same, but her steam turbines produced 27,000 shp, driving her four shafts to achieve 21 knots. Her belt was 50 mm (1 31/32 inch) deeper at 280 mm (11 1/32 inches), but like all the other designs her deck armour is listed at 48 mm (1 7/8 inch). She was a twin funnel design.

Her 30.5 cm 50 cal were mounted in a combination of triple and twin turrets, all mounted on the central line. Turrets '1' & '4' were triple and the super firing '2' & '3' were twin. This gave her a broadside of ten and five firing over either the bow or stern. Her broadside would equate to 4500 kg (9920 lb).
 She had sixteen 15 cm 50 cal guns mounted into casements and eight 10 cm 50 cal guns similarly presented. She is also possibly to have mounted two single 17 cm 45 cal guns in turrets '2' & '3'. she might also have had four single 53 mm underwater torpedo tubes.

Theodor Novotny's Proposal (1910)

Item	Description
Dimensions:	155 (wl) x 27 x 8,6m
Displacement:	20.000tons (standard)
Engines:	27.000shp Steam Turbines, 4 shafts
Speed:	39km/h (21knots)
Armour:	48mm Deck, 280mm Belt
Armament:	2x3, 2x2 30,5cm/50 Cannons 16x1 15cm/50 Casemated Guns 8x1 10cm/50 Casemated Guns 2x1 7cm/45 Guns (Probably) 4x1 53cm Underwater Torpedo tubes (Probably)

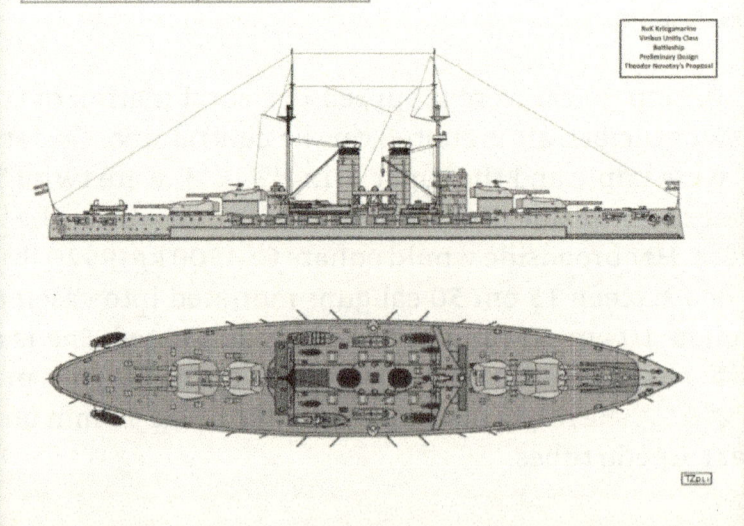

APPENDIX C: THE MILTARY HISTORY MUSEUM, VIENNA (ILLUSTRATIONS).

(PHOTO CREDIT ANDREW WILKIE COLLECTION WWW.VIRIBUSUNITIS.CA)

In the Museum of Military History in Vienna there is a cut-away model of the *Viribus Unitis*. The model is in a scale of 1:25 and has a total length of over 19 feet (6 mtrs). It was built between 1913 and 1917 by eight craftsmen of the shipyard Stabilimento Tecnico Triestino.

ANDY SOUTH

THE BOW PORTION OF THE MODEL. ALTHOUGH THE CLASS OFFICIALLY HAD A BOW RAM, THE CELLULAR NATURE SHOWN HERE DOES RAISE A QUESTION AS TO HOW IT WOULD HAVE FAIRED IN USE?

KEY

A = SEGMENTED BOW/RAM.
B = BOW TORPEDO COMPARTMENT.
C = TORPEDO RESERVES
D = ANCHOR CHAIN STORAGE.
E: HATCH FOR BRING TORPEDOES BELOW DECKS.
F = STORES
WC = TOILET.

THE TEGETTHOFF CLASS.

THE FORWARD 12 INCH TURRET PORTION OF THE HULL.

KEY

1. THE ARMORED DOME OF THE RANGEFINDER (THE RANGEFINDER ITSELF IS MISSING FROM THE MODEL). 2. THE TOWER COMMANDER'S SWIVEL CHAIR. 3. THE TELESCOPIC CHARGING ROD IS RETRACTED. 4. LOADED LOADING WAGON, THE BOTTOM OF THE PROJECTILE, THE TOP OF THE CHARGE. 5. MIDDLE GUN EXHAUST FAN. 6. 280 MM THICK BARBETTE ARMOR. 7. THE BULLET TRACK AND ITS SUBSTRUCTURE ON WHICH THE ROTOR OF THE GUN TURRET RESTS. 8. MECHANICS OF TOWER ROTATION. 9. WEDGE LOCK FOR THE MIDDLE 30.5 CM CANNON. 10. COMPRESSED AIR REPELLENT FOR THE MIDDLE 30.5 CM CANNON. 11. COMMON SHAFT OF THE MAIN AMMUNITION ELEVATORS OF THE LEFT AND CENTER CANNONS. 12. 98 HP ELECTRIC MOTOR FOR TOWER ROTATION. 15. ANCHOR CHAIN STOWAGE.

THE BOILER ROOMS WITH THEIR FUNNEL UPTAKES. NOTE THE LADDER FITTED
TO THE INTERIOR OF WHAT WOULD HAVE BEEN A DARK, SOOTY CLIMB.

KEY

A = TURBINES
B = FUNNELS WITH INTERNAL LADDERS.
C = FURNACE GRILLS
E = INTERANAL LADDER TO CROWS NESTS ON MAST
G = ARMOURED ACCESS TRUNK TO CONNING TOWER.

THE TEGETTHOFF CLASS.

THE REAR MIDSECTION OF THE HULL.

KEY

A = TURBINES
B = POSSIBLE ASH LIFT TO REMOVE BOILER WASTES
D = RANGE FINDER
E = AFT CONNING TOWER
F = FURNACE GRILLS
G = FUNNEL UPTAKES

ANDY SOUTH

THE STERN PORTION.

APPENDIX D: THE PHOTOGRAPH ALBUM

THE VIRIBUS UNITIS

THE TEGETTHOFF.

THE TEGETTHOFF CLASS.

PREVIOUS PAGE. THE STERN OF THE SZENT ISTVAN WHILE SHE IS AT ANCHOR.
THE PHOTO MAY BE IN HER DAYS OF CAPTIVITY GIVEN THE LACK
OF A STEN ENSIGN AND A NEAR BARE MAST?

THE LIGHT CRUISER HELIGOLAND IN DRY DOCK, BUT BEHIND HER IS THE
BOW OF THE VIRIBUS UNITIS, BOTH VESSELS ARE IN SEPARATE DRY DOCKS.
PHOTO COPYWRITE OF INTERNATIONAL RESEARCH ORGANIZATION.

ANDY SOUTH

THE VIRIBUS UNITIS IN DRY DOCK, AS ITS EITHER FLOODED OR DRAINED.
COPYWRITE OF INTERNATIONAL RESEARCH ORGANIZATION

THE TEGETTHOFF CLASS.

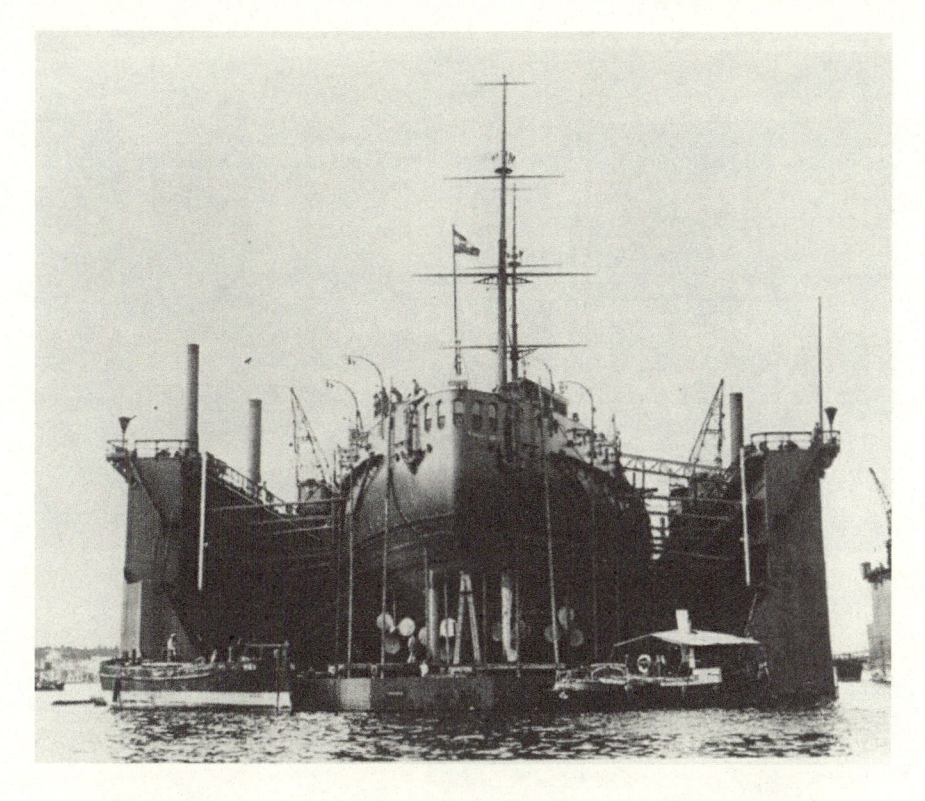

THE VIRIBBUS UNITIS IN DRY DOCK DURING 1913, HAVING BEEN COMMISSIONED ONLY THE YEAR PRIOR. COPYWRITE OF INTERNATIONAL RESEARCH ORGANIZATION

THE VIRIBUS UNITIS IN DRY DOCK, COPYWRITE OF INTERNATIONAL RESEARCH ORGANIZATION

ANDY SOUTH

A PHOTOGRAPH NOTED AS THE INTERIOR OF THE TEGETTHOF?

"S.M.SCHIFF SZENT ISTVAN 1914"

S. M. SCHIFF "SZENT ISTVÁN" - 1914 -

"THE S.M.SHIP SZENT ISTVAN -1914-"

S. M. S. »SZENT ISTVÁN«

ERBAUT AUF DER WERFTE DER MASCHINEN-, WAGGON- UND SCHIFFBAU-
AKTIENGESELLSCHAFT GANZ & COMP.-DANUBIUS ZU BERGUDI BEI FIUME

NACH DEN PLANEN DES K. U. K. GENERAL-SCHIFFBAUINGENIEURS
SIEGFRIED POPPER

DURCH DEN SCHIFFBAUDIREKTOR DER WERFTE, K. U. K. SCHIFFBAU-OBERINGENIEUR D. R.
JOHANN MASURKA

UNTER AUFSICHT DES K. U. K. SCHIFFBAU-OBERINGENIEURS
ALEXANDER TITZ

DIE MASCHINEN WURDEN NACH DEN PLANEN DES MASCHINENBAUDIREKTORS DER WERFTE,
K. U. K. MASCHINENBAU-OBERINGENIEURS D. R.
JOSEF ZIMNIC

UNTER AUFSICHT DES K. U. K. MASCHINENBAU-INGENIEURS
JOSEF PROKOP

AUSGEFÜHRT

ANDY SOUTH

"BUILT ON THE SHIPYARDS OF THE MACHINES WAGON AND SHIPBUILDING
CORPORATION COMPANY DANUBIUS TO BERGUDI FIUME

ACCORDING TO THE PLANS OF THE K.U.K SHIPBUILDING ENGINEER SIEGFRIED POPPER

BY THE SHIP DIRECTOR OF THE SHIPYARDS K.U.K SHIPBUILDING SENIOR
ENGINEER D.R JOHANN MASURKA

UNDER THE SUPERVISION OF THE K.U.K. ALEXANDER TITZ
THE MACHINES WERE DESIGNED IN ACCORDANCE WITH THE MACHINE
CONSTRUCTION DIRECTOR OF THE SHIPYARDS K.U.K MECHANICAL ENGINEERING
CHIEF ENGINEER D.R JOSEF ZIMNIC
UNDER THE SUPERVISION OF THE K.U.K MECHANICAL ENGINEER
JOSEF PROKOP
EXECUTED"

STEPHAN DER HEILIGE EMPFIEHLT UNGARN DEM SCHUTZE
DER HEILIGEN JUNGFRAU
NACH DEM GEMÄLDE VON JULIUS BENCZUR
MIT GENEHMIGUNG DES UNGARISCHEN KUNSTVERLAGS-A.-G. KÖNYVES KÁLMÁN, BUDAPEST

THE TEGETTHOFF CLASS.

PREVIOUS PAGE "STEPHAN THE HOLY RECOMMENDS HUNGARY TO THE PROTECT OF THE HOLY VIRGIN, TO THE PAINTING BY JULIUS WITH THE PERMISSION OF THE HUNGARIAN ART PUBLISHER A.G. KONYES KALMAN"

ANSICHT DER WERFTE DER MASCHINEN-, WAGGON- UND SCHIFFBAU-AKTIENGESELLSCHAFT GANZ & COMP.-DANUBIUS ZU BERGUDI BEI FIUME

"VIEW OF THE MACHINES., WAGGON. AND SHIPBUILDING CORPORATE GANZ O COMP.-DANUBIUS ON BERGUDI AT FIUME"

S. M. S. »SZENT ISTVÁN«.

Baumaterial: Stahl.	Länge: 151 m.		12 Stück 30'5 cm G. L./45.	2 Stück 8 mm Mitraill.
Tonnengehalt: 20.331 t.	Breite: 27'2 m.	Armierung:	12 » 15 cm G. L./50.	4 Torpedolancierapp.
Maschinenleistung:	Bemannung: 950 Mann.		18 » 7 cm G. L./50.	2 Stück 7 cm Landungs-
25.000 Wellen-Pferdekräfte.			2 » 47 mm S. F. K. L. 44	geschütze L./18.

TECHNICAL DETAILS FROM THE 1914 SOURCE.

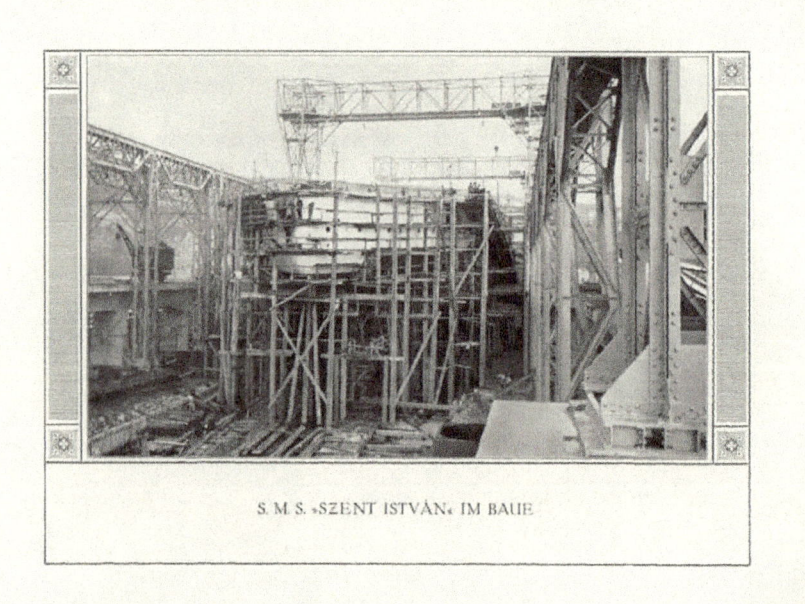

S. M. S. »SZENT ISTVÁN« IM BAUE

THE TEGETTHOFF CLASS.

"SMS SZENT ISTVAN UNDER CONSTRUCTION".

ANDY SOUTH

*PREVIOUS PAGE: FOUR IMAGES SHOWING EACH OF THE INDIVIDUALS STERNS.
(PHOTO CREDIT ANDREW WILKIE COLLECTION www.VIRIBUSUNITIS.CA)*

THE ERZHERZOG FRANZ FERDINAND AND TEGETTHOFF OFF VENICE IN MARCH 1919.

THE PRINZ EUGEN UNDER FRENCH OWNERSHIP. HER GUNS HAVE BEEN REMOVED AND SHE IS READY FOR HER FINAL ROLE SERVING AS AS A TARGET SHIP.

THE TEGETTHOFF CLASS.

POLA SHORTLY AFTER THE ARMISTACE. THE SHIPS IN PORT FROM LEFT TO RIGHT ARE THE ITALIAN CRUISER SAN MARCO, A RADETZKY CLASS PRE-DREADNOUGHT, THE PRINZ EUGEN, THE TEGETHOFF & THE FRENCH CRUISER WALDECK ROUSSEAU. AN ARCHIVES.

APPENDIX E: THE FILM ARCHIVE

At the time of inclusion all hyper-links were up to date and worked. But websites change and videos get deleted, so if the link declares "404" and the links not found, I apologize but sadly its beyond my power to remedy.

Andy South

DEATH AT DAWN, THE EMPEROR'S LAST BATTLESHIP.

THE TEGETTHOFF CLASS.

SMS TEGETTHOFF

CONSTRUCTION OF THE SZENT ISTVAN

SMS ISTVAN (GERMAN AUDIO)

SINKING OF THE SZENT ISTVAN

THE TEGETTHOFF CLASS.

1912 LAUNCH OF THE SZENT ISTVÁN & SCENES ON TEGETTHOFF

SMS VIRIBUS UNITIS - ANSCHIESSEN

1915 SZENT ISTVAN GUNNERY EXERCISES.

THE SZENT ISTVAN LAUNCH DAY.

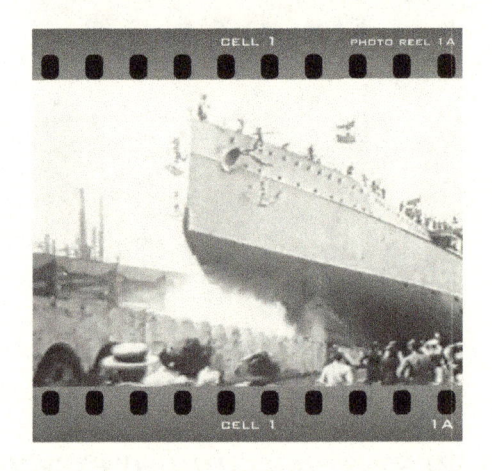

THE SZENT ISTVAN'S LAUNCH

THE TEGETTHOFF CLASS.

THE SZENT ISTVAN SINKS

THE ITALIAN ATTACK (CRITICICAL FILMS)

APPENDIX F: THE PLUMBING

BERIESELUNGSANLAGE. (SPRINKLER SYSTEM)

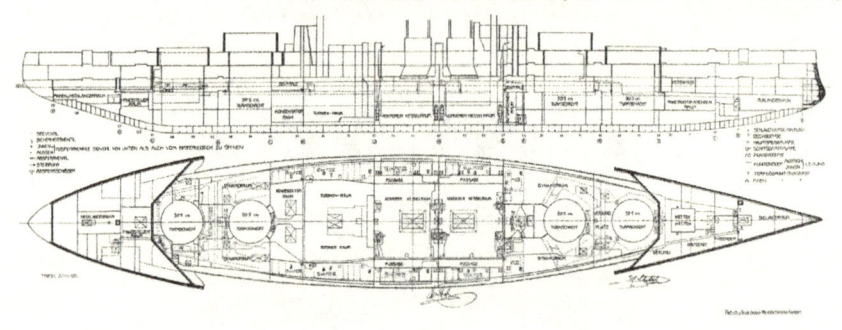

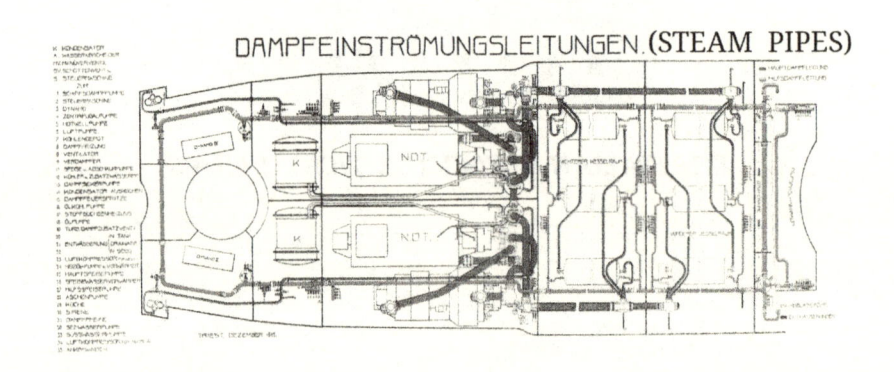

DAMPFEINSTRÖMUNGSLEITUNGEN. (STEAM PIPES)

THE TEGETTHOFF CLASS.

DRAINAGE-PLAN.

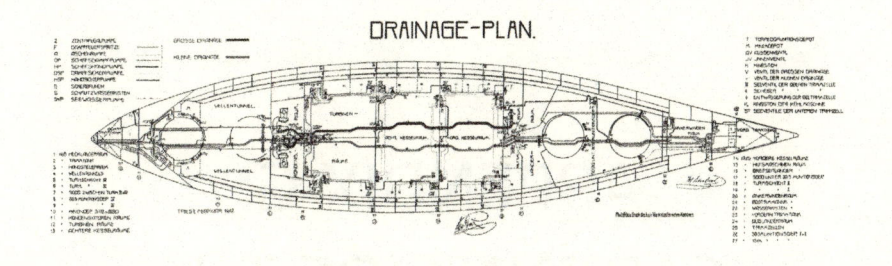

ENTWÄSSERUNGS-LEITUNGEN. (DRAINAGE PIPES)

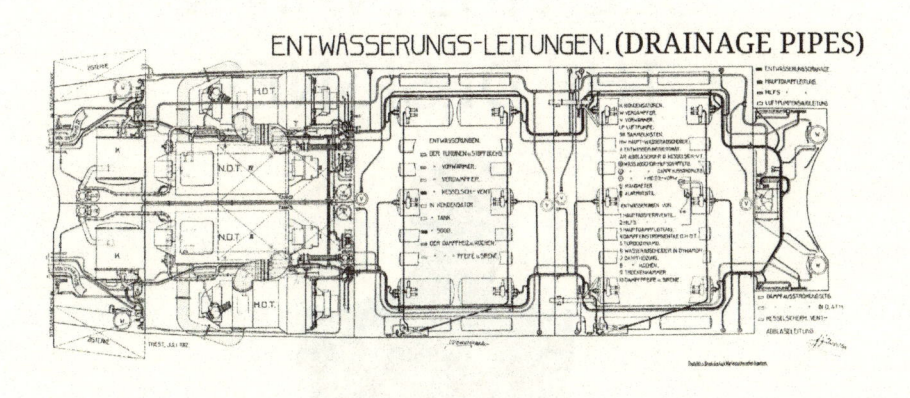

SPEISELEITUNGEN. (FEED LINE)

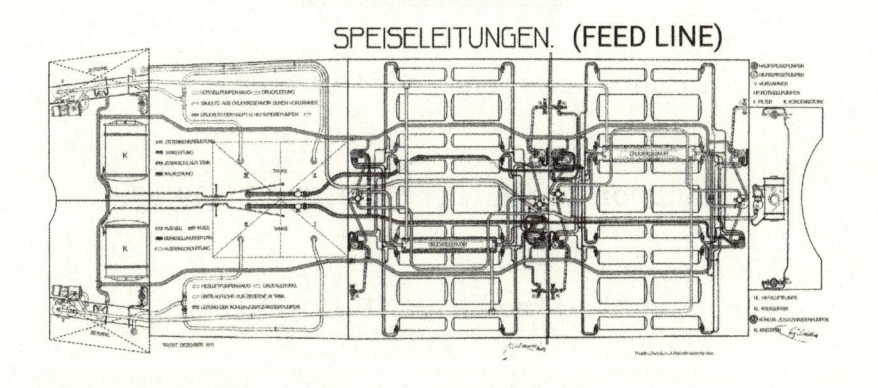

APPENDIX G: CAPTAIN'S OF THE SZENT ISTVÁN & THE DESIGNER

Edmund Grassberger: 28.10.15 - 04.93.17.

Franz von Teichgräber : 04.03.17 - 29.09.17.

Franz Karl Lauffer: 01.10.17 - 11.03.18.

Heinrich Seitz von Treffen: 11.03.18 - 10.06.10.06.18.

◆ ◆ ◆

THE TEGETTHOFF CLASS.

The ships, despite Austrian claims, had a poor reputation as a design. Its main constructor of the class and the chief designer was the former Admiral and General-shipping civil engineer Siegfried Popper (1848-1933). He was nearly blind at the design stage and was to be retired before the ships were launched due to his poor eyesight. In addition, he suffered a level of deafness. Many consider him to be responsible for the poor quality of the Tegetthoff class and after his retirement he was to spend much of his time translating Hebrew literature into German. It was because of his deafness that he was run down by a tram, (he did not hear or see coming), in Prague and was to die several days later, on the 19th April 1933.

LITERATURE & SOURCES

I must acknowledge and pay tribute to several sources without who the extracts and much of the information just would not have been available.

If I have omitted anyone I apologize, it was not intentional. If you contact me the omission will happily be corrected. Thank you:

Krámli Mihály: Az Osztrák-Magyar Monarchia csatahajói 1904-1914. HM HIM, Budapest, 2018.

Krámli Mihály: A Tegetthoff-osztály születése. Az osztrák-magyar dreadnought-program. In: Hadtörténelmi Közlemények 2005/1-2

Krámli Mihály: A győri Magyar Ágyúgyár Rt. felállítása. In: Hadtörténelmi Közlemények 2010/4

Monthly of the Naval General Staff, Nos. 4–9, 1914

The Maritime Collection, 1912–1914

W. Aichenburg, L. Baumgartner, FF Bilzer, G. Pawlik, F. Prasky, EF Sieche. Die Tegetthoff-Klasse: Österreich-Ungarns grosste Schlachtschiffe. - Muenhen: Bernard and Graeve Verlag, 1981. S. 104

R. Greger. Who Was Responsible for the Faults of the Tegetthoff Class? // "Warship", Vol. IV, 1980, pp. 69–72

PG Halpern. A Naval History of World War I. - London: University College press Ltd., 1994, p. 591

PJ Kemp. Austro-Hungarian Battleships. - London: ISO Publishers, 1991, p. 112

F. Prasky. The Viribus Unitis Class // Warship, Vol. II, 1978, pp. 104–115

F. Prasky. Faults of the Viribus Unitis Class // "Warship", Vol. III, 1979, pp. 47

RF Shelma de Heere. Austro-Hungarian Battleships // Warship International, No. 1, 1973, S. 11–97

EF Sieche. Die Schlachtschiffe der KuK Marine // "Marine Arsenal" No. 14, S. 48

EF Sieche. Szent Istvan, Hungaria's Only and Ill-Fated dreadnought // "Warship International", No. 2, 1991, pp. 112–146

HH Sokol. Oesterreich-Ungarns Seekrieg 1914-1918. - Wien, 1933. Vol. I, II

Ufficio Storico della Regia Marina: La Marina Italiana nella Grande Guerra. - Finennze, 1938-1942. Vol. I – VIII

Appendix to the magazine "Modelist-Constructor" "Marine Collection" - No. 3 (39) - 2001

Austria-Hungarian Battleships 1914-18 (New Vanguard Book 193) Kindle Edition by Ryan K. Noppen.

A Fleet in Being: Austria-Hungarian Warships of WW1 Kindle Edition by Russell Phillips

Austria-Hungarian Warships of World War I by Rene Greger

K.U.K Flotte 1900-1918 by Wladimir Aichelberg

Austro-Hungarian Naval Policy, 1904-1914 By Milan Vego

The Millstone by Geoffrey Miller.

The Imperial & Royal Austro-Hungarian Navy by Sokol RGAVMF, f. 401, 418, 441, 876.

Monthly of the Naval General Staff, Nos. 4–9, 1914

"Marine collection", 1912-1914.

W. Aichenburg, L. Baumgartner, FF Bilzer, G. Pawlik, F. Prasky, EF Sieche. Die Tegetthoff-Klasse: Österreich-Ungarns grosste Schlachtschiffe. - Muenhen: Bernard and Graeve Verlag, 1981. S. 104

R. Greger. Who Was Responsible for the Faults of the Tegetthoff Class? // "Warship", Vol. IV, 1980, pp. 69–72

PG Halpern. A Naval History of World War I. - London: University College press Ltd., 1994, p. 591

PJ Kemp. Austro-Hungarian Battleships. - London: ISO Publishers, 1991, p. 112

F. Prasky. The Viribus Unitis Class // Warship, Vol. II, 1978, pp. 104–115

F. Prasky. Faults of the Viribus Unitis Class // "Warship", Vol. III, 1979, pp. 47

RF Shelma de Heere. Austro-Hungarian Battleships // Warship International, No. 1, 1973, S. 11–97

EF Sieche. Die Schlachtschiffe der KuK Marine // "Marine Arsenal" No. 14, S. 48

EF Sieche. Szent Istvan, Hungaria's Only and Ill-Fated Dreadnought // "Warship International", No. 2, 1991, pp. 112–146

HH Sokol. Oesterreich-Ungarns Seekrieg 1914–1918. - Wien, 1933. Vol. I, II

Ufficio Storico della Regia Marina: La Marina Italiana nella Grande Guerra. - Finennze, 1938-1942. Vol. I – VIII

Appendix to the magazine "Modelist-Constructor" "Marine Collection" - No. 3 (39) - 2001.

www.viribusunitis.ca/viribus-unitis-class

web.archive.org

www.kriegsmarine

www.croatian-treasure.

www.warshipsresearch.

www.regiamarina.net

www.naval-encyclopedia.com

www.navweaps.com

naval history and heritage command.

wk1.staatsarchiv.at/seekrieg/die-flottenpolitik-von-grossadmiral-anton-haus/

WWW..tmg110.tripod.com/austria1.htm

Super-Drawings In 3D. The Sms Viribus Unitis, Austro-Hungarian Battleship

In 1907 the navy of the dualist, multinational Austro-Hungarian Empire placed an order for a new class of warships, whose design was based on the "all big gun" concept pioneered by HMS Dreadnought. Eventually four Tegetthoff class vessels were laid down, including the flagship Viribus Unitis, Tagetthoff, Prinz Eugen and Szent Istvan. The last warship of the class was not completed until well into World War I. The vessels' careers were not especially eventful. They spent most of their service lives as a "fleet in being" anchored in a well-protected port of Pola with only occasional trips to the Fažana Channel (well-screened by Brijuni Islands) for gunnery practice. During the war the ships were manned mainly by reservists, while the most promising and experienced members of their crews were detached to serve onboard submarines or torpedo boats, or assigned to land-based units. The second ship of the class ended her career in rather dramatic circumstances, which is why she perhaps deserves a more detailed treatment.

Hmas Sydney : The Birth Of Australia's Fleet (1913) (Vol 1)) (Warships Of World War One Book 2)

HMAS Sydney is famed for destroying the Sydney. But there was much more to here tale. The 13 months of peace time service, the capture of Germany's Pacific colonies, service in the Atlantic hunting the great Tran-Atlantic liner and commerce raider the, Kronprinz Wilhelm and over two years as part of the Royal Navy's Grand Fleet.

The first volume in this series tells the story of those first 13 months when on her maiden voyage, she visited South Africa, toured eastern Australia and escorted the two submarines AE1&2 from Singapore to Sydney.

The narrative draws on the ship's log, crew members journals and the local Australian newspaper archives. It tells the tale of the ship but also the story of those crew men who served in her. Of their sporting achievements, and of the controversy over the gunnery shield. The tales travels from the laying down of her keel, to the eve of the war. Volume 2 will tell the tale, in depth of her war service and will draw on a number of sources that until now have been largely ignored.

The narrative is chronological, allowing the reader to follow events in the order they occurred and to see the ships timeline laid out in a logical order.

The Suicide Club

"There have been several books written about the 'K' Class Submarines in the past however, most of them have concentrated solely on their poor safety record and the many fatal accidents involving Submarines of the Class. This new Book, as well as describing the many accidents and incidents, also looks into the decision-making process behind the design, why steam propulsion was chosen, the complexity of the design and many of the characters who commanded these 'Fleet' submarines .Much of the information comes from the Ships Covers, Ships Logs, Court Martial and other Records held at the National Archives at Kew, and also contemporary personal records by some who served in 'K' Class boats. One letter quoted (from the Royal Archives at Windsor) was written by HRH Midshipman the Duke of York (the future King George VI) to his father describing the near disastrous diving incident to Submarine K3 in Stokes Bay in the Solent in December 1916. Luckily Stokes Bay is quite shallow - otherwise British history might have been quite different. The book contains many photographs, charts and drawings (many not seen before) which assist with understanding the 'K' Class story.

Andy South has managed to pull together a wide range of technical detail, contemporary first-hand accounts and other information into a readable form helping to explain the history of the 'K' Class boats and coming to a conclusion that the 'Fleet Submarine' concept - whilst understandable - could not be safely supported by the technology available in the early 20th Century". Barrie Downer. The Submariners Association.

AUTHOR NOTE: This is the second volume of The Suicide Club; its predecessor having been a trouble creature and withdrawn. There were in that original publication's technical issues in uploading the file, problems which even Amazon could not resolve. A 'work-around' I devised resulted unintentionally in an early draft, that had yet to be proofread being published.

The Suicide Club has been proofread once more, new material added and the appendix vastly expanded. It is a huge piece of work based on over 2000 pages within the National Archives at Kew.

Armour Comparisons

	Belt	Turrets	Deck	Casements	Conning tower
Tegetthoff	6"-11" (150-280 mm)	2"-11" (60-280 mm)	1" to 2" (30-48 mm)	7"1 (80 mm)	1"-2" (60-280 mm)
Dante Alighieri	10" (254 mm)	10" (254 mm)	1.5" (38 mm)		12" (305 mm)
Corbet	10"6' (270 mm)	11'8" (300 mm)			11'8" (300 mm)

Made in United States
Orlando, FL
13 December 2021

11627899R00268